AISLING

About The Author

∞

Jeremy Schewe has been leading international sacred site retreats, socio-economic service trips, and conservation-based eco-adventures for 10 years. He is an ecologist, botanist, tree keeper, and community activator who has worked around the world for the past 15 years with indigenous and at-risk communities. Jeremy is an avid outdoorsman and athlete, and he has 23 years of experience practicing and 15 years teaching Qigong and Tao-Yin meditation.

In addition to these many talents, Jeremy is a carrier of the Light of Erin, or Solas Gael na hÉíreann in Irish, which is a Connacht branch of the Celtic Twilight, rekindled in the nineteenth century by WB Yeats, Lady Gregory, AE Russel, Edward Martyn, and more. Through this, Jeremy helps sustain a bridge between the Celtic Otherworld and the contemporary one. Jeremy has also been fully immersed in studies, fieldwork, and teaching of ecology, botany, herbology, shamanism, and Qigong, as well as Nordic, Sami, Hindu, and Mayan traditional ecological and mythological knowledge for over 21 years. He is also a certified herbalist.

In 2017, Jeremy published his first book, *Ports of Entry*. His second book, and his first title with Crossed Crow, is *Aisling: Discovering Keys in the Irish-Celtic Mysteries*.

AISLING

Discovering Keys in the Irish-Celtic Mysteries

JEREMY SCHEWE

CROSSED CROW BOOKS

Chicago, IL

First Edition. 2023.

Paperback ISBN: 978-1-959883-17-3
Library of Congress Control Number on file.

Cover design by Wycke Malliway.
Typesetting by Mads Oliver.
Edited by Becca Fleming.

Disclaimer: Crossed Crow Books, LLC does not participate in, endorse, or have any authority or responsibility concerning private business transactions between our authors and the public. Any internet references contained in this work were found to be valid during the time of publication, however, the publisher cannot guarantee that a specific reference will continue to be maintained. This book's material is not intended to diagnose, treat, cure, or prevent any disease, disorder, ailment, or any physical or psychological condition. The author, publisher, and its associates shall not be held liable for the reader's choices when approaching this book's material. The views and opinions expressed within this book are those of the author alone and do not necessarily reflect the views and opinions of the publisher.

Published by:
Crossed Crow Books, LLC
6934 N Glenwood Ave, Suite C
Chicago, IL 60626
www.crossedcrowbooks.com
Printed in the United States of America.

Other Books by Author

Ports of Entry, 2017

∞ Acknowledgments ∞

Ochone, cuisle mo chroidhe.

Ochone, solas geal na hEireann.

Seanmháthair, Máthair Mhór –

Táimid ar thuras, táimid ar aistear:

Deoraí Dé, Deoraí Bandia.

Thank you, Mother. You always thoroughly emphasized the importance of honing the mind, but more so, encouraged following the heart in the responsible pursuit of dreams. You gave me a sense of home, belonging, and place as a springboard to pursue the clues through the labyrinthine dreams of life. Our Mother country, Ireland, heard the beauty and purity of your prayers and made way for the Great Queen, Kathleen ní Houlihan, to call me home and into Her service. Thank you to all those before me who rallied to reclaim Her freedom, and to all those who will be called to maintain Her sovereignty for generations to come.

All reverence to the Celtic Twilight and the Order of Celtic Mysteries for demonstrating the power of devotion to a cause beyond our increasingly isolated and self-contained worlds. Your inspiration incited the emancipation of the Irish nation. Thank you to my friend and guide, the greatest Celtic faërie historian of the twenty-first century, Steve Blamires. And special gratitude to my loving wife, Lumi Ketto, my life partner, playmate, and fellow dreamer: thank you for keeping me fed while I dive down into rabbit holes in pursuit of elusive clues or burn the midnight oil in the scriptorium. Thank you for riding the waves of change with me and the rediscovery together of the power of loyalty and devotion.

Thank you to all my *aislingí*, mentors, allies, guides, and friends of the seen and unseen. Specifically, Sinéad de Búrke, thank you for helping me stitch together the visions of my dreaming with the sacred landscape of Ireland. Delfina Rose, thank you for helping me to navigate the gentle journey of rewriting my relationship to both mental and social constructs into a richer, harmonious relationship with my Celtic heritage. Thank you to Ralph Dehner and Dennis Thoman for teaching me *Flying Crane* as a tool for gardening the life force moving through my body and precipitating wholesome change via discipline. To Fr. Ferone and Fr. Milbourne, thank you for encouraging me further along the pilgrim's path and honoring the communion of saints. And thank you to all the amazing souls who have journeyed back and forth with me to Ireland for the past ten years, especially Angele Mason, James Mayfield-Smith, Patricia Leas, River Bryant, and Alex de la Barre—we do it again and again and again. Oh, the clues we find!

Finally, thank you to all those who directly helped this book evolve from a dream into reality, including the steadfast efforts of my editor, Rebecca Fleming, at Crossed Crow Books. A big thank you must also go out to Bernie Pháid, Sam "Fergus" Brett, and Morgan Daimler for help with Gaeilge pronunciation, grammar, and etymology along the Way. And finally, I must offer a big gratitude to all the members of the Grove of the Light of Erin for digesting the early versions of all the chapters contained within this book. Thank you for all your tireless faith and enduring long hours of Irish chanting, walking mountains, blessing holy wells, and drinking from the firehose. *Go raibh maith agat!*

"Out of imagination that is fire of the brain; out of tenderness that is magic of the heart; out of a hard endurance that is pride of the body we are building—all of us, great and small—the Ireland that our poets have dreamed of and our seers foretold. Ireland herself—the substance, for our dream is but a shadow of her—Ireland herself, the Sacred Land, the Dark Rose, for ever lovely and beloved blesses the work, enlightening our minds and our hearts, and strengthening our hands."

~ Ella Young, *Flowering Dusk* (1945)

∞ CONTENTS ∞

∞ Foreword ∞

There are countless books dealing with the esoteric facets of Celtic spirituality and practice, some complex and academic, others simple and weightless. This clearly begs the question; do we need another one? For my part, the answer is yes, we do. This one.

Much of Jeremy's writing deals with material that will be familiar to people with an inkling for the Celtic Mysteries, however, it quickly becomes apparent that everything herein is written with such passion and excitement, it is like being exposed to it for the first time. There is a fresh impulse within these pages that is lacking in much of the Celtic-oriented material already in print. Each chapter seamlessly weaves together important mythological knowledge, accurate historical data, and often ignored archaeological details in a way that makes sense, is relevant, and is not there just to impress.

Jeremy writes of the various deities, heroes, and heroines both historical and mythological as if they are old and deeply respected friends. His words are backed by extensive and comprehensive personal experiences. He assumes the reader has an interest in the subject but does not talk down insultingly and neither does he write at a level designed for university papers.

He manages to encapsulate within these pages the culture, belief system, and history of the Irish-Celtic people wherever they were and, importantly, still are. He avoids criticizing other belief systems and does not fall into the trap of telling the reader what they must or must not do. It is all given in the form of sage advice from an old, trusted friend.

This is a work that requires several readings to fully absorb the layers of interconnection that weave and twist and wander in the background like never-ending Celtic knotwork.

Enjoy the journey.
Steve Blamires
New York
March 21, 2021

Introduction

"Tír gan teanga is tír gan anam."

~ Irish Saying

The essence of all things Celtic and Irish is summarized in this saying. *Tír gan teanga is tír gan anam.* In English, it means "a land without a language is a land without a soul." I believe that this holds true for all people of the Earth, not just the Celts. Any people who consider themselves indigenous to a place—where the sacred and secular dovetail as one—know that language and song are the cultural codices that shape the world. In tracking the heart of the etymology of the word *indigenous*, we can uncover the true essence of the intention behind crafting the landscape and human consciousness that gave it birth. *Indigenous* comes from Old Latin, a Greek derivative of the words *indu*, meaning "within, in," and *gignere*, meaning "to beget or produce." Thus, the essence of the word *indigenous* can be translated as "creation from within."

Gaeilge, or Irish, is the native tongue in Ireland and is a modern evolution of one of the oldest language groups still being spoken on the planet: Gaelic.[1] Irish is a variant of Gaelic as is Manx, Scottish, Welsh, and Breton. The Irish word that most strongly associates with the Latin-Greek word "indigenous" is *dúchas*. Yet, the root of the ancient Gaelic language group is as old as Greek and perhaps Hebrew, and of course, has its own essence derived from thousands of years of culture in relation with the land. The Irish word *dúchas* can refer to a hereditary right or even birthplace while at the same time meaning an ancestral home or native place. Deeper, it reveals a sense of traditional or kindred affection and natural affinity to a place. Finally, it also refers to a natural, wild state of being, like a poet or mystic's wildness and madness.

[1] Irish-Gaelic is in the top ten to fifteen oldest languages still spoken in the world amongst others, including Tamil, Basque, Finnish, and more.

The Celtic people and our music are twined in an interdependent and reciprocal relationship like Celtic knots—no beginning, no end. The Celtic revolution of the living, breathing knotwork of art and music is derived directly from this relationship with the Irish-Celtic people and Ireland herself. In these modern times, the Celtic path calls not only to those with a direct Celtic heritage, but it calls to many who seek to awaken and contribute to the harmonic relationship between people, spirit, and the land.

The Irish-Celts speak frequently of the Otherworld, most frequently as *Tír na nÓg*, essentially a heaven on earth that is neither here nor there, neither up nor down, neither small nor vast…yet ever-present and waiting for us. Herein, flowers are in eternal bloom, life is eternally youthful, and there is no lack of sustenance, good cheer, music, and the company of illuminated beings. This "otherworld" realm, or parallel plane of existence, is sometimes referred to as "the Summerlands" in English—the land of eternal nectar. The guardians of *Tír na nÓg* are ever seeking to reunite with Middle Earth, the world of humanity we know so well with all its suffering and bliss. Often, to those imbued or struck by the magnetism of *dúchas*, emissaries of *Tír na nÓg* will appear as Faë beings (light elves or faëry in a non-diminutive form), sometimes seen as saints, angels, goddesses, beautiful women/men, and more. In Irish, these sightings, whether in sleep or waking state, are called an *aisling*. These world walkers and emissaries from the other side show up in our lives with a purpose: to invite the one having the vision to visit them in the Summerlands, follow them to some sacred destination to complete a task, or perform some service to bridge their world with ours more wholly.

The Summerland is the realm of the immortals, or the Good People, typically referred to in Irish as the *sídhe*. An *aisling* is an expression or family branch of the *sídhe*. At times, they are birthed amongst us as humans, or changelings are set consciously among us to hasten the resurrection of life within—to embrace the fullness of humanity or untwist a complicated puzzle or riddle. During visions, often repetitive, such as that of an *aisling*, the form that a *sídhe* takes on is in a form that the recipient of the vision will understand and be most moved by—depending on their mental and spiritual constructs. To some, they appear as almost extraordinarily beautiful human-like elves. To others, they appear as gods, angels, or saints. Some people see them as little faëries, leprechauns, *púcaí*, selkies, and more. For some folks, they may appear as tricksters, demons, or goblins. Some people may see them as aliens, star people, demigods, or archetypal superheroes. Choose your lens. If they want your attention, they will find you. The *sídhe* and *aislingí* are intermediaries between our world and the eternal. For those who may not have the knack for clairvoyance, or that may be undeveloped, the *sídhe* will find other ways to communicate with you.

As dreamers, poets, and mystics magnetized by the throb of our *dúchas* to follow the soul's longing through the invitation of visions and dreams, our *aislingí*, we are constantly receiving invitations from the *sídhe* to braid together the seemingly disparate worlds of humanity and the eternal. That is the heart of this book: to help navigate the journey of the *aislingí* riddles through which they call you home to Ireland in respect to spirit, the sacred landscape, and the flowering of the soul's expression incarnate.

By no means is this book intended to be an academic foray into the vast archive of the Irish literary mountain. I will leave that to the academics, to whom I am forever grateful for their vast works, specifically the ancient Irish texts of the medieval period to the powerful translations from Irish to English in the mid-nineteenth century. These translations heavily influenced the Celtic Literary Revival of the late nineteenth and early twentieth centuries. The Celtic Literary Revival, frequently referred to as the "Celtic Twilight," not only propelled the timeless knowledge of our Irish, Scottish, and Welsh heritage forward into the modern age, but it also gave spiritual fuel to national pride that sparked the liberation of the Irish Republic from the British empire. Standing in the centennial celebration of the reclamation of the Irish heritage at the foot of Cnoc Bréanainn in the west of Ireland, I bow in gratitude to the works of my teacher's teachers, William B. Yeats, Maude Gonne, Lady Gregory, Fiona Macleod, Ella Young, Kenneth Morris, Æ Russell, and many more. As Æ Russell so aptly put it, "divine poets [make] known the paths between heaven and earth."[2]

◇◇◇◇◇◇◇◇◇◇◇◇◇◇

2 Æ Russell, *Song and its Fountains*, 1932.

This book is a living invitation from the Celtic Twilight, from *Solas Geal na hEireann*, the living Light of Erin—Ireland's nurturing spirit and living spiritual heritage—to braid the ever-evolving mythos of our dreams and visions into an Irish-Celtic cultural context and to thus express one's service into the world in a deeper harmonic way in respect to the soul. Perhaps along the way, the twenty-first-century healers, shamans, poets, and mystics will unravel or deepen their own mysterious relations with the unseen. Erin, the sovereign goddess of Ireland, and the *sídhe* and *aislingí* are reaching across the void from *Tír na nÓg*.[3] They are calling. Heed the call. Reach out your heart and hands, embrace the mystery of Erin's invitation in its complex yet simple Celtic knotwork of dreaming. As Ella Young said, "*The outstretched hand is the hand that is filled the fullest.*"[4] Herein is an invitation for those in pursuit of their own personal Irish-Celtic riddles and beyond. Awaken the soul in respect to spiritual or hereditary sovereignty, your *dúchas,* in respect to the richly complex dance of humanity. Throughout the book, contextual references and a bibliography will help the reader better understand the source material. A glossary including a pronunciation guide is provided at the back of the book for easy reference.

All wayward sons and daughters of Erin are invited into her living light, the Light of Erin, in an ever-evolving journey of intertwining myth and legend. The quest is yours. In each moment, we have a choice between life and death. And each moment is an invitation to pick up your sword, your pen, your wand, or your cross, and claim your sovereignty...not claiming power over others but claiming an inner knowledge and glow that directs the path of the soul through the waves of confrontations, hurdles, and conflicts in life. Ultimately, this leads to victories that are beyond the normal construct of reality: mystery, magic, and miracles. In the living Celtic heart, there is no separation between the secular or mundane and the sacred or magical. There is no separation between the

3 *Erin*, or *Éire*, is the modern form of *Ériu*, the ancient goddess whose name is given to Ireland: *Ériu-land*. She is symbolized in the modern world via the Celtic harp, specifically the "Brian Boru" harp in the old library, The Long Room, at Trinity College, Dublin.

4 Ella Young, *Celtic Wonder-Tales* (Maunsel & Company, Ltd., 1910).

divine and nature. The dichotomy of the seemingly separate worlds is wed as one in the heart through imagination and intuition. The marriage of logic and vision is the loom of the soul, housed in these temples we call our bodies. This sacred marriage emboldens the weaving of the tapestry of our lives for the betterment of all beings to be free from suffering.

Time is irrelevant in the stitching of the worlds. The illuminated, living light of the soul paints its masterpiece where *Tír na nÓg* and our world meet. Allies and enemies alike will ride into the fray of our lives, looking for entry into the creation of our living mythology—through both tempest and calm. Something is born and dies in us with each breath, and yet, the evolving eternal spirit remains. Spirit or divinity—the *sídhe* and *aislingí*—seek to know each of us and become related to us both collectively and individually. Specifically, throughout life, they will seek to bind you to "contracts," especially if you excel in skill sets attractive to the work they are seeking to complete—much like getting a job. In this respect, a "contract" is an agreement between an individual and the divine as the *sídhe* or *aislingí*. In Irish, this type of contract is sometimes referred to as a *géis,* like a vow or taboo. These contracts are received by an individual in a heightened state of consciousness, such as a plant medicine journey, shamanic journey, dreams, and even through loss, pain, or disease. As recipients of possible contracts from the *sídhe* or *aislingí*, we consciously or unconsciously choose to accept or reject the tasks or missions of those visions depending on our own human filtering. In some instances, a *géis* is like Indian *karma*, a malediction directed at us from another source or derived from poor choices from the past. In this case, as individuals, there may be no choice other than to complete the requirements, follow a set of taboos, or complete a task to be free of or live in respect to that *géis.*

When we have the choice of contracts at the crossroads in life, we can understand from a place of inner freedom and clarity that some aspects of eternity are worth serving, and we can clearly say "yes" to those tasks. Most contracts offered are better left behind as they will be mere distractions away from our true path into harmony. Just because we are offered a job does not mean we have to take it. Only you can know which contracts to say "yes" to, and thus, which turns in the labyrinth of life to make. Such is the journey of life: a series of choices, freedom, agreements, services, redemption, illumination, and completion. Somewhere along the path, as seekers, we pushed off from an unknown dock and sailed seas wrought with sea serpents, Vikings, and corsairs. Your quest brought you here now. Be not afraid of the path before you, though it be wrought with its mysteries and monsters. They are like the forge fire and will shape you into a better instrument to be played at the leisure of the divine.

Step through the mists. The invitation to the living Celtic soul is to embrace life with a vibrant and unvanquishable spirit. Do not kowtow to complacency, security, and short-term safety in exchange for a form of existence that is devoid of life. *Tír na nÓg* is calling us to live fully and to be emissaries between the Blessed Realm and the density of human life. We are the living bridge between the eternal and the mortal. Each moment, we have an opportunity to walk that bridge—to carry over the ever-changing gold to be poured in ovations on the temples that feed and sustain the living. Irish poet James Joyce of the Connemara in Ireland embraces it fully as he shouts from the top of Ben Bulben in County Sligo, Ireland:

> *"Welcome, O life! I go to encounter for the millionth time the reality of experience and to forge in the smithy of my soul the uncreated conscience of my race."*[5]
> ~ James Joyce, 1916

There are infinite doors to the inner sanctuary and the Celtic grove. There are infinite probabilities weaving throughout the multiverse. Hold close the center—the chalice of the heart-mind. Come not to the realm of mysteries seeking the absolute, but instead, to be on a quest seeking a refinement of the questioning and the riddles that unfold. Come hungry and thirsty, for we shall find both feast and famine.

Ireland is a pure gate and the heart of the planet. It is a place to refine, deepen, and listen. If you are looking for absolutes, The Light of Erin is not the access gateway for you. This is a temple of dreaming, intuition, and critical thinking where the ever-evolving riddle of the soul is refined and remade to keep the mind, heart, and soul ever pliable,

[5] James Joyce, *A Portrait of the Artist as a Young Man* (B.W. Huebsch, 1916).

ever reverent, and ever seeking wonder and awe. Do not come to the Irish-Celtic path seeking answers to your small questions. Come here seeking better questions that illuminate your eternal nature.

As you read this book, you will be invited again and again to polish different lenses, clear off windows, and open doors to look through. Only you will know if you are looking from the mundane into *Tír na nÓg* or if you are looking from the sweet Summerlands back into the world of the mundane. Perhaps, at times, your viewpoint will shift from one to the other. Through this, you may be reminded of tools and personal capabilities that perhaps you have known only from dreams. You may remember capabilities that perhaps you had mastered in another world or parallel life. This is truly the Mystery of the Celts. Life is not linear. Life does not end when you pass over—you simply take a break in the Summerlands and come back when called. Sometimes you will bring parts of yourself back that were not present when you left, or the world may look quite different, like when Oisín came home from the Blessed Realm because he missed Ireland and his comrades of the *Fianna*.

The heart of this book is not to glorify an ancient pre-Christian past, nor is it to exonerate the Celtic-Christian or later Catholic traditions of the Irish people. The purpose of this book is to seamlessly tie together the essence and spirit of Ireland, the Light of Erin, like Fionntán, the sole survivor of the first settlement of Ireland by Cessair. Fionntán is Ireland's Greenman, *fear uaine,* a shapeshifter who weaves in and out through over six millennia, changing forms ever in devotion to pure spirit and the Light of Erin. The magic and majesty of the Irish people have taken on many forms, but the line of true service to the divine is unbroken. The invitation in this book is to honor where we have come from and where we are going. By looking through the Irish-Celtic lens into the past, we can better create a map of the probable futures that we are diligently working toward. The timeless oracle and the council of elders are inviting you to take your seat in circle, add your voice to the song of songs, and amplify the strength of the rainbow bridge between the worlds.

The final invitation of this book is, as you read, to enter a journey on a pilgrimage to Ireland. When going on a journey, we might gather maps, translators, and try to understand the nature of place. We may look at the lay of the land and the current or historical traditions of those who have gone before us. This book will provide you with some guidance from what I have learned over the past twenty-five years in the sacred grove of my ancestors and with the teachers and mentors who have gone before me. When going on a pilgrimage, we leave behind the secular and embrace the divine. *Aisling: Discovering Keys in the Irish-Celtic Mysteries* may provide some entry as well as exit portals for you on your own journey as an emissary of the living Light of Erin. You will know them when you find keys and/or doors or as they find you. May you find all the sacred talismans and disparate pieces, like the *Sons of Tuireann* on their sacred quest around the world, or transmit hallowed objects of a previous age, like the four gifts the *Tuatha Dé Danann* brought to Ireland from their sacred cities now beneath the sea.[6]

Come then, friend, turn your tears to gold. Come and braid your pain into ecstasy. Embrace the fullness of the spectrum of living light and exonerate the gorgeous and fertile darkness from whence the light issues forth. Let us build of ourselves vessels of sound, prayer, craft, and lore that we can become a bridge between the eternal and the mortal. The drum at the prow is the heart, the mast the spine, and the helm the mind, but ever the wind in our sails is the breath of the divine.

You are invited to bring alive the mythos of your soul not as an independent nebula floating in the void, but instead, deeply immersed in the living knotwork of life. You are charged with writing the autobiography of your life. The guardians of Ireland, the *sídhe*, are calling you to tell the story of the Blessed Realm through your lens. They have been calling to you throughout your entire life via your own personal *aislingí*—asking you to play your part in the creation and management of the harmonic symphony of life. They are calling to you to be an emissary of the living light of the eternal.

◇◇◇◇◇◇◇◇◇◇◇◇◇◇

6 The *Sons of Tuireann* comes from *Oidheadh Chlainne Tuireann*, the Irish title for the prose narrative of the Mythological Cycle known in English as *The Tragic Story of the Children of Tuireann* or *The Fate of the Children of Tuireann*; The *Tuatha Dé Danann* were a tribe of pseudo-mythological beings introduced later, and spoken of frequently, in this work.

May the living Light of Erin ever find a home in your heart. May you remember the immortal song of your heritage. May the ancient forests of yesteryear, today, and tomorrow—that are just around the mountain, a thousand miles away, and in your backyard—stir your memories lived and those yet to be. May you remember the *sídhe* in the temple of your soul. May you ever climb the divine—above, below, and within—bringing the fruits of your abundance to the hungry, rich soil to the ungrounded, and strength of limb to the weary. May you climb a Mystery every day and always find your way home to the sweet Summerlands.

IRELAND'S MYTHOLOGICAL AND HISTORICAL CONTEXT

Chapter One

IRISH MYTHOLOGICAL CYCLE PRIMER

Before we climb anything, albeit a mystery, a tree, scaffolding, a ladder, or a long set of stairs through the rainbow castle of our souls, the most important thing is to make sure that we have a sturdy structure to climb. In what substrate is this tree, this mystery of our heritage, rooted? Before we climb, let us smell the soil and identify the mineral rocks that sustain the life of the tree and enable it to weather any raging storm that is thrown at Erin's shores. Dive in and explore the power of the roots with me. Track with me Ireland's story across time. This is an invitation to better understand the majesty of the beautiful path before us. Do not worry. We will not get lost in the weeds of mental tomfoolery—yet, respectfully, we will honor the acumens of our cultural heritage as it has been passed down to us over the millennia. We will infuse ourselves with the essence of the Irish-Celtic heritage via a sweet hazelnut collected from an ancient hazel hanging heavy with nuts over a bubbling spring on Connla's hill or near Nectain's lair. Let the hazelnut feed the fire in the head, our *ímbas,* illuminate the pathway and bring our eyes to the crucial branching of the roots that give the Irish heritage its beautiful, restorative, and steadfast nature.

Let us initiate our journey through time at the beginning of the Irish archives with an overview of Ireland's main settlements and invasions over time. This can be studied in great detail in the *Irish*

Book of Invasions or *Lebor Gabála Érenn*.[7] Ireland, a fairly remote island compared to the cradle of Western civilization around the Mediterranean Sea, has been settled by a series of cultural invasions since the end of the last ice age, largely catalyzed by prehistoric global climate change. This is a scientifically proven global phenomenon. In the first 4,500 years of the Holocene epoch, entire sections of most continents were lost due to sea level rise, and in Europe, the "sinking" of what is known as "Doggerland" underneath the North Sea, as well as massive swaths of lowlands under what are now the English Channel and the Irish Sea, created islands of much of what we now know as the British Isles and Ireland.[8] Modern antiquarians, scientists, journalists, and New Age philosophers believe a great maritime civilization was lost during the flood that resulted due to global climate change.[9] The prehistoric "invasions" of Ireland likely correspond with the loss of the rich forests, farmlands, and this lost "Atlantean" civilization due to the slow inundation of the land by rising sea levels over thousands of years. People needed somewhere to go. This phenomenon of flooding can be viewed in Figure 1.

After the conclusion of the last major ice age 12,000 YBP (years before present), or 10,000 BC, Doggerland was a vast heartland of lowland forest and wetlands across northern Europe. All in all, a lot of land was lost, and people were on the move looking for a new home. Most readers will be familiar with the lost island of Atlantis. While Atlantis is not directly part of the Irish story per se, it is believed by many in the Avalon traditions that the Mysteries of the druids were the encoding of this greater maritime civilization prior to the flood. They were tasked with guarding the wisdom of this ancient civilization before it was buried beneath the waves. The Brittonic-Celtic Otherworld is often correlated with Avalon, while the Irish-Celtic Otherworlds

◇◇◇◇◇◇◇◇◇◇◇◇◇◇◇

7 R.A. Stewart Macalister, *Lebor Gabála Érenn* (Irish Texts Society, 1938–1956).

8 David Cabot, *Ireland: A Natural History* (HarperCollins, 1999); The Holocene is the current geological epoch. It began approximately 11,650 years before the present, after the last glacial period, which concluded with the Holocene glacial retreat followed by the slow sinking of Doggerland.

9 Graham Hancock, *Fingerprints of the Gods* (Penguin Random House, 1995).

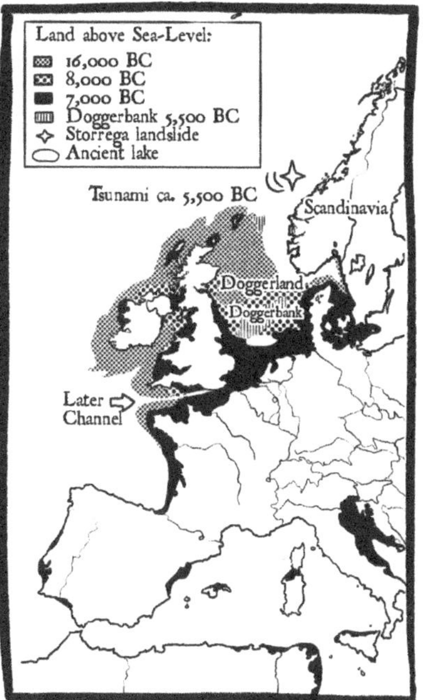

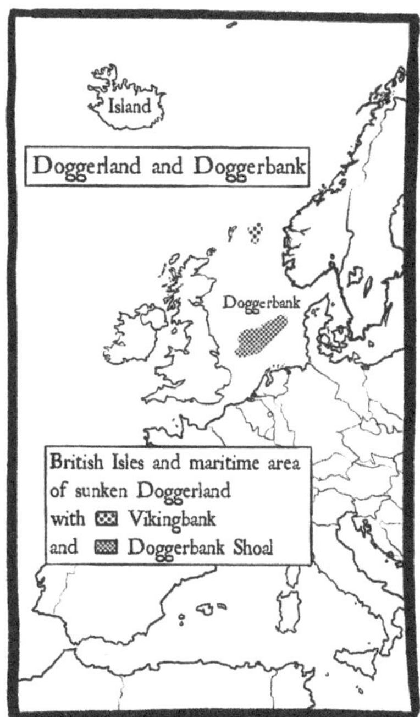

Figure 1: The Sinking of Doggerland

Figure 1: The Sinking of Doggerland

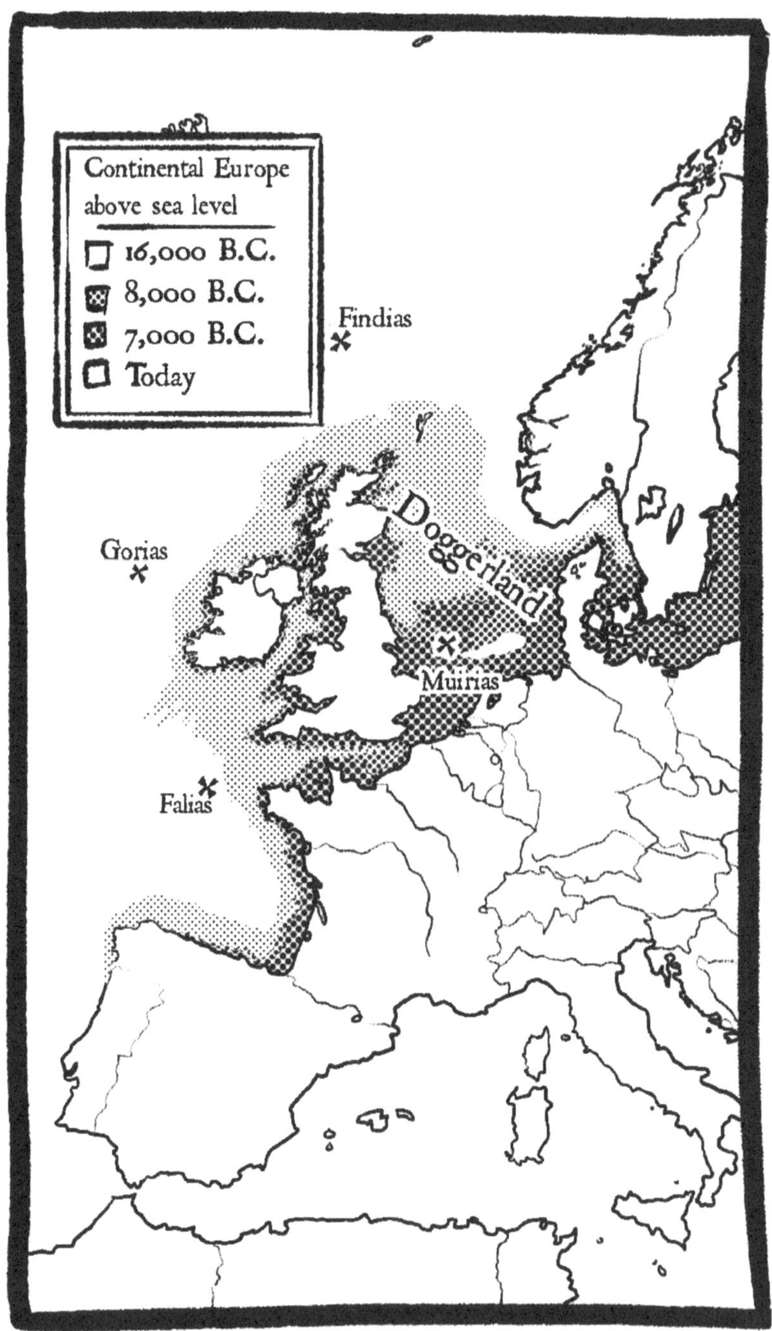

Figure 2 Pre-Diluvian Cities Projections

of *Tír na nÓg* and *Tír fo Thuinn* (among other names) are reflections of this high, pre-Diluvian civilization (Figure 2) contained in the mythological archives of the Celtic worldview. The Greeks, by way of Plato, called this land "Atlantis," while archaeologists call the lands inundated by rising sea levels in northern Europe "Doggerland."

The Irish have close ties with several ancient cities that are now "beneath the sea," and received four legendary treasures via the *Tuatha Dé Danann* from these four cities respectively. From the *Lebor Gabála Érenn*, we know of a great white fortress or city that was once found to the north called *Findias.* Knowing that there was not much to the north of Ireland during the ice age, it makes you wonder if this "bright white fort," as it translates, was built into the very heart of the glacier or upon any of the northern islands inundated by ice and no longer found above sea level. From Findias, our treasure is *Claíomh Solais,* or the Nuada's Sword of Light.

Found to the east of Ireland, which would be in the direction of Doggerland proper, was the great island city of Muirias or the "fort of the sea," as the name translates. As sea levels rose, Doggerland gave way to the North Sea, and an island formed. We call it "Doggerbank" now (though it, too, is now beneath the North Sea), and it was still a huge island 7,500 YBP.[10] Prior to the rest of Doggerland and Doggerbank being inundated, Muirias may have been similar to many of the cities in the Swiss Alps—near a large lake surrounded by mountains. Naturally, the inhabitants would have begun to search for something a little more promising for long-term habitation to sustain their culture. It also happens that this period corresponds with the same antiquity as the first archaeological remains found in Ireland in the Sligo region and around Lough Gur in County Leinster. From Muirias, the treasure brought to Ireland was *Coire Ansic,* or the Dagda's Cauldron of Plenty.

The third city beneath the waves was Falias, or the "city of the gods" found to the south of Ireland. This city also seems to have played a crucial role in Irish evolution, both in history and prehistory. From Falias, the Stone of Destiny (*Lia Fáil*), the most important of the four legendary

---

10 Benjamin Kessler et al., *Doggerland—The Europe That Was* (National Geographic Society, 2023).

treasures of Ireland, was brought to the Hill of Tara. *Lia Fáil* was said to roar or scream with joy when the rightful High King of Ireland put his feet on it.

The fourth and final city, Gorias, to the west, can be geophysically associated with Hy-Brasil. The island or island group of Hy-Brasil is often cited as the source of much of Connacht's mysterious druidic knowledge, where even in the sixteenth century, learned Irish scholars still received in-depth learning from the residents of Gorias at Hy-Brasil.[11] Hy-Brazil was identified for centuries with the modern islands of Terceira or Flores in the Portuguese Azores. Modern studies as well as nineteenth-century expeditions off of the west coast of Ireland now associate Porcupine Bank, a shoal in the Atlantic Ocean west of Ireland, with Hy-Brasil. Similar to Doggerbank, this shoal now sits 200 meters below sea level, indicating that prior to 7,500 YBP, Porcupine Bank was a cluster of islands at least 100 meters above sea level.[12] Gorias translates to "the burning fort," perhaps in respect to the setting sun. From Gorias comes *Gáe Assail*, the Spear of Destiny, or the Spear of Lugh, which is said to be unvanquishable.

The Five Prehistoric Invasions of Ireland

In the Celtic tradition, there is no creation story. Some believe that perhaps it has been lost over the eons. Others believe that perhaps it has yet to be rediscovered within the archives of thousands upon thousands of ancient Irish scrolls and texts waiting to be translated from Old Irish and Latin into modern languages.[13] I believe none of it. The Celts do not have a creation story because we know that we have always been here and there never was a beginning. The universe is constantly creating, destroying, and recreating itself through the dynamic birth and death of all things passing on and changing forms.

---

11 O'Lee, *The Book of O'Lees (Book of Hy-Brasil)*, or *Leabhar Mhuintir Laidhe nó Leabhar Ua mBreasail* (Collections at the Royal Irish, Fifteenth Century AD).

12 Justin Winsor (1889), W. Frazer (1883), and P. Shannon, et al. (2001).

13 Ella Young's telling of the Celtic creation myth in her *Celtic Wonder-Tales* is a gorgeous recreation of Celtic creation lore.

The world, or more specifically, Ireland, was always here and the Celts immigrated as needed. The mythology of the invasions of Ireland states that, before the Celts, there were five waves of invaders or settlements. Each had a profound effect on the land and mythology. Some believe that the predecessors to the Celts came from another star system in spaceships, or rode into this world on the backs of dragons or cloud eagles. The *Tuatha Dé Danann* are said in the *Lebor Gabála Érenn* to have resided in "the northern islands of the world"—at the four cities described above—where they were instructed in the magical arts, before finally riding on dark clouds to Connacht in the west of Ireland to settle and conquer those that came before them.[14] Let us take a look at the first five invasions of Ireland.

Five successive groups of invaders are said to have arrived in Ireland before the present-day Celts arrived in the sixth century BC. The first three groups are known by the names of their respective leaders and the last two by the names of the races involved. These five invaders were:

1. Cessair
2. Partholón
3. Nemed
4. The *Fir Bolg*
5. The *Tuatha Dé Danann*

Let us look at their stories.

First Invasion—The Arrival of Cessair and Her Cohort of Women

The first invasion was that of Cessair, a woman who arrived with mainly female companions before the great flood. The flood is considered to be the same as the flood in *The Tora* or *The Old Testament*. She was said to be a granddaughter of Noah and he, with his inside information, warned her of what God had up his sleeve for the wicked people of this world. She fled to Ireland because, "She thought it probable that

[14] R.A. Stewart Macalister (1938–1956), Alexei Kondratiev (1999), Tom Cowan (1993), and Steve Blamires (2012).

a place where people had never come before, and where no evil or sin had been committed, and which was free from the world's reptiles and monsters, that place would be free from the Flood."[15]

Either way, it is likely that the Noah bit was added in to connect the Irish to Canaan of old, but then again, who knows? More than likely, Cessair and her cohort of women came from Doggerland—an area threatened by rising sea levels. In approximately 6225–6170 BC, three massive submarine landslides took place, likely catalyzed by earthquakes at the edge of Norway's continental shelf. The collapse involved an estimated 180-mile (290 km) length of coastal shelf, with a total volume of 840 cubic miles (3,500 km^3) of debris collapsing into the ocean, which caused a powerful paleotsunami in the North Atlantic Ocean.[16] It sounds to me like a woman of high stature; priestess, queen, demi-god, or oracle had a clear vision that flood was coming and gathered up a group of her best priestesses and headed to Ireland. Let us go further into her story from the *Lebor Gabála Érenn*:[17]

> *"She arrived forty days before the deluge, but two of her three ships were wrecked and she eventually came ashore at Corca Dhuibhne which is the Dingle Peninsula in County Kerry, Ireland. The total crew of the ship that survived was fifty women and three men. These men were Cessair's father Bith, son of Noah; Ladra the pilot of the ship; and Fionntán. They are also credited with bringing the first sheep to Ireland and perhaps settling around Lough Gur. Cessair divided the women amongst the men. Among Fionntán's women was Cessair herself. The other two men soon died, as it is said, of excess of women. Fionntán, horrified at the prospect of having to see to the ministrations of fifty women on his own, fled the*

15 R.A. Stewart Macalister, *Lebor Gabála Érenn* (Irish Texts Society, 1938–1956) 202-203.

16 Alastair G. Dawson, et al., "Reconciling Storegga Tsunami Sedimentation Patterns with Modelled Wave Heights: A Discussion" *Shetland Isles Field Laboratory, Sedimentology, International Association of Sedimentologists*, vol. 67, issue 3, 2020, pp. 1344–1353.

17 As translated by R.A. Stewart Macalister (1941), *Lebor Gabála Érenn*, Chapters 26–29, and interpreted by Steve Blamires.

scene. Cessair consequently died of a broken heart and soon after all the other women died too, leaving Fionntán all alone in this new country.

Fionntán, the sole survivor of Cessair's expedition, lived to be 5,500 years old and during these long years he took on various forms including that of a salmon, an eagle, and a hawk. During his various shape-shiftings he witnessed all the great events that took place in Ireland and he passed on this knowledge to the historians before he eventually died. That is why we know of Cessair and her companions and all of the many events that took place long before writing came to Ireland's shores."

So much for the first invasion and the conquest of Ireland! It sounds like the women's enclave overwhelmed their seed bank before they could settle. And, we have also the first hint of longevity due to withholding by Fionntán as later discovered by the Chinese in their Taoist sexual practices.

Second Invasion—The Arrival of Partholón of Greece

Ireland then lay in a purely wild state for several hundred years after Cessair and her companions died, while Fionntán explored his capabilities of withholding and shapeshifting, becoming the ancient derivation of the *Fír Uaine*, the Irish Greenman. Eventually, a Greek named Partholón arrived with his followers. *Partholón* is a corruption of the original form of the name *Bartholomaeus* which was said to mean "son of him who stayed the waters," and consequently, he is associated with the post-deluge invasion of Ireland—whereas Cessair was the pre-flood invader. More specifically, his arrival in Ireland is associated with the period around 5300 BC which correlates with further sea level rise and land loss in Doggerland, Canaan, Italy, and Greece.

According to the *Lebor Gabála Érenn,* Partholón fled Greece after killing his father and mother in an unsuccessful attempt to take kingship from his brother.[18] After seven years of wandering, he arrived in Ireland with his wife, three sons, and their wives. Of Partholón's three sons, it

---

[18] R.A. Stewart Macalister, *Lebor Gabála Érenn* (Irish Texts Society, 1938–1956) 253–273.

is said that Beoil made the first guesthouse in Ireland, Brea instituted cooking and dueling, and that Malaliach was the first brewer who made ale from alder. Partholón also brought with him four oxen which were thus the first domesticated cattle to be brought to Ireland. At the time he and his followers arrived in this Ireland, there was only one clear plain (field) across the entire island, so they set about making more room for themselves and cleared another four plains (which became the classic "fields" or kingdoms of Ireland—Ulster, Leinster, Munster, Connacht). At this stage in ecological history, Ireland was otherwise completely covered with forests and was much less rainy than it is today.

After only thirty years in Ireland, Partholón eventually died. His survivors and descendants continued to inhabit the country for a further 520 years, by which time they numbered over 9,000 inhabitants.[19]

They were all overtaken by a plague; however, and all died "between two Mondays in May." All, that is, except a character called Tuán mac Cairill, a son of Partholón's brother Starn. He seems to have been very similar in nature to Cessair's Fionntán in that he too lived for a very long time and took on various forms, including a salmon, a stag, a boar, and an eagle (which also happen to be the four most important animals to the Irish-Celts, corresponding with the four kingdoms). Perhaps he ran into Fionntán in the extensive forests of Ireland, apprenticed with him, and decided that conjoining the shapeshifter of Ireland was the way.

And so, this is how the second illustrious invasion came to an end with a bit of a successful human establishment occurring. Ireland now also has sheep, oxen, and a couple of shapeshifting demigods roaming the countryside.

Third Invasion—Nemed's Temptation and Eventual Invasion of Ireland

A settlement that took place between the invasions of Partholón and Nemed is not held as important to the historical narrative other than in regard to the arrival of a supernatural race of primordial beings known as the *Fomors* or the *Fomoire* (similar to the *Jötunn* of Norse mythology).

[19] R.A. Stewart Macalister, *Lebor Gabála Érenn* (Irish Texts Society, 1938–1956) 253–273.

Did Fionntán and Tuán invite them in or sire them from wild beasts? The *Fomors* are often portrayed as hostile and monstrous beings who come from the sea or underground. Later, they were portrayed as giants and sea raiders. Either way, the source of their arrival in the country is unknown and, from my perspective, makes the coming story the first true invasion of Ireland, as prior to that, no invasions occurred, just settlements.

Nemed, which is an old Celtic word for "a holy or sacred place"—thus giving him druidical connections—arrived thirty years after Partholón's people had been wiped out by the plague. He had a fleet of numerous ships that set forth from their great isle (perhaps Muirias on Doggerbank before it slipped under the sea), but on their journey, they came across a tower of gold in the sea (perhaps the remains of Gorias).[20] Greedy for the gold, they went to take the tower, but the sea rose in a great torrent and swept them all away except for one ship. The ship that was saved was Nemed's own, and onboard the vessel was his wife Macha, his four sons, their wives, and twenty other people. After a year and a half of wandering, they eventually landed in Ireland (giving them enough time to breed a small army onboard).

By the time Nemed and his immigrants had arrived, Ireland was already the home base of the *Fomors*. After three great battles, Nemed and his faction defeated them and built himself a strong fort in the south of Armagh. Nemed eventually died from the plague and the *Fomors* returned and imposed heavy taxes on his survivors. After a while, the survivors of Nemed's original people decided they had had enough of the *Fomor's* oppression, and they staged a revolt. They put up a good fight but were eventually overpowered. Only one ship managed to escape from Ireland with a crew of thirty warriors aboard, sailing back to what was left of Muirias on Doggerbank, and some then set off to the Mediterranean.

According to tradition, later groups of settlers in Ireland were descended from these fleeing warriors. One grandson of Nemed's, Semeon, went to Greece where his progeny later became the *Fir Bolg;* another grandson, Beothach, fathered the race that would become the *Tuatha Dé Danann.* and one of his sons, Fearghus Leathdearg,

---

20 R.A. Stewart Macalister, *Lebor Gabála Érenn* (Irish Texts Society, 1938–1956) Chapters 39–47.

went to Britain and fathered the race that would later be known as the *Brittonic Celts.*

So ends the third invasion, swept over by the primordial *Fomors* and sent packing back to Doggerbank, the Mediterranean, or both. Something must be done as the last bastion of Doggerland is being inundated by sea levels rising and no one seems to be able establish themselves in Ireland.

Fourth Invasion—The Fir Bolg Immigrate to Ireland from Greece

The word *fir* in Irish means "men" and the Irish word *bolg* means "belly" or "bag," so the name *Fir Bolg* may mean "Men of the Bag" or "Men of the Belly" and there are various legends explaining how they got this curious name. One legend says that while in Greece, they were under bondage to the Greeks and were forced to carry good soil to the high places and infertile regions in order to make Greece more suitable for agricultural development. They moved this good earth around in large leather bags and hence earned the name "Men of the Bags." Another tradition claims that while in Greece, they carried with them little bags containing soil from Ireland which had the effect of warding off the numerous poisonous snakes and reptiles which they encountered in Greece. Another meaning of the word *bolg* is "spear." It could be the *Fir Bolg* means "Men of the Spear" or "spear-throwing warriors." This, to me, seems much more likely, especially as in one later legend, specific mention is made of their very effective spear utilization.

When the *Fir Bolg* arrived in Ireland, which was mostly destitute of people, five brothers divided the land amongst them, and this explains the five-fifths of Ireland (Ulster, Leinster, Munster, Connacht, and Meath). It is also said that during their captivity in Greece, they became very numerous and split into three main sections including the *Fir Bolg* proper, the *Gaileoin*, and the *Fir Domhnann.*[21] According to tradition, the *Gaileoin* got their name, which means "Javelins of Wounding," from the two words *gai,* a javelin, and *leoin*, to wound, because they dug the hard

[21] R.A. Stewart Macalister, *Lebor Gabála Érenn* (Irish Texts Society, 1938–1956) IV.

clay of Greece with these short stabbing javelins. The *Fir Domhnann* are purportedly named after the depth of the clay they had heaped on the bare Greek rocks while performing their involuntary services. In Irish, the word for "deep" is *domhain,* which shares a similar root, *dumno,* which means both "deep" and "the world," with *Fir Domhnann*—to the "Deep Men" or "World Men."[22]

In reality, we can compare these mythical peoples with actual, known Celtic tribes. The *Fir Bolg* would appear to have been the Belgae people who occupied modern-day Belgium and parts of southern Britain. Perhaps instead of Greece, the descendants of Nemed who fled from the *Fomorians* settled in modern Flanders looking for the remnants of Doggerbank.[23] The *Gaileoin* group is associated with the *Laighin,* the main tribe of present-day Leinster.[24] The *Fir Domhnann* were the tribe who occupied vast parts of Britain and Western Europe.[25] Even at these early stages, we are able to identify elements amongst the mythology that are confirmed by history and the archaeological record.

Unfortunately, the *Fir Bolg* were only allowed stress-free possession of Ireland for thirty-seven years before the *Tuatha Dé Danann* invaded and drove them out to Islay, Rathlin, the Isle of Mann, and Arran. Much later, the Picts drove them out of Scotland, and they ended up back in Ireland. And so ends the fourth mythological invasion.

Fifth Invasion—The Invasion of the Tuatha Dé Danann

This last wave of pseudo-mythological invaders, the *Tuatha Dé Danann,* are the most interesting from a mythological point of view. It is largely members of this mysterious race who make up the Irish-Celtic pantheon. The meaning of their name is open to interpretation, although it is

[22] P.W. Joyce, *The Origin and History of Irish Names of Places Vol. 1–3.* 6th ed., (M.H. Gill & Son, 1893).

[23] John T. Koch, *Celtic Culture: A Historical Encyclopedia* (ABC-Clio, 2006) 749–750.

[24] T. F. O'Rahilly, *Early Irish History and Mythology* (Dublin Institute for Advanced Studies, 1946).

[25] John T. Koch, *Celtic Culture: A Historical Encyclopedia* (ABC-Clio, 2006).

most commonly given as "the people of the goddess Danu," or more specifically "the tribe of the goddess Danu." The word *tuatha* means "people" or "tribe," though specifically, it refers to rustic people. It is the root of the word *tuath*, from which the present-day Irish words for "lay person" or "rural/farmer" are derived, specifically a countryman, *fear tuaithe*.[26] *Tuatha* also means "north," and in the main legend dealing with the arrival of the *Tuatha Dé Danann* in Ireland, *"Cath Maige Tuired"* or the Battle of Moytura, it is specifically stated that they came from the north. The *Tuatha Dé Danann* also went on to further clear some of the extensive forests of Ireland and thus expand the agricultural potential of the island.

Danann refers to Danu and *Dé* is the Irish genitive singular word for "god," though it literally means "smoke" or "breath"—the People of the Breath of Danu.[27] It was this same goddess who gave her name to the Danube River and the country of Denmark. The Celtic people are known to originate from the headwaters of the Danube in the Alps (Hallstatt and La Tène cultures), so it would make sense that these invaders, the predecessors of the Celts, would be known as the "people of the goddess," the river of Danu, from whence they came.[28] In addition, all of the Irish-Celtic deities had specific functions and associations and one of Danu's main associations was with craftsmanship and artistic ability. Because a deity's name was often interchangeable with their function, it may well be that *Tuatha Dé Danann* means the "people of the goddess of craftsmanship" or, to put it a bit more simply, "the Artistic People." Judging by the amazing Celtic artifacts and works of art in the form of jewelry and intricately prepared weapons, the Celts were certainly an artistic and highly flourishing people. Like many languages, elements of all of these various scholarly interpretations hold true. I am of the People of the Breath of the Goddess Danu, renowned for our Artistic Craft and Mysteries: *Tuatha Dé Danann.*

◇◇◇◇◇◇◇◇◇◇◇◇◇◇

[26] Niall O'Donaill, *Focloir Gaeilge-Bearla/Irish-English Dictionary* (Oifig an tSolathair, 1977).

[27] Ibid.

[28] Eugene O'Curry, *On the Manners and Customs of the Ancient Irish* (Williams and Norgate,1873); J. Collis, *The Celts: Origins, Myths and Inventions* (Tempus Publishing Ltd., 2003).

The Arrival of the Celts: The Milesians

It seems most likely to me that the arrival of the Celts in Ireland and the British Isles came in waves, partly due to the inundation of many of the fertile lands in Doggerland that had been sustaining them for thousands of years. The colonization by Cessair, Partholón, the *Fomors*, Nemed, the *Fir Bolg*, and the *Tuatha Dé Danann* were merely the first waves. The *Fir Bolg*, the primordial *Fomors*, and the *Tuatha Dé Danann* happened to be the only ones who were successful in landing, settling, and establishing long-term residency status. The accepted, officially Irish-Celtic academically-stamped arrival of the Celts or Gaels[29] in Ireland is set around the same time as the first golden age of the Celts in Europe, the La Tène and Hallstatt cultures, or between 600–450 BC. The Celts arrived to find thousands of megalithic structures (cairns, stone circles, portals, henges, court cairns, etc.) already in place, long before built by the *Tuatha Dé Danann* and their forebearers.

The arrival of the Celts is placed into a nice biblical context to tie the heritage of the Irish with that of the Abrahamic traditions of Canaan.[30] Whether this is accurate to the telling, we may never know. The theory seems to carry some grain of truth, as does any myth. Yet, it also seems likely that as the *Tuatha Dé Danann* are related to the Celts: there was likely trade between the people as well as marriages, and again, global climate change and growing populations encouraged people to migrate to Ireland. [31] Or perhaps even deeper, Ireland herself was ushering forth a calling…a calling to come home to Ireland. For Ireland is truly the last bastion of all things Celtic and in ancient times, was the end of the known world to most of the world's populations. But let us tell the story of the invasion of the Celts.

Doggerland, and its remains of Doggerbank, were long under the waves when the Celts answered the call of Ireland. The Sons of Mil, or the Milesians, what the *Lebor Gabála Érenn* refers to the Celtic people as, purportedly arrived in Ireland from the northwest of Spain in present

29 *Gael* in Old Irish was borrowed from an archaic Welsh word *guoidel*, meaning "forest people," "wild men," or, later, "warriors."

30 R.A. Stewart Macalister, *Lebor Gabála Érenn* (Irish Texts Society, 1938–1956).

31 Ella Young and Maude Gonne, *Celtic Wonder-Tales* (Maunsel & Company, Ltd., 1910).

day Galicia.[32] After many adventures and battles, they eventually took possession of it from the defeated *Tuatha Dé Danann*. The Sons of Mil are said to be the forefathers of the Gaelic people, both Irish and Scottish, and their descendants are therefore technically still in charge of Ireland.

Mil's full name was *Míl Espáine* which simply means "soldier of Spain" in Latin.[33] This association with Spain is attributed to the fact that the Celts had settled far into the west of Europe.[34] The story of Mil's arrival in Ireland, or strictly speaking, his son's arrival, is also told in the *Lebor Gabála Érenn*.

According to the ancient Irish myth so eloquently revealed in *Lebor Gabála Érenn*, the people of Scythia were descended from Noah's son, Japheth, and one of their members was Fenius the Ancient, who was amongst the architects who built the Tower of Babel.[35] Fenius was also a great linguist and when the languages were separated by God, he alone retained knowledge of them all. His grandson was called *Gaedheal Glas*, and he fashioned the Irish language out of the seventy-two languages in existence. Gaedheal and his descendants lived in Egypt and Gaedheal himself was friends with Moses. According to one story, Moses saved Gaedheal's life after he had been bitten by a serpent by touching the affected part with his staff. The skin turned green at this place and hence his name *Gaedheal Glas* which means "green." Moses also then proclaimed that Gaedheal would forever be safe from serpents, and in whichever land he finally settled, there would be no serpents there to molest him or his descendants.[36]

After many years and different adventures, the descendants of Gaedheal left Egypt and traveled around the Mediterranean Sea for a long time before they arrived in Spain which they subjugated by force. Their king at that time, Breoghan, built a great tower to protect their newly acquired territory and, one clear evening, his son Ith saw Ireland from that tower.

32 R.A. Stewart Macalister, *Lebor Gabála Érenn* (Irish Texts Society, 1938–1956); Annette M.B Meakin, *Galecia: The Switzerland of Spain* (Methuen & Co. 1909).

33 William Gunn and John Allen Giles, *Historia Brittonum* (1848).

34 Annette M.B Meakin, *Galecia: The Switzerland of Spain* (Methuen & Co. 1909).

35 R.A. Stewart Macalister, *Lebor Gabála Érenn* (Irish Texts Society, 1938–1956).

36 R.A. Stewart Macalister, *Lebor Gabála Érenn* (Irish Texts Society, 1938–1956).

Mil was Breoghan's grandson, and he left Spain curious to learn about his ancestors' homes of Scythia and Egypt. His first wife died in Scythia, but when he was in Egypt, he remarried the pharaoh's daughter who was called Scota.[37] It was she who gave her name to the tribe who later became the Scots.[38] Between Mil's two wives, he fathered no less than thirty-two sons. Eight of these sons, Eibhear, Amhairghin, Glungheal, Ir, Colptha, Erannan, Donn, and Eireamhoin later play an important part in the taking and naming of Ireland from the *Tuatha Dé Danann.*

Receiving word of his uncle's vision from the tower, Mil set sail for Ireland but stopped on the way in Spain and, unfortunately, was killed before he had a chance to resume his journey. Meanwhile, Ith had already set sail for Ireland and landed with his party just as the kings of the *Tuatha Dé Danann* were holding a counsel to determine how best to divide the land amongst themselves.

Ith came up with a suggestion which, on the surface, seemed very fair but on his way back to his boats, the *Tuatha Dé Danann* became suspicious of his motives and killed him. His followers returned to Spain and allied with the Sons of Mil to return to Ireland and take it by force.[39]

As the Sons of Mil approached Ireland, Erannan climbed the mast to have a better look at the Emerald Isle, fell, and was killed. Another of Mil's sons, Ir, rowed ahead but his oar broke; he fell backward into the sea and drowned. Finally, the remaining Sons of Mil landed at *Inbhear Sceine* (Kenmare Bay in County Kerry) and Amhairghin was the first to set foot on Irish soil after his famous oration known in English as the *Song of Amergin.*[40] The Sons of Mil encountered the three *Tuatha Dé Danann* goddesses Banba, Fódla, and Eriu, each of whom asked that Ireland be named after her in turn. This was granted and then the Sons of Mil met the respective husbands of the triple goddess, whose names were MacCuill, Mac Ceacht, and Mac Gréine (which means "son of Áine," the sun goddess).[41]

37 R.A. Stewart Macalister, *Lebor Gabála Érenn* (Irish Texts Society, 1938–1956).

38 Joseph Lennon, *Irish Orientalism: A Literary and Intellectual History* (Syracuse University Press, 2004).

39 R.A. Stewart Macalister, *Lebor Gabála Érenn* (Irish Texts Society, 1938–1956).

40 Lady Gregory, *Gods and Fighting Men* (John Murray Publishing, 1904).

41 James MacKillop, *A Dictionary of Celtic Mythology* (Oxford University Press, 2004).

These three gods asked that they be allowed to keep the kingship of Ireland for a mere three days more and that during that time, the sons of Mil should return to their ships and wait off the Irish coast at a distance of nine waves.[42] The Sons of Mil agreed to this, but while sitting out in their ships, the *Tuatha Dé Danann* druids caused a great storm to spring up, which swept them further out to sea. The ships were in danger of being swamped until Amhairghin sang a magic verse which calmed the seas, and they were able to return.[43] In a fit of anger, Donn threatened to kill everyone in Ireland once they arrived there and, at this, the wind blew up again and he and his brother, Aireach, were drowned. The surviving Sons of Mil eventually landed in Ireland at the Boyne estuary and after a great battle against the *Tuatha Dé Danann* at Tailtiu (Teltown in County Meath), the Sons of Mil were victorious. From the remaining Sons of Mil, it is claimed, are descended the present-day inhabitants of Ireland and Scotland, known collectively as the Gaels.

The magic song which Amhairghin sang to calm the waves is very similar to the shapeshifting tales recounted by Fionntán (from Cessair's immigration party) and Tuán (from Parthalon's immigration party). Shapeshifting and weaving the mysteries is thus an integral part of assuming the kingship and sovereignty of Ireland. Lady Gregory's partial translation of this potent song and powerful lorica has come down to us today as follows:

I am the wind on the sea.
I am the wave of the sea.
I am the bull of seven battles.
I am the eagle on the rock.
I am a flash from the sun.
I am the most beautiful of plants.
I am a strong wild boar.

---

42 R.A. Stewart Macalister, *Lebor Gabála Érenn* (Irish Texts Society, 1938–1956).

43 Lady Gregory, *Gods and Fighting Men* (John Murray Publishing, 1904).

I am a salmon in the water.
I am a lake in the plain.
I am the word of knowledge.
I am the head of the spear in battle.
I am the god that puts fire in the head.
Who spreads light in the gathering on the hills?
Who can tell the ages of the moon?
Who can tell the place where the sun rests?[44]

From this amazing diversity of ideas and pseudo-history mingled with known factual history, we can begin to see why Irish mythology is so vast and complex. This brief look at the invasions of the Celtic peoples and the Irish "coming into being" legends should also serve to point out that it is useless to talk in the all-encompassing terms of "the Celts" or "Celtic," as these words must be refined before we can even begin to understand just what people are being referred to and, consequently, which pantheon of deities is involved, which corpus of legends surrounding them, and of course, which magical system is being discussed.

The Historic Invasions

The Celts, in the form of the Sons of Mil, came to Ireland between 600–450 BC and found a well-established culture of Neolithic farmers, aristocracy, druids, and temple builders. The Celts moved in, eventually mixed with the natives (*Fir Bolgs* and *Tuatha Dé Danann*) and became the root of the Irish people as we know them today. Let us review to create some historic context:

1. ***Prehistory (Megalithic/Neolithic Culture)***
   Approx. 6,000 BC–2,500 BC
   Cessair, Partholón, the *Fomors*, and Nemed all settle and begin to change the land, creating megaliths.

[44] Lady Gregory, *Gods and Fighting Men* (John Murray Publishing, 1904).

2. ***Bronze Age (First Golden Age of the Celts)***
   Approx. 2,500 BC–600 BC
   The *Fir Bolgs* and *Tuatha Dé Danann* settle in deeper and add to the complexes of stone and clearing forests.
3. ***Early Iron Age (Celtic Expansion)***
   Approx. 600 BC–AD 400
   The Sons of Mil arrive and claim sovereignty of Ireland, expanding across Ireland until the dawn of the Christian era.
4. ***Iron Age (Multiple Waves of Invasions)***
   Approx. AD 400–1850
   a. "Invasion" of Christianity: Approx. AD 400
   b. Viking Invasions and Settlement: Approx. AD 900–1169
   c. Anglo-Norman Invasion: Approx. AD 1169–present

Of course, Ireland has been able to reclaim her relative sense of freedom from the English crown as of 1917, which also falls under the continual Anglo-Norman Invasion. Typically, this invasion refers to the period of AD 1169–1536.[45]

In 2022, the Republic of Ireland celebrated her first 100 years of freedom since the Anglo-Norman Invasion in the late twelfth century AD.

The Mythological Context

We have summarized the general prehistory and pseudo-history as a way to prepare for the massive, sweeping changes that are felt across Ireland during the Middle Ages, or late Iron Age, as it is often referred to in Irish history. Ireland played a key role in the Dark Ages and is said to have been the "great light in the West" where all manner of knowledge was retained while the rest of Europe grew "dark" (in reference to the global cooling that took place at this time).[46]

[45] Thomas Cahill, *How the Irish Saved Civilization* (Anchor, 1996).

[46] Thomas Cahill, *How the Irish Saved Civilization* (Anchor, 1996).

The various ages of Ireland previously listed can be directly correlated with major periods or cycles of mythology. The classic breakdown of Irish mythology is grouped into four cycles:

1. Mythological Cycle
2. Fenian Cycle
3. Ulster Cycle
4. Cycles of Kings or Historic Cycle

Each of these can be directly associated with an invasion wave, or more specifically, changes in climate, technology, and culture. As each wave of culture with its new technologies immigrated to Ireland, they were smitten by her deep magic, rich ecology, and layered mythology while also bringing their new technologies, tools, and crafts. Each wave also had its mad character (druid, shapeshifter, shaman, wildsoul) that was called to a deeper sense of presence and surrender to the potent currents that flow in and through Ireland.[47] Cessair's lover Fionntán, Partholón's nephew Tuán, Mil's son Amhairghin,[48] and later, Lugh of the *Tuatha Dé Danann*, Fionn mac Cumhaill,[49] and Cú Chulainn[50] were specifically called to give themselves fully to Ireland, as many of her sons and daughters have been called again and again throughout history. Let us not forget Nemed. Though he died in Ireland, his great love for the Emerald Isle was so great that it drew the rest of the immigrants to Ireland over the next three invasions.

[47] Gerard Murphy, *Duanaire Finn: The Book of the Lays of Fionn, Part II* (Simpkin Marshall, 1933); J.G. O'Keefe, *Buile Suibne: The Frenzy of Suibhne, A Middle Irish Romance* (Irish Text Society, 1913).

[48] Lady Gregory, *Gods and Fighting Men* (John Murray Publishing, 1904).

[49] J.G. O'Keefe, *Buile Suibne: The Frenzy of Suibhne, A Middle Irish Romance* (Irish Text Society, 1913).

[50] Eleanor Hull, *Cuchulain: The Hound of Ulster* (George G. Harrap & Co., 1913)

Changes in climate, culture, and technology brought different ways of interacting with the world, with the Mysteries, and with other cultures.[51] That which held power and sway in one cycle may become diminutive in another or gain even more power.

The mythological cycles of Ireland can be thus roughly correlated as such:

Cultural Age	*Approximate Years*	*Mythological Age*
Neolithic Age	6,000–2,500 BC	Early Mythological Cycle
Bronze Age	2,500–600 BC	Mythological Cycle
Early Iron Age	600 BC–AD 400	Fenian Cycle, Ulster Cycle
Late Iron Age	AD 400–1850	Cycles of Kings

Cessair, Partholón, the *Fomors*, and Nemed all settled in Ireland in the broad band of prehistory known as the Neolithic Age, which includes the late Stone Age, the Copper Age, and the early Bronze Age.[52] Many of Ireland's megalithic sites were built during this time, including dolmens, court cairns, and chambered cairns (located at Newgrange, Loughcrew, and Carrowkeel).[53] The powers that seemed to have held sway were

51 Eugene O'Curry, *On the Manners and Customs of the Ancient Irish* (Williams and Norgate, 1873).

52 Jack Roberts, *The Sacred Mythological Centres of Ireland* (Bandia Publishing, 2016).

53 Cary Meehan, *The Traveller's Guide to Sacred Ireland* (Gothic Image Publications, 2002).

primordial—close to the Earth and the human relationship therein. This period of Ireland's history was also much warmer and drier than historic and modern conditions. The warmer and drier climate would have been much more conducive to cereal agriculture, population expansion, and economic growth.[54] The mythology of this period reflects a rather misty sense of the past and magical, almost untouchable realities.

During the lengthy transition of the Neolithic into the Bronze Age, we can track a slow transition of technology and power. This is due in part to the climate remaining mild and the next wave of the invaders (*Fir Bolg* and *Tuatha Dé Danann*) already having some cultural ties to the native inhabitants, though it is often made very clear that the *Fomors* are distinctive and clearly of a different race or culture altogether. This is where the bulk of the greatest stories in the Mythological Cycle emerge. The *Fomors* often overpower the *Tuatha Dé Danann* initially, except when the *Tuatha* utilize their magical implements gathered from the four cities inundated under the Atlantic and the North Sea.[55] The *Fomors*, eventually defeated, retreat to their northern strongholds on islands off the north coast of Ireland.[56] Archaeological evidence, along with some stretching of the imagination, points to the connection between the *Fomors*, the Picts, and the ancestors of the Scandinavians. Who knows? Perhaps the ancient Scandinavians were the evil giants and trolls or the *Fomors*, who battled the *Tuatha Dé Danann*. And vice versa—perhaps the *Tuatha Dé Danann* were the ice giants and trolls (Jötunn) who waged war on the ancient gods of the Norse. Some of the most classic stories from the Mythological Cycle include:

1. The Children of Lir
2. Wooing of Etain
3. The Dream of Aengus
4. First and Second Battles of Moytura (Cath Maige Tuired)

◇◇◇◇◇◇◇◇◇◇◇◇◇◇

54 Peter Wyse Jackson, *Ireland's Generous Nature* (Missouri Botanical Press, 2014); David Cabot, *Ireland: A Natural History* (HarperCollins, 1999).

55 Ella Young and Maude Gonne, *Celtic Wonder-Tales* (Maunsel & Company, Ltd., 1910).

56 Lady Gregory, *Gods and Fighting Men* (John Murray Publishing, 1904).

5. The Curse of the Macha
6. Morrígu and the Dagda—Ride of the Morrígu

During the Bronze Age, we see the tradition of megalith buildings continuing, especially with the explosion of stone circle creation.[57] Most of the stone circles of Ireland were built in the transition period of the Neolithic and well into the Bronze Age. There are more known stone circles in Ireland and Scotland than anywhere else in the world (there are 851 remaining, to be exact).[58] The stone circles are of all different sizes and variations. There are many ideas of what these stone circles' functions were: plotting the stars, the moon, seasons, galactic portals, open-air temples, cemeteries, and so on. Some truth, I am sure, can be found in all of these speculations.

Figure 3: Map of La Tene Cultural Expansion

57 Jack Roberts, *The Sacred Mythological Centres of Ireland* (Bandia Publishing, 2016).

58 Ibid.; Cary Meehan, *The Traveller's Guide to Sacred Ireland* (Gothic Image Publications, 2002).

The end of the Bronze Age (around 600 BC) seems to have coincided not only with the invasion of Ireland by the Sons of Mil but also with the incursion of the technology of iron and a significantly measurable change in global climatic conditions. The global climate change brought wetter and colder conditions to Ireland and most of the Northern Hemisphere, much more akin to what we observe in Ireland today. During this time, the Celtic people in Europe were still thriving in the First Golden Age as the La Tène culture and were making a serious mark on the world—sacking Rome a few times as well as Delphi—mostly through the arts, iron works, precious metals, and more. It is also during this period that most of the continental Celts slowly succumbed to the might of Rome or were absorbed into the Germanic people of the north, as they too were fleeing climate change and seeking a better life further south across the Rhine and Aare Rivers.

In the mythological context, the Bronze Age and early Iron Age stories are my favorite and where some part of my soul resonates deeply in the telling. The infiltration of iron into Irish mythology and culture had a tremendous impact on how the world was viewed by our ancestors. Degraded upland agricultural fields had turned into acidic bogs due to soil exhaustion and the increase in rainfall with climate change. Iron gave inhabitants a more efficient tool for clearing the ancient forests of the lowlands. And for many, this meant growth, while for others, it meant the loss of a way of life. When the Sons of Mil defeated the *Tuatha Dé Danann* at the Plain of Tailtiu, the spirit of the ancient land was chased underground. As it is said in the *Lebor Gabála Érenn*:

> *"After the battle, the* Tuatha Dé Danann *were defeated beyond any hope of recovery. They decided not to stay with the Sons of Mil, who were dividing Ireland in half so that Eremon and Eber Donn could rule it together. Instead of staying where they would have to pay taxes and tributes to the conquerors, they retreated, and shrouded themselves in invisibility, taking all of their magic with them. They took ownership of the hills, the forests and the waterways of Ireland, where they lived forever more. And thus they became the* sídhe.*"*[59]

[59] R.A. Stewart Macalister, *Lebor Gabála Érenn* (Irish Texts Society, 1938–1956).

As Ireland transitioned into the Iron Age and the *Tuatha Dé Danann* moved into the earth, under the sea, and to the Blessed Isles to the west, the narrative of the magical folk begin to change. Many of the stories began to focus on shapeshifting, traveling between worlds, great journeys, interactions of gods and humans, and the courting of humans or demi-gods into the Otherworld, or the land of *sídhe*—the new term for the *Tuatha Dé Danann.*

The stories in the late Bronze Age into the early Iron Age revolve around a hero, Fionn mac Cumhaill, and his warrior druids the *Fianna*. They gathered among them the best of the remaining druids, warriors, healers, and bards, roaming the countryside in pursuit of adventure, quests, and the protection of Ireland, while also training in the above-mentioned arts.

It is believed that if ever Ireland has need of her ancient heroes, Fionn will be one of the first to awaken to defend the country at the sounding of the *Dord Fiann*, the horn of the *Fianna.*[60] Here are some of the classic stories of the Fenian Cycle:

1. Fionn and the Salmon of Knowledge
2. Fionn and Sadbh
3. Fionn and The Giants Causeway
4. Fionn, Diamuid, and Gráinne
5. Oisín in *Tir na nÓg*

With the incursion of the Celtic version of Christianity (by way of Saint Patrick, Saint Secundinus, Colm Cille, and others) into Ireland in the fifth century AD, the stories once again morph and change. The *Tuatha Dé Danann* are no longer just underground or under the sea, but they begin to become more diminutive, further away, and harder to reach as well as sometimes seen as dark or tempting forces...but not too much yet. The forests of Ireland were cleared more in this time, and the matrilineal relationship between family and inheritance was beginning to shift into a patrilineal system. Many of the place names and family names we know to be traditional

[60] J.F. Lynch, "The Legend of Birdhill," *Journal of the Cork Historical and Archaeological Society,* Cork Historical and Archaeological Society, vol II, 1896, p 188.; Ella Young, *The Tangled-Coated Horse and Other Tales* (David McKay Company, Inc. 1967) 73.

Irish names began to emerge or solidify at this time.[61] Stories begin to take on a more human and almost historic context in what is called the *Ulster Cycle* or the *Red Branch Cycle*. Many of these stories revolve around the warriors and druids of Ulster, and in particular, the Hercules-like hero Cú Chulainn.[62] Some of the most important stories from the Ulster Cycle include:

1. The Birth of Cú Chulainn
2. *Táin Bó Cúailnge* or "Cattle Raid of Cooley"
3. The Tragedy of Deirdre
4. The Elopement of Emer
5. Morrígu and Cú Chulainn
6. The Battle of Fergus and Conchobar

As we move into the historic era or the Historic Cycle, the weavings of ancient tales take on an entirely new measure, which often means it was the profession of a druid, bard, and/or priest (a hybrid of all three in one person was often the case) to weave the tales of their benefactors. It was part of the responsibility of the medieval Irish bards to record the history of the family and the genealogy of the king they served. This they did in poems that blended the mythological and the historical to a greater or lesser degree.[63] The resulting stories form what has come to be known as the Historic Cycle, and there are a number of independent groupings. Often, the purpose of these great works was to show that the sovereigns, the patrons of the authors, were somehow tied to both the ancient past as well as having Christian heritage. Here are some of the classics from the early Historic Cycle, or the Cycle of Kings:

1. Cormac Mac Art
2. Conaire Mór
3. Niall of the Nine Hostages
4. Brian Boru (who finally casts off the yoke of the Vikings)

---

61 P.W. Joyce, (1891); Edward MacLysaght, *Irish Families: Their Names, Arms and Origins* (Crown Publishers Inc., 1957).

62 Eleanor Hull, *Cuchulain: The Hound of Ulster* (George G. Harrap & Co., 1913).

63 George Sigerson, *Bards of the Gael and Gall* (T.F. Unwin, 1897).

It was during this period that the Vikings began to invade Ireland and set up colonies along the coast (the Irish tended to live in the central part of Ireland and not as much along the coast).

Figure 4: Viking Settlements in Ireland (c. AD 950)

For the first time, the concentration of secular power began to draw to the coast more than the midlands. The re-emergence of an Irish High King correlated with this period as well, and the story of Brian Boru focuses on the Irish reclamation of power from the *Lochlannach*, or who we know in English as the Norse.[64] However, it was not long after the Irish reclaimed sovereignty from the Norse that the Anglo-Normans invaded from England and Wales by papal decree.[65] Regardless, the Irish had not truly been conquered yet. The priests and bishops of the Celtic and Ionian Church held almost as much power as the Roman Church. Many of them were more druidic and respectful of nature, which is the way of the Celts, as opposed to being subservient to the Bishop of Rome, who tended to be more imperial and secular.

Tales from this period of the Viking invasions and beyond became so convoluted that it is difficult to track them all. On one side, you have high-end and professional bards mastering the weaving of prose and stories of antiquity into a thread or spell in the ancient art of persuasion or marketing. On the other side, there are the cottagers and keepers of deep forest magic whose tales of the Otherworld begin to weave into fragmented or diminutive deities, now seen as faëries and *sídhe,* emerging into the world of humans to meddle and cross-pollinate.

It has been shown that high human civilization has already been achieved at the end of the last ice age.[66] Ireland was settled, first as an extension of Europe as Doggerland, and then, eventually, as an island settled by the Celts and their ancestors (and gods). The ebb and tide of humanity and its interactions with the power and abundance of Ireland is echoed through the mythologies as we know them today, likely containing the essence of the original tales as they were passed down in the oral tradition up into the historic age.

Along the pathway through the scrambled pseudo-historical past shrouded in the mists of mythology, the stories of our ancient past coagulated into the delicious and extensive archives of our Irish heritage that we feast on today in the promulgation of our cultural and natural heritage into the twenty-first century and beyond. You too

◇◇◇◇◇◇◇◇◇◇◇◇◇◇

64 Ella Young, *The Tangled-Coated Horse and Other Tales* (David McKay Company, Inc. 1967); Niall O'Donaill, *Focloir Gaeilge-Bearla/Irish-English Dictionary* (Oifig an tSolathair, 1977).

65 T. F. O'Rahilly, *Early Irish History and Mythology* (Dublin Institute for Advanced Studies, 1946).

66 Graham Hancock, *Fingerprints of the Gods* (Penguin Random House, 1995).

are part of the journey of the renewal of the spirit of Ireland[67]—the ever-regenerating soul of Kathleen ní Houlihan as she strides the hills of Erin and calls her children home to serve the Emerald Isle.[68] Technology helped the various waves of immigrants and conquerors to establish themselves as sovereign, but never without paying respect first to the land and the Goddess in her various forms. The true keepers of the lore, the druids and their predecessors, were shapeshifters whose relationship with the Otherworld left a lasting impression on those who followed them, including the Celtic Church, and even the localized Catholic Church, albeit the Irish version of the Catholic Church was always getting into trouble with Rome historically, hence the papal decree to invade Ireland in the late twelfth century. With the Anglo-Norman invasion of Leinster in 1169, we are left with a map of Ireland that looks something like Figure 5 in 1171.

67 W.B. Yeats, *Cathleen Ni Houlihan* (Shakespeare Head Press, 1911).

68 Maude Gonne-MacBride, *A Servant of the Queen: Reminiscences* (Victor Gollancz, 1938).

Figure 5: Map of Ireland in 1171

Chapter Two
IRISH HISTORICAL PRIMER

In the previous chapter, we took a journey together from the beginning of the Holocene, the end of the last ice age, all the way up to the Viking invasions and the High Kings of Ireland. Here, we begin with the Anglo-Norman invasion of Ireland in 1169 up to the present. The Anglo-Norman invasion is a crucial turning point in the history of Ireland as it begins the intermittent English occupation and the beginnings of the classic Irish struggle for autonomy and freedom under *Sassenach* influence. From the Anglo-Norman invasion on, the histories become so complex that it would truly require an in-depth study or course entirely focused on this part of Ireland's history to truly grasp the complexities. I am going to draw your attention to some key moments and portray an underlying certainty: indigenous people, including the Celts of Ireland, have most often been completely destroyed or enslaved by colonization. Perhaps just as important, indigenous traditions have an allure that draws people to merge with or emulate them which we see throughout Irish history. Through it all, somehow, the Irish have survived and, for the most part, other than some very dark times, as a people and a nation, they have thrived. Here are the crucial events and timeline in the last 800 years of Irish history since the Anglo-Norman invasion:[69]

[69] Most of the following is derived from Seán Duffy, *Atlas of Irish History* (M.H. Gill & Company, 2011) and Thomas Cahill, *How the Irish Saved Civilization* (Anchor, 1996).

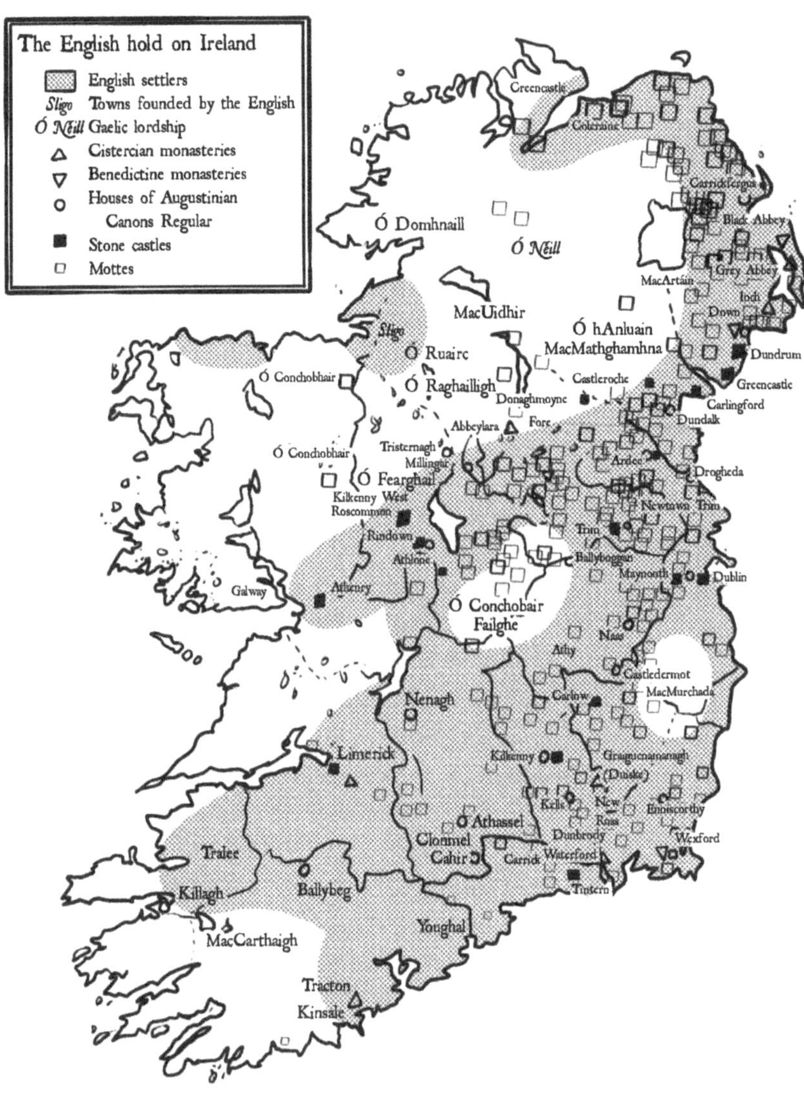

Figure 6: Map of Anglo-Norman influence

1. Anglo-Norman invasion and settlement of Ireland in the late twelfth century (AD 1166–1171)

This began with the expulsion of the King of Leinster (Dermot MacMurrough) from Ireland by the Irish High King in 1166. Dermot was granted permission by the Anglo-Norman King of England to raise forces to retake Leinster, which he did in 1167 at Wexford. Many of those who answered the call were Marcher lords and crusaders returning from Palestine, looking for a new place to settle, including one of my likely distant relatives, Oliver Martin, who arrived in the cohort of Richard "Strongbow" FitzGilbert. By 1171, much of eastern Ireland had been subjugated and brought under the English crown, either through direct conquest or subjugation. To be clear, the High King, Rory O'Connor, never bent his knee to the invaders.

The Normans built walled towns, castles, and churches. They also increased agriculture and commerce in Ireland. The Anglo-Norman invasion was not only an invasion of conquest but an invasion with the purpose of stimulating long-term economic growth and colonization of Ireland. Figure 6 depicts the area of colonial Anglo-Norman influence and the areas still held by the Celtic kings and chieftains. Generally speaking, the Irish resistance in the century after the English arrived was sporadic, uncoordinated, and prompted by local rather than national concerns, but it did ensure the survival of the most important native families, traditions, lore, language, and the Irish-Celtic culture.

2. The Gaelic Revival (end of the twelfth century to end of the fifteenth century)

The greatest threat posed to the English by the Irish was not militaristic but was the Irish-Celtic culture itself. The Anglo-Norman settlers began to identify with the indigenous culture more so than their own English heritage within less than 100 years after the initial invasion and colonization. The adoption of Irish-Celtic traditions became so extensive that legal measures were attempted to thwart the cultural uprising. In 1366, the Statutes of Kilkenny were created in a futile attempt to legally prohibit the English settlers from speaking the Irish language, marrying Irish partners, or fostering their children with Irish families. The educated families of the Irish thrived on this cultural uprising and the abundant economy that came with it, embarking on a 300-year period of tremendous energy in the production of poetry, legal commentaries, medical treatises, genealogy, Irish history, smithcraft, jewelry, and the establishment of Celtic religious centers (monasteries, etc.).

Figure 7 depicts a mountain of information including the effect of the black plague (which arrived in Ireland in 1348), and more importantly, the connection of Irish families with their heritage, lineage traditions, and homes. In essence, this map holds a key to one of the founding principles of the Light of Erin, and the living spirit of Kathleen ní Houlihan. What we are looking at in this map opens a wave of connectivity in conscious thought and tangible history. To be specific, each family had its own lineage-based knowledge to uphold, foster, and ward. Families were keepers of one or two branches of knowledge including law, poetry, martial arts, science, history, music, arts, etc. It was their responsibility to pass on all inherited lore to the next generation.

This is the living cultural tradition of the druids and their ancient oral traditions, drawn forward into the present in a tangible and traceable way. It was the eldest child's duty to increase the economic virility of a family, while it was the second child's duty to carry on the lore or tradition inherent to their particular lineage. For example, it would be my duty as the eldest son to increase the trade and fortunes of my kin, and perhaps to marry the daughter of another lineage holder to increase both family fortunes. I would thus be most focused on the secular, business, and trade elements of life. My brother would then be tasked in this life to become the inherited lore and tradition carrier, and myself to philanthropically support him and the lineage. He would thus dive into one of these professional lines with my family's patronage. During this Gaelic Revival in Ireland, his choices would be based on what our family lineage was, such as a poet/musician (bard), a law keeper, physician, ecologist, geologist, or perhaps a monk or bishop. My Irish heritage—the Kilmartins, Martins, Gilmartins (as Anglesized) through my mother's line—were primarily druids, bards, and (later) monks and bishops.

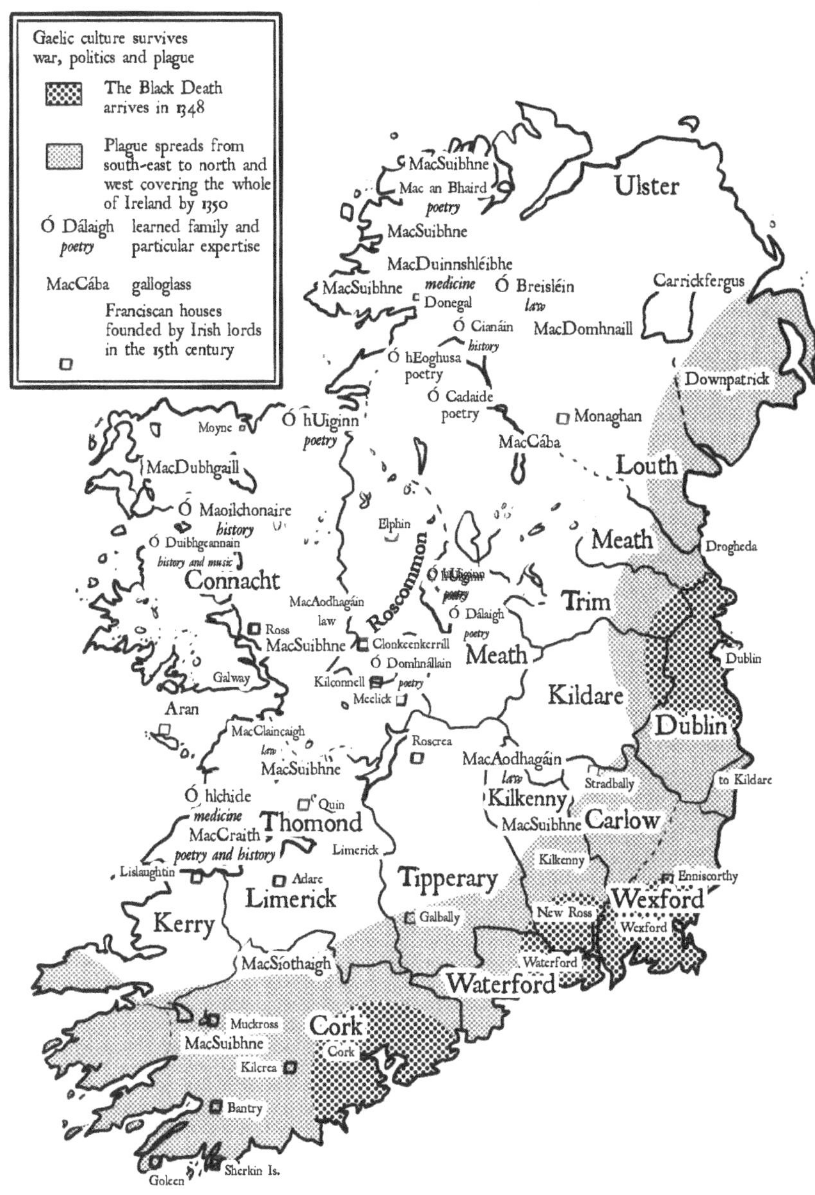

Figure 7: Map of Gaelic Revival Learned Lineages

3. The Protestant Reformation & Plantations (1517–1648)

The Reformation was introduced into an Irish Church containing divisions similar to those in the Irish secular or socio-political sphere. Keep in mind that the Roman Church still did not hold sway over Ireland or the Irish or Celtic Church as it was relatively independent from the rest of Christendom until the Second Council of Nicaea in AD 787. While ecclesiastical institutions and practices of the Irish Church were similar to those in much of pre-Reformation Europe, what made Ireland and other parts of the Celtic world unique was that clerical positions were hereditary with respect to the families who were wardens of the traditions and holy places. Most families preferred to worship in the old ways in their homes and conserved their ecclesiastical temporalities for the later endowment of continentally trained Catholic priests.

Furthermore, it was at this time that King Henry VIII of England declared himself Supreme Head of the English Church in 1534, and then claimed to be King of Ireland in 1541. The religious rift with Rome eased the way for his children (two of his successors) Edward VI and Elizabeth I to not only reform the Church of England but also to destroy the Gaelic strength in Ireland. This was conducted by a policy known as "surrender and regrant," whereby Irish (both Gaelic and Anglo-Norman) would submit to his authority, and in return, their lands would be restored and held in trust under English law. King Henry's eldest daughter, Mary Tudor (Catholic), initiated the first plantations of English settlers on Irish lands after she came to the throne in 1553. If a Gaelic chieftain failed to submit and was then conquered either economically or in battle, they were disgraced and removed. Either all or a grant of their lands was then given to an English overlord—as first took place in 1556 with the failed O'Connor and O'More uprising of the midlands (County Offaly and County Laois). This continued for the next 150 years and ultimately proved to be the death sentence for the ancient Irish-Celtic aristocracy with few exceptions.

Irish tower houses were built during this era, both by the English settlers and the Gaelic and Irish-Norman families. Many of these structures were positioned within sight of each other, and a system of visual communication is said to have been established between them based on the line-of-sight from the uppermost levels, although this may simply be a result of their high density. In Ireland, there are well over 2,000 tower houses extant, and some estimate that there were as many as 8,000 built during the Middle Ages. Most are in disrepair or ruin, but some are still home to contemporary Irish people—there are currently a few for sale, if you are in the market for a small castle from this era.

Hundreds of thousands of acres were given away in what is known as the *Jacobean Plantations* to what became known as "English undertakers," mostly English gentlemen, courtiers, and servitors. Many efforts were made by the Irish to resist, including the revolt of the Barony of Idrone (Irish-Norman, 1569), the Earl of Desmond's revolts (Irish-Norman, 1569–1573 and 1579–1583), the Nine Years War (Irish, 1593–1603), and O'Neill's Rising in 1601. Failed resistance expedited the plantation process, furthering the loss of Irish-Celtic power in Ireland. Only four groups of people were able to become undertakers of these plantations, including the English, Scottish (Protestant), "deserving" Irish, and the Church. Most of Ireland had been "planted" by the 1590s by any of these four groups. Native Irish people were allowed to stay as servitors or tenants. Somehow, some of my Kilmartin/Martin ancestors were granted this "deserving" classification and were able to retain family lands at Feá Órga near Tobercurry (Tobar an Choire) in County Sligo.[70]

4. Cromwell Campaigns and Administration (1649–1659)

The military campaigns of Oliver Cromwell may be one of the most brutal conquests of indigenous peoples until the Spanish reached the New World and the Portuguese came to Africa. Oliver Cromwell was a ruthless English general and Puritan zealot. He came to Ireland determined to stamp out military resistance to English authority, wreak vengeance on the Irish people (for their support of the "wrong" side, the nonparliamentary forces in the English Civil War), convert the entire population to the Protestant faith, and destroy what remained of the Gaelic traditions. As one travels the countryside of Ireland, you see the

◇◇◇◇◇◇◇◇◇◇◇◇◇◇

70 *Tobar an Choire* translates into English as "Holy Well of the Cauldron," an ancient oracle site in historical County Mayo in modern County Sligo off the N-17 near Kesh, Ballymote, and Temple House. Ireland's St. Attracta is the matron saint of the area.

remains of much of the wake behind Cromwell's campaigns and to this day, his name is a harbinger of evil tidings and that which would destroy all that is free and good in the Irish world. Anywhere Cromwell met resistance, he destroyed what lay in his path. This campaign was the first time canons were ever used in Ireland. Many tower houses, castles, estates, and small holdings were destroyed either by Cromwell's forces or by those who would rather self-destroy what they had in order to deny the approaching Cromwell forces the honor. In general, Cromwell was wildly successful and completely changed the face of Ireland for hundreds of years, causing many of the old Gaelic and Irish-Norman families to hide, go rogue, or flee to continental Europe.[71] In December of 1659, the Cromwellian regime collapsed as a result of an army coup.

5. From Plantations to Penal Laws (1685–1798)

As we have seen with the Cromwell campaigns, the seventeenth century was a bloody one in Ireland. The violence continued into the latter part of the seventeenth century in the Williamite Wars (1689 to 1691) pitting Catholics (the Jacobites, mostly Irish) against Protestants (mostly English). During this time, a Catholic king, James II, came to the English throne in 1685. The Irish army and government were Catholicized, and the Protestant plantations threatened to be deconstructed. James was pitted against his son-in-law, William the Orange (a Protestant), in a battle for the crown that waged across Ireland. William won, once again leaving the country in shock as the temporary return to Catholic power and the possible deconstruction of the English plantations came quickly to a close, culminating in the imposition of an even harsher Protestant regime under the Penal Laws. These laws set about disempowering Catholics, denying them, for example, the right to take leases or own land above a certain value, outlawing Catholic clergy, forbidding higher education and entry to the professions, and imposing oaths of conformity to the Church of Ireland (now an extension of the Church of England). During the latter part of the eighteenth century, strict enforcement of the Penal laws eased, but by 1778, Catholics held only about 5% of the land in Ireland.

71 Known as the *Flight of the Wild Geese.*

My family, the Martins/Kilmartins/Gilmartins, sided with the Catholics and lost power and prestige, but once again retained lands in County Galway and County Mayo, largely through the oration and diplomatic skills of Colonel Richard Martin (1754–1834) in the Irish House of Commons in the late eighteenth century.[72] Colonel Richard Martin was an Irish politician and campaigner against cruelty to animals. He was commonly known as "Humanity Dick" or "Hairtrigger Dick," as he was a leading exponent of dueling in Galway, with over one-hundred successful duels with sword and pistol.[73] Richard promoted Catholic emancipation in Ireland (his father was a Jacobite leader in Ireland) and was a strong supporter of the amelioration and abolition of Slavery throughout the British Dominions in the early 1800s.

6. Rebellion and Union with Great Britain (1798–1844)

In 1782, a Parliamentary faction led by Henry Grattan (a Protestant) successfully agitated for a more favorable trading relationship with England and for greater legislative independence for the Parliament of Ireland. However, London still controlled much of what occurred in Ireland. Inspired by the French Revolution, in 1791, an organization called the *Society of United Irishmen* was formed with the ideal of bringing Irish people of all religions together to reform and reduce Britain's power in Ireland. Its leader was a young Dublin Protestant called Theobald Wolfe Tone who is memorialized to this day in many a rowdy Irish rebel song. The United Irishmen were the inspiration for an armed rebellion in 1798 with French support. Despite the help from the French, the rebellion failed, and in 1801, the Act of Union was passed, re-uniting Ireland politically with Britain as the United Kingdom of Great Britain and Ireland. In 1829, one of Ireland's greatest leaders, Daniel O'Connell, known as "the great liberator," was central in getting the Act of Catholic Emancipation passed in Parliament in London. He

72 Shevawn Lynam, *Humanity Dick Martin "King of Connemara" 1754–1834* (Lilliput Press, 1989).

73 Burke and Fox-Davies, *A Genealogical and Heraldic History of the Landed Gentry of Ireland* (Harrison & Sons, 1912).

succeeded in getting the total ban on voting by Catholics lifted and they could now also become Members of Parliament in London (Colonel Richard Martin served at this time and helped with the passing of the Emancipation).[74] After this success, O'Connell aimed to cancel the Act of Union and re-establish an Irish parliament. However, this was a much bigger task and O'Connell's approach of non-violence was not supported by all. Such political issues were overshadowed, however, by the worst disaster and tragedy in Irish history—the Great Famine, when most of my family and many other families like yours emigrated to the United States and Canada.

7. The Great Famine and Emigration (1845–1911)

The Great Famine (in Irish: *an Gorta Mór*), or the Irish Potato Famine, was a period of mass starvation, disease, and emigration in Ireland between 1845 and 1852. Potatoes had become the staple food of a growing population at the time, as two-fifths of the population was solely reliant on this cheap crop (originally imported from the Andes Mountains in the New World). The potato had allowed Ireland's population in the latter eighteenth and early nineteenth centuries to almost double. Unfortunately, the Irish were predominantly growing only one type of potato variety called "the Lumper." When the blight, *Phytophthora infestans*, a form of plant disease imported from Mexico in 1844 struck potato crops nationwide in 1845–1847, and through 1852, disaster followed. Potatoes were inedible and people starved to death. An Irish population of over 8 million souls was reduced to half in just over ten years due to death or emigration.

Imagine a landscape filled with dazed, starving people, not unlike a zombie apocalypse in modern twenty-first-century films: Destitute men lined the roads in their rags, sleeping in crude shelters dug into roadside ditches. People ate dogs, rats, and tree bark. Reports of cannibalism were frequent and perhaps accurate. Entire families died in their homes and were eaten by feral pets. Disease picked off the survivors. Mobs of

---

[74] Shevawn Lynam, *Humanity Dick Martin "King of Connemara" 1754–1834* (Lilliput Press, 1989).

homeless, half-naked, famished creatures besieged the homes of the wealthy, calling for alms. So many people died that their bodies were interred in mass graves. Starving men stole into fields to steal turnips while farmers dug mantraps in the ground to stop them. Landlords evicted tenants in mass numbers, tore down their homes, and burned them. Neighbor fought neighbor for food and shelter.

The response of the British government also contributed to the disaster—Irish trade agreements were still controlled by London. Some historians believe that this may be one of the largest concise cultural genocides after the Holocaust of World War II, and purportedly, the British saw the blight as an opportunity to reform Ireland by emptying Ireland of the Irish. While millions of Irish people were suffering from extreme hunger, Ireland was forced to export abundant harvests of wheat and dairy products to Britain and further overseas. The population of Ireland has never since reached its pre-famine level of approximately 8 million. It is the only modern, developed country in the world to have a smaller population (seven million in 2023) than it did 200 years ago. Ireland's history of emigration continued from this point onward, with the majority of Irish emigrants going to the USA, many of them landing just in time to be thrown into military units in the American Civil War (1861–1865) on behalf of the Union. Interestingly enough, they were pitted against the Scotch-Irish Protestants of the Confederacy, continuing the age-old conflict of Catholics versus Protestants. According to my family history, Mary Martin sold off the entire 200,000-plus acre track of the family land in southern Connemara (west of Galway) piecemeal throughout the famine to help feed the people of the estate until she finally sold the home (*Ballynahinch*) in 1852 and emigrated to New York City and other family members emigrated to Canada.[75] Those who remained in Ireland grappled with another kind of anguish. As surviving inhabitants tried to come to terms with a significantly emptier landscape, they were also wrestling with a sense of guilt: that they had survived, and a great number of their neighbors had not. In so many cases, their survival had been at their neighbors' expense. This sense of survivor's guilt was something that inevitably became embedded

[75] Shevawn Lynam, 1989.

in the Irish psyche. One castle remained in a branch of my family at this period in Irish history, Tulira Castle, located southeast of Galway, owned by Edward Martyn (1859–1923), one of the critical players in the Irish Literary Revival, or the Celtic Twilight, in the late nineteenth and early twentieth centuries. He was close friends with William B. Yeats, Lady Gregory, Ella Young, and many more.

8. Home Rule & Easter Rising (1912–1919)

There was little effective challenge to Britain's control of Ireland until the Home Rule efforts of Charles Stewart Parnell (1846–91). At the age of 31, he became the leader of the Irish Home Rule Party, which became the Irish Parliamentary Party in 1882. While Parnell did not achieve Home Rule (or self-government), his efforts and widely recognized skills in the House of Commons earned him the title of "the uncrowned king of Ireland." The impetus he gave to the idea of Home Rule was to have lasting implications. In Ulster, in the north of Ireland, the majority of landholders were Protestants. They were concerned about the prospect of Home Rule being granted as they would become a Protestant minority in an independent Ireland with an otherwise Catholic majority. They favored continued union with Britain. The Protestant Unionist Party was led by Sir Edward Carson. Carson threatened an armed struggle for a separate Northern Ireland if independence was granted to Ireland. A Home Rule Bill was passed in 1912, but fatefully, it was not brought into law. The Home Rule Act was suspended at the outbreak of World War I in 1914. Many Irish nationalists believed that Home Rule would be granted after the war if they supported the British war effort (see the film *Black '47* for a taste of the times).[76] John Redmond, the leader of the Irish Parliamentary Party, encouraged people to join the British forces, and many did.

A minority of nationalists did not trust the British government, leading to one of the most pivotal events in Irish history, the Easter Rising. On April 24 (Easter Monday) 1916, two groups of armed rebels, the Irish Volunteers and the Irish Citizen Army, seized key locations in

---

76 *Black '47*. Directed by Lance Daly, performances by Hugo Weaving, James Frecheville, and Stephen Rea, Elemental Pictures, 2018.

Dublin. The Irish Volunteers were led by Padraig Pearse and the Irish Citizen Army was led by James Connolly. Outside the General Post Office in Dublin City Centre, Padraig Pearse read the Proclamation of the Republic which declared an Irish Republic independent of Britain. Battles ensued with casualties on both sides and among the civilian population. The Easter Rising finished on April 30th with the surrender of the rebels. The majority of the public was actually opposed to the Rising, however, public opinion turned when the British administration responded by executing many of the leaders and participants in the Rising. All seven signatories to the proclamation were executed including Pearse and Connolly. Two of the key figures involved in the rising who avoided execution were Éamon de Valera and Michael Collins. In the December 1918 elections, the *Sinn Féin* party, led by Éamon de Valera, won a majority of the Ireland-based seats of the House of Commons. On the 21st of January 1919, the *Sinn Féin* members of the House of Commons gathered in Dublin to form an Irish Republic parliament called *Dáil Éireann*, unilaterally declaring power over the entire island.

9. War of Independence and Civil War (1919–1923)

What followed is known as the "War of Independence" when the Irish Republican Army—the army of the newly declared Irish Republic—waged a guerilla war against British forces from 1919 to 1921. One of the key leaders of this war was Michael Collins. In December 1921, a treaty was signed by the Irish and British authorities. While a clear level of independence was finally granted to Ireland, the contents of the treaty were to split Irish public and political opinion. One of the sources of division was that Ireland was divided into Northern Ireland (six counties) and the Irish Free State (twenty-six counties) established in 1922. Such was the division of opinion in Ireland that a civil war followed from 1922 to 1923 between pro- and anti-treaty forces (pro- and anti-division between Northern Ireland and the Republic), with Collins (pro-treaty) and de Valera (anti-treaty) on opposing sides. The consequences of the Civil War can be seen to this day where the two largest political parties in Ireland have their roots in the opposing sides of the civil war—*Fine Gael* (pro-treaty) and *Fianna Fáil* (anti-treaty). A period of relative political stability followed the civil war.

10. Formation of Northern Ireland (1920–Present)

Under the same Government of Ireland Act of 1920 that created the Irish Free State, the Parliament of Northern Ireland was created. The Parliament consisted primarily of Protestants, and while there was relative stability for decades, this was to come to an end in the late 1960s due to systematic discrimination against Catholics. In the year 1968, Catholic civil rights marches in Northern Ireland began (inspired by the Civil Rights Movement in the USA) which led to violent reactions from some Protestant loyalists and the Protestant police force. What followed was a period known as "the Troubles," when nationalist/republican and loyalist/unionist groups clashed, oftentimes violently. In 1969, British troops were sent to Derry and Belfast to maintain order and protect the Catholic minority. However, the army soon came to be seen by the minority Catholic community as a tool of the Protestant majority. This was reinforced by events such as Bloody Sunday in 1972 (U2's song "Sunday Bloody Sunday" commemorates this) when British forces opened fire on a Catholic civil rights march in Derry, killing thirteen people. An escalation of paramilitary violence followed with many atrocities committed by both sides. The period of the Troubles is generally agreed to have finished with the Belfast (or Good Friday) Agreement of April 10th, 1998. Between 1969 and 1998, it is estimated that well over 3,000 people were killed by paramilitary groups on opposing sides of the conflict. Since 1998, considerable stability and peace have come to Northern Ireland. In 2007, former bitterly opposing parties, the Democratic Unionist Party (DUP) and *Sinn Féin,* began to cooperate in government together in Northern Ireland.

11. Republic of Ireland (1920–Present)

The 1937 Constitution re-established Ireland as the Republic of Ireland. In 1973, Ireland joined the European Economic Community (now the European Union). In the 1980s, the Irish economy was in recession and large numbers of people emigrated for employment reasons. Many young people emigrated to the United Kingdom, the United States of America, and Australia. Economic reforms in the 1980s and 1990s, along with membership in the European Community (now European Union), created one of the world's highest economic growth rates. Ireland in the 1990s, so long considered a country of emigration, became a country of immigration, due largely to the North Atlantic Free Trade Agreement (NAFTA), which opened up agreements with many American pharmaceutical and tech companies. Thanks, Bill Clinton! This period in Irish history was called the "Celtic Tiger," which collapsed with the economic recession of 2008.

12. The Celtic Twilight (Late Nineteenth–Early Twentieth Century)

The Celtic Twilight, also referred to as *the Celtic Revival*, began in the late nineteenth century and was fueled largely by ancient Irish manuscripts translated from Irish, or Middle Irish, into English in the mid-eighteenth century. The Celtic Twilight was a renewal of interest in Irish and Celtic culture. Artists and writers drew on the traditions of Irish, Welsh, and other Gaelic literature and Celtic art.

The Celtic Twilight can also refer to a group of Celtic Mystery and lorekeepers led by William Butler Yeats, Lady Gregory, Æ Russell, Ella Young, Maude Gonne, William Sharp, Fiona Macleod, Edward Martyn, Edward Plunkett, and more who gathered for high magic in one of the Galway branches of my family's heritage at Tulira in Gort, County Clare. The heart of this group, under the auspices of the Order of Celtic Mysteries (OCM) and spearheaded by Yeats, seeded much of the twentieth-century revival of literature, fantasy, magic, theater, occult, scrying, and more. The rise of OCM and the Celtic Twilight coincides with the major revolutionary changes happening on the Earth at the time, including the translation of Egyptian hieroglyphics, the rise of Kabbala teachings to non-Jewish people, the influence of Eastern Indian spiritual traditions in the West. Additionally, it coincided with the advent of the Hermetic Order of the Golden Dawn, the collapse of the world's royalty leading to World War I, the rapid expanse of capitalistic-driven democracy, and the rise of socialism and communism. The Celtic Twilight also fueled and amplified the spirit behind the liberation of Ireland from the English crown—in the heart of Kathleen ní Houlihan or the spirit and "Light of Erin." *Solas geal na hEireann* is rooted not only in the workings of our grandfathers and grandmothers from the Celtic Twilight, but also in the heart of the living spirit of Ireland:

Kathleen ní Houlihan. She has asked that I write this book as a *seanchaí*, or lore keeper, with her blessing, to help all her wayward children in the navigation of remembrance, returning home, and braiding dreams.

There are currently more people who claim Irish descent in the United States alone than in all of Ireland and Northern Ireland combined. In the past 800 years of Ireland's history, Ireland and her people have suffered continuous beatings by the English (as has much of the world), and yet, somehow, have been able to continue to rebound, survive, and at times, to even thrive. As a tribute to the Celtic spirit, reverence for life and nature, Ireland's president from 1997 to 2011, Mary McAleese, spoke at the University of Notre Dame's commencement in 2006 on the Irish love for freedom: "The love of freedom is the essence of the 'Fighting Irish.' It reflects the Irish people's indomitable spirit, and commitment, never tentative, always fully committed, to life itself."[77]

A note on the Irish National Flag: The green represents the older Gaelic tradition (Celtic, Catholic, etc.), the orange represents the followers of William the Orange (Protestant), and white represents the lasting truce between the orange and the green—the Protestants and the Catholics. The Celtic Lion-Dog is a mystical beast that braids together the heart of the Irish people: the fierceness of the lion and the loyalty of the dog. Fierce and loyal are the defining adjectives and the heartbeat of the Irish-Celtic people. This is the mythological creature that is sculpted into the heads of the torcs of initiates of the grove of *Solas geal na hEireiann.* Éirinn go Brách! Let us climb the mystery together via the Light of Erin. Together, let us remember our dreams and follow the trails of our *aislingí* in discovering the keys and clues they are leaving for us to find our way Home into Deep Peace.

[77] Mary McAleese (2006).

SOVEREIGN GODDESSES OF IRELAND

Chapter Three

IRISH-CELTIC CODEX

"May the road rise up to meet you.

May the wind be always at your back.

May the sun shine warm upon your face;

The rains fall soft upon your fields... until we meet again,

May God hold you in the palm of His hand."

~ *Fiona Macleod*

Welcome to the Irish-Celtic Mysteries in the living Light of Erin, a silver-blue apple branch emerging from the Celtic Twilight in the dreams of the Order of Celtic Mysteries. Perhaps stepping across the threshold into the mysteries for you was led by intuition or dreams. Perhaps you have been guided by divine intervention or illumination. Or, perhaps, your heart and intellect are ripe for knowledge that spans the realms of logic and intuition simultaneously. Whatever the catalyst to nudge you forward on this path, I bid you welcome.

Welcome to the journey of Irish-Celtic dreamers and wisdom keepers, that of the *fear feasa, bean feasa,* and *seanchaí,* where we braid reason, logic, and Celtic tradition with intuition, dreaming, mythology, and lore craft.[78] Within this fluid braiding, often depicted artistically as Celtic knot work, lies the essential truth and discovery of life's riddles. The art of the bard and lore craft is alive and strong. Between the fire of your soul's passion and the compost of life's hardships, we will heat the raw materials of life into a malleable epic tale that is your own for the telling. On this anvil of life's purpose, we will reshape and refine until you are an embodiment of your eternal nature. Let us find our allies with all the seen and unseen, crafting life accordingly.

You stand at a threshold. The thin layer between the worlds is elusive and intertwined with the fabric of your heart-mind-soul. There are many Mystery Traditions all over the planet from hundreds of philosophies, cultures, and faiths. Walking through a Mystery Tradition brings us closer to a philosophy, culture, and faith; or the mysteries may usher us completely away on the hunt for answers elsewhere. Seeker, it is an honor to meet you at the metaphoric crossroads of life here in all things Celtic. I pray that you may find nourishment in the Irish-Celtic garden. May it propel you toward your Ancient Future Self. I trust when you begin to see living, breathing, swelling, undulating Celtic knots twining through all animate and inanimate beings, that you will have nourished your intuitive thirst for the living essence of the Light of Ireland—*Solas geal na hÉireann.* An invitation: become or remember yourself as a *seanchaí*: a Celtic bearer of ancient and timeless lore promulgating the sacred river of our Great Mother forward until the end of days.

The beauty of Ireland is thus: the ancient pre-Christian traditions and the modern Christian ones are iterations of the same essence, though reverence has shifted from a Mother Goddess culture to a Father God culture. The Emerald Isle has a way of thwarting false agendas from taking root in anyone who sojourns in a sacred and respectful manner. Furthermore, a respectful relationship with the sacred landscape of Ireland will catalyze the alchemy of spirit, mind, and body in the progression toward an authentic and powerfully heartfelt disposition. In the Celtic tradition, nature and the divine are inseparable. People and the land are inseparable. All things are connected, and if one has yet

[78] *Fear feasa* is a male wisdom keeper, *bean feasa* is a female wisdom keeper, and a *seanchaí* is a traditional Celtic storyteller or knowledge keeper.

to see the relationship, one simply must surrender and allow Ireland's medicine to settle in. Trust, for Ireland constantly invites the seeker to open to grace.

As we continue this journey together, let us remember that all things are inseparable. Let us remember that as we progress through the seasons of the year, thousands of generations have done so before us. They have left us with little tidbits of information, keys, or codices that truly can only be understood through solving the riddles life presents. And our forebearers have left us with some powerful knowledge that spans time—giving us a "map" to navigate the twists and turns of life.[79] On top of that, our predecessors ask us to learn and contribute to the whole—for *the future*—so that all beings may benefit from our progression in the promulgation of the Light of Erin.

Let us remember as we move through the Wheel of the Year that we also progress through various seasonally appropriate modes and moods. Our consciousness shifts with the seasons, and this is perfectly healthy. So too, we move through the wheel of life. However we look at the Wheel of the Year, or of life, the metaphor and road map remains similar. When it is spring, we are chipper and open to quick growth. In summer, we play and work to develop the best fruits within our labors of life. In autumn, we begin to turn within, revealing our true colors and harvesting what we have sewn. Come winter, we reflect, refine, and look to our accomplishments (and shortcomings) in hopes that those who follow us will be more successful.

I love many things about Ireland. I could sing a thousand songs of my reverence for my motherland and never exhaust the distinctive gold of Ireland's beauty: her landscape, sea, people, music, unbroken traditions, pure water, ancient forests, waterfalls, mountains, sea caves, thick mists,

79 Our forebearers from the Celtic Twilight—Æ Russell, William B. Yeats, Fiona Macleod/William Sharp, James Joyce, Standish James O'Grady, Edward Martyn, Lady Gregory, Maude Gonne, Kuno Meyer, Ella Young, John Duncan, Kenneth Morris, Dion Fortune, Alexei Kondratiev, John Michell, and many more who rose to the occasion of Celtic sovereignty and the promulgation of our heritage, dreams, language, mythology, culture, music, and so much more. We stand on the shoulder of giants.

and on goes the list. Yet, what sings to me most and contains the very seed of the Irish-Celtic Mysteries codex is the intact interrelationship between the sacred year, the land, and her people—and we can map it. It is as simple as that. The land *is* a map to the sacred covenant that Ireland, or *Erin's land*, has sustained with her people since the beginning of time. Map in hand, Ireland under our feet, and her spirit singing in our soul, it is our responsibility (if you so choose to grow into a *seanchaí*) to usher her sacred mysteries forward in perpetuity. The Irish-Celtic codex is hidden in plain sight within the symbolic map of Ireland, within the flag of the provinces of Ireland, within the seasons, and within the sovereign goddess of the land.

Ireland may be the only developed country in Europe that is truly capable of claiming an unbroken lineage of Mystery Keepers from the prehistoric up into the present, as well as boasting an intact relationship of sacred sites with respect to the turning of the great wheel of time. This fact is so engrained in the Irish everyday social construct that many Irish natives may not even be fully conscious of the seamless traditions. But who am I kidding? The Irish people know, especially in the *Gaeltacht*.[80] In Ireland, the land is her people and is a physical reflection of the divine. There is no separation. Ireland is the humble yet proud heart of indigenous consciousness and traditions in the Western world.[81]

Through faith, we can see the beauty, power, and grace of Ireland and how she has affected her children throughout the world—or those that have or claim Irish heritage via ancestral or spiritual connections. Beyond faith, the Irish heritage also invites us to absorb and propagate her wisdom teachings. Through deep dives into mythology, ecology, history, music, art, athletics, theology, geology, and religion, we can track the roots of the Irish-Celtic archive like knotwork through a rich contextual fabric of unending riddles, geomythology, and an endless

◇◇◇◇◇◇◇◇◇◇◇◇◇◇◇

80 *The Gaeltacht* is the Irish term referring to the areas of Ireland where the Irish language *(Gaeilge)* is still spoken as a community language in everyday speech, and traditional Irish culture and traditions are alive and thriving.

81 Noting that the Sámi people in the northern Scandinavia region, called *Sápmi*, are also a beautiful indigenous culture in the Western world.

repertoire of legends. Let us open our hearts and minds together. Let us walk into the timeless and ancient groves. Let us walk into the stone circles, cairns, dolmens, *rátha*, *clocháin*, churches, cathedrals, castles, caves, loughs, and mountains.

There are more than 138,800 known sacred sites in Ireland as of June 21, 2022.[82] That is over 138,800 sites in a country not much larger than the state of Ohio in the United States, and these 138,800 sites are only the locations recorded by the Archaeological Survey of Ireland in the national database. More sites are found every year. Multiple significant sites were newly discovered in the summer of 2018 during a very dry and warm period. The Irish of antiquity understood that the interface of the landscape and the divine was not only intertwined but also symbiotic. This living relationship with the land is sustained by many contemporary Irish who still visit their sacred sites on a routine basis. Everywhere you go in Ireland, you see the signs of a thriving culture intertwined with the land and the divine: prayer ties on elder or hawthorn trees, coins/votive offerings left at holy wells/springs, notes tucked under standing stones and crucifixes, Brigid's crosses over doors/prayer niches, and so on.

As an American from a country where most of the sacred sites of our indigenous heritage have either been farmed or paved over, it has been a powerful discovery to find that many places in the world do not separate the sacred and the secular, nor the prehistoric and contemporary. Perhaps we can blame our American plight on belligerent colonialism, Puritanism, and Manifest Destiny, or on the flawed pretense that there were not massively significant indigenous high cultures in the Americas prior to colonization.[83] However, this is not my focus for this book as plenty of people have written volumes of material on this very subject. I instead seek to focus on the excitement, discovery, power, and beauty

82 From the Archaeological Survey of Ireland (ASI), a unit of the Irish National Monuments Service. The ASI was established to compile an inventory of the known archaeological monuments in Ireland constructed prior to AD 1700.

83 Charles C. Mann's theory is that there were more people in North America in 1491 than there were in Europe.

of over twenty-four years of immersion in the Irish heritage as an orienteering journey for any of the 70 million people who claim Irish lineage or are magnetized to her rich spiritual heritage. Furthermore, this book is written for those who dream across time, who quest for a key to open doors of intuition, long to return home *(éolchaire),* track the force of personal *dúchas*, follow *aislingí* for the illumination of the soul, or tune into the song of the *sídhe.*

As with any map or model, that which is provided herein is simply a tool to navigate unfamiliar territory. The archive of the Irish heritage is massive. The spirit essence that is the emanating Light of Erin calls her *seanchaí* to help her children find their way home. May you find some navigational assistance in the pages ahead, and if you do not, I suppose you could always light a good fire with the book pages and scry what you find in the flames therein. On behalf of Ireland and the Light of Erin, know that you are very welcome. *Céad míle fáilte.*[84]

The Irish-Celtic Codex

The beauty and true magic of Ireland is revealed with the ancient classical map or the Irish-Celtic codex: the map of Ireland is the Wheel of the Year and of life. The land, her people, and the divine are truly inseparable. In the following chapters, we will look at this through both the lens of pre-Christian and Christian Mysteries. If we were to take a slice in time across the map of Ireland, in any era after the settlement of Milesians, the slice would yield similar patterns in respect to the codex. Albeit the names of local deities may become national deities in one slice; local deities may evolve (or devolve) into *púcaí*, *beansídhe*, or leprechauns in another slice; or even morph into saints or historic figures in another. Songs may change in theme, but not in essence. The language may vary slightly. Styles of clothing may shift. Offerings left at sacred sites may change as well. Yet, one thing truly remains through it all: Ireland is alive and well—filled with mystery and magic that is waiting to be celebrated, discovered, honored, and revered.

---

84 *Céad míle fáilte* literally means "a hundred thousand welcomes."

Figure 8: Five Sacred Kingdom Centers

All of Ireland is ruled by the sovereign goddess of Ireland—Ériu. Politically and spiritually, Ireland consists of the four classic kingdoms and one central kingdom. Each kingdom is associated with a season of the year and thus one of the traditional Celtic high holidays or cross-quarter fire holidays. A sacred and secular center is located in each kingdom, within which the local sovereign would rule only through the authority of a sovereign matron deity intimately interconnected to the land and to the respective season. Each matron deity—Morrígu, Brigid, Áine, and Macha—is the sovereign goddess of the land (Connacht, Leinster, Munster, and Ulster respectively) and thus, the Great Mother of its mysteries. Ériu (modern Irish: *Éire* or English: *Erin*) is the eponymous matron goddess of all Ireland centered in Meath. The English name for Ireland comes from the name *Ériu* and the Germanic (Old Norse or Old English) word "land," thus her name: *Éire-land*—Ireland.

Each of the traditional kingdoms and their inherent mysteries are stewarded by timeless keepers of traditions, the *seanchaí*. From the Celtic Golden Age (fourth and fifth centuries BC), through the Irish Gaelic Revival (end of the twelfth century to the end of the fifteenth century AD), the Celtic Twilight (late nineteenth to early twentieth centuries), and into the modern Celtic Revival, the Mystery Keepers were druids, bards, Christian druids, and Christian mystics—both women and men. Well into the Christian era, the monasteries and convents were, in many cases, archives and transcribers of the ancient Irish-Celtic Mysteries. The custodians of these centers were and remain the spiritual and secular councilors to the Irish people.

In respect to sustaining the interconnection of the sacred land with her people, the *ollamhs* and later the bishops, in company with the high royal Irish court, would have made an annual pilgrimage around Ireland to all the kingdoms in their seasonal respective order for the cross-quarter festivals.[85] In Irish, this annual pilgrimage was known as an *óenach*, which was both the actual procession between the sites and the assembly which often would last up to fourteen days at the respective sacred center. The *óenach*, also known as a *feiseanna*, would attract everyone from the surrounding hosting kingdom as well as the movers

◇◇◇◇◇◇◇◇◇◇◇◇◇◇

85 An *ollamh* (literally meaning "most great") was a poet or bard of literature, law, music, mythology, medicine, astronomy, and/or history. Each chief or *tuath* (tribe) had its own *ollamh*. Over all of the provincial *ollamhs* was the *Ard-Ollamh* (*Rí-Ollamh, Rí-Eigeas, Príméces*) who held the official post of *Chief Ollamh* of Ireland or *"Ollamh Érenn."* His social status was equal to the High King of Ireland, and he had his own official residence and a large retinue of about thirty *ollamhs* together with their staff and students. The *ollamh* had a gold bell-branch held above him, the *anruth* had a silver bell-branch, and the other poets had a bronze bell-branch. The post was partly hereditary, as *Uraicecht na* states that a poet can only attain *ollamh* rank if he stems from a family of poets. Originally, the *ollamh* was appointed by the king, but by the sixth century AD, it had become an elected post that was voted for by the other *ollamhs*. One of my distant ancestors, Giolla Earnáin O'Martin, was *Ard-Ollamh* of Ireland in Ulster and Meath through the early thirteenth century.

and shakers from across the entire countryside. An *óenach* was a time to celebrate, sell crafts, goods, and services, as well as trade in livestock, conduct business transactions, make marriage arrangements, contend in athletic competitions or war games, compete in bardic competitions, and celebrate the high holy days of Samhain, Ímbolc, Bealtaine, and Lughnasadh. During times of peace, the *óenach* was a place of joy and celebration of life with respect to the seasons. Economics, traditions, religion, and lore craft all thrived on the community coming together for the gatherings. The cross-quarter holidays in the Irish-Celtic tradition are the most important traditional holidays of the year. Midwinter and Midsummer follow thereafter. According to mentor and pre-Christian Celtic ritual reconstructionist Alexei Kondratiev, the equinoxes had little significance to the Irish-Celtic people but have become more so in contemporary times due to its mixing with other Earth traditions such as those of Native American cultures.

The most important role of the *óenach* was the promulgation of a unified cultural continuum of the Irish-Celts which was symbolically reignited at every turn of the season. Specifically, at every cross-quarter on the eve of the high ceremony and celebration, every household across Ireland would bank out their hearth fires. The ash from the cold hearth was returned to field and forest. Meanwhile, back at the respective sacred site for the holiday, the *ollamhs* would be preparing the way for the return of the sacred fire gifted from the sovereign goddess of the land and her intermediaries from the Otherworld, *Tír na nOg*. During the culmination of the ceremony, runners would light torches from the ritual fire. They would then run with the sacred fire on their brands like Olympic torch bearers to light the fires at the sacred centers of the other respective kingdoms. Once the fires were lit at the sacred centers of the other kingdoms, new runners would light brands from those fires (and the origin flame at the site of the respective holy day). Hefting their brands, these runners would disseminate out across the land to regional sacred sites to spread the holy flame. In turn, these regional sacred centers would have runners to convey the flame to local sacred sites, great houses, villages, towns, enclaves, schools, monasteries, and convents until eventually every cold, darkened hearth across Ireland was relit from the one flame of the Otherworld at its sacred source, birthed from the seasonal sovereign matron deity.

And so it was: four times a year. Darkness temporarily prevailed until it was pushed back with the light of the divine, the Light of Erin—renewing all hearts and minds. And it all begins at the Celtic New Year at Samhain. The image below depicts the seed of the Irish-Celtic Codex. The numbers correspond to the flow of the *óenaig* (plural of *óenach*) through the year and in their respective locations in Ireland from the map on Page 69.

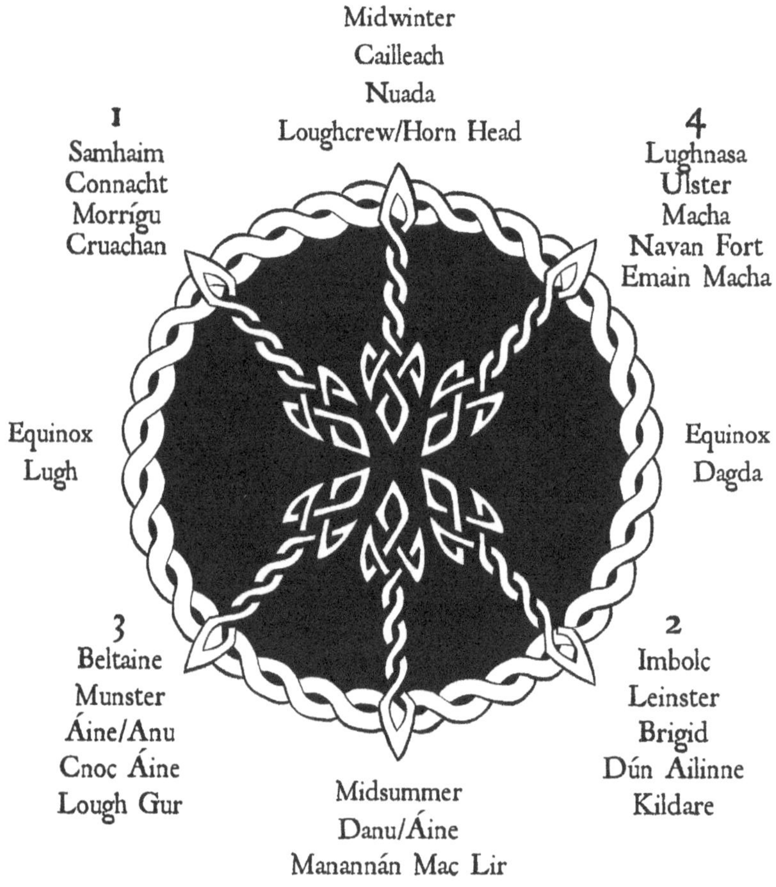

Figure 9: Irish-Celtic Codex

First Cross-Quarter Holiday: Samhain
Date(s) of Fire Festival: October 31–November 1
Traditional Realm: Connacht (Irish: *Connachta*)
Matron Deity: Morrígu (Morrígan)
Sacred Center: Cruachain (*Ráth Cruachan*)
Traditional Cultural Roles: Druids[86]

The Wheel of the Celtic Year begins at Samhain. Samhain (*samhfhuin*), as translated by most Irish scholars in Irish literally means "end" (*fhuin*) of "summer" (*sam*).[87] All things Celtic, as we see with the tradition of the *óenaig* and the relighting of the sacred fires, begin in the dark and grow towards the light. Call the Celts optimists if you will, but we must remember that they originated in the forested northlands of the Mother Goddess culture. Therefore, all things begin in the dark womb at the seed of the beginning of winter: at Samhain—when the sun rises beneath the belt of Orion (the Celtic origination stars) pointing toward

◇◇◇◇◇◇◇◇◇◇◇◇◇◇

86 R.I. Best, editor and translator. *The Settling of the Manor of Tara*, vol. 4, Royal Irish Academy, Dublin, Ireland, 1910. Irish families passed down traditional knowledge from one family to the next, and most regions were known for certain skill sets. Though it is not all-encompassing, each kingdom was also known for certain lineage-familiar traditions or cultural roles. In Connacht, the classic role is and was often with respect to druids (bards, healers, geologists, ecologists, mythologists, genealogists, musicians, lawyers, etc.). Though druids, of course, were from all over Ireland, Connacht was known to produce many of the best, with many *ollamhs* hailing from Connacht.

87 *Sam* is the Old Irish word for "summer," "light," and "daytime" ("light half"). It is often referred to in the pan-Celtic world as *samos*. Modern Irish for *summer* is "*samhradh*." The Old Irish word *gaim* indicates the opposite: winter, dark, nighttime (the dark half), and is often referred to in the pan-Celtic world as *giamos*. Modern Irish for *winter* is "*geimhreadh*." One of my teachers, Alexei Kondratiev, leans into this heavily with respect to the Celtic Mysteries in Celtic Rituals. *Fhuin*, the second half of the *Samhfhuin* (the "fh" is silent) means to "end," and, written here as *ain*, means "un." Thus, Samhain also can mean to "un-summer."

the constellation of Pleiades. The modern-day festival of Halloween originates from the ancient Celtic ritual of Samhain that coincided with the midnight culmination of the Pleiades cluster. It was believed that the veil dividing the living from the dead, and this world from the other, is at its thinnest when the Pleiades reaches its highest point in the sky at midnight.

In respect to the codex of the Irish-Celts, the kingdom associated with the great *óenach* feast of Samhain is Connacht. Its sacred and secular center is Ráth Cruachan near Tulsk in County Roscommon, where the kings of Connacht would have married the Goddess and the land in the ancient rite of *ban feis* where the king was bestowed the temporal right to rule on behalf of the sacred land, the Goddess, and Her people. It was also at Ráth Cruachan that the fires of the other cross-quarter holidays would be relit by the torch runners for distribution across Connacht. The matron deity, who surprisingly never became a saint (but was instead diminished to the queen of *beansídhe*), is the goddess Morrígu. The Morrígu is a northern battle goddess, often called a "dark goddess." As all things Celtic come in trinities, she is in a triplet relationship with her sisters, the other northern goddesses, the Macha and the Badb (synonymous with the Cailleach), collectively known as *the Morrígna*. The Morrígna are also synonymous with the three land goddesses Ériu, Banba, and Fódla, and are goddesses of sovereignty. I cannot find any references in anything translated into modern English that will verify this, but intuitively, I track that the Morrígu is Ériu, while Áine/Anu is also Ériu. Morrígu represents the dark, winter, guardian half of Ériu, while Áine represents Ériu's bright, summer, and radiant half. Ériu (and therefore, all of Ireland) is thus the balance of summer and winter, light and dark.

The Morrígu is often portrayed as a lusty battle goddess with crows as her totem or assistants. At other times, she is portrayed as a crone: sometimes in finery and sometimes in rags. She is often compared to the Valkyries, the Norns, or the Fates. Her sacred places in Connacht are located at Carrowkeel, Keshcorran, Carrowmore, and Oweynagat (at Cruachain). The Morrígu dwells within these caves and cairns, or at least touches our world therein—allowing movement between our world and the Otherworld, especially at Samhain. As the winter voice of Ireland, she directs our attention to the vital issues we have to face in order to grow. She does not care much for our personal agenda unless it is truly in line with the divine, and she will let you know when it is out of alignment. She does not beat around the bush with flowery speeches. She will bring your eye and heart directly to whatever it needs to look at—now. She is not patient. Tackle the problem and move on. This is her way of navigating the mysteries, and for me, this is often a breath of fresh air. At other times, the way she directs my attention leaves me with a feeling of "wow, I have to look there again?!"

Connacht was renowned for its druids. Often seen as the mistiest and most mysterious of the four kingdoms, Connacht's vast vales in the east of the realm, and the sweeping mountains and fjords of the west, bred some of Ireland's finest mystics, both as druids and later as priests, monks, and nuns. In contemporary times, the majority of the Celtic Twilight emerged from Connacht (and Munster)—or called it home for part of their lives.

Second Cross-Quarter Holiday: Ímbolc
Date(s) of Fire Festival: February 1–February 4
Traditional Realm: Leinster (Irish: *Laighin*)
Matron Deity: Brigid (Bríg, Brid)
Sacred Center: Kildare (Dún Ailinne)
Traditional Cultural Roles: Craft & Tradespeople

From Samhain, the *óenach* moves through Midwinter (winter solstice) where we pass through the sacred center of Ireland on the solar return towards Ímbolc, the second cross-quarter fire holiday. *Ímbolc*, in Old Irish, means "in (or of) the belly," as this is a time when sheep begin to lactate (their udders fill), fields are tilled, and the grass begins to grow. Although Ímbolc—from a contemporary view unconnected to the changes in nature—seems to sit in the heart of winter, it is truly a celebration of the beginning of spring. Remember, all things Celtic begin in the dark. And thus, Ímbolc is the "light half" of the dark half the of the year.

At Ímbolc, the *óenach* travels into the southeast of Ireland to the lands of the summer goddesses (imploring that they help restore the balance of light in the dark of winter) into the kingdom of Leinster, at the sacred center at Dún Ailinne, and later at nearby Kildare. For here in Leinster, a "summer" fire goddess rules: Brigid. In relational triplet with the summer goddesses Áine/Anu and Áine/Danu, Brigid is a triple goddess in her own right—being a matron of inspiration (poets/bards), refinement (smiths/metal workers), and of the hearth (homemakers). Both as a goddess and later as a saint (Saint Brigid of Kildare), she often is depicted wielding symbols for the triple aspects mentioned above: a lamp (poets/bards), a hammer (smiths), and an eternal flame (hearth and home).

Brigid was also a matron goddess and saint of the poor and destitute. She brings nourishment and warmth where it is needed most. Her sacred sites are at Kildare, Dún Ailinne (at Cnoc Ailinne), St. Brigid's Well (near the Cliffs of Moher in County Clare), and holy wells across Ireland. It was at Dún Ailinne where the kings of Leinster would have married the goddess and the land through *ban feis*, and the fires of the cross-quarters would be relit for distribution across Leinster. During the early Christian era, the sacred center of Leinster was moved to Kildare.

Though she is a "summer" fire goddess (pushing back the mantle of winter), Brigid is also the matron of dozens of holy springs all over the country. At Ímbolc, families bless the sources of their spring or well water on outings including picnics, prayers, and offerings (of coins, Brigid crosses, and more). The Irish weave the traditional equal-armed Brigid's crosses from rushes (*Juncus spp.*) collected near the holy wells and springs to give to friends, share as offerings, or hang over their doors to bless visitors (and keep out unwanted guests). The modern-day festival of Saint Brigid's Day (Groundhog Day in the United States) originates from the ancient Irish festival of Ímbolc. While certainly the feast of Saint Brigid (*Lá Fhéile Bríde* in Irish) still honors the holiday, having a goddess reduced to a groundhog in the United States is certainly something to ponder.

Leinster is renowned for its craftspeople. Being situated in the southeast of Ireland, sea trade with Wales, England, France, and Spain was quite straightforward via ship. Additionally, Leinster is the only realm in Ireland where the soft, fertile earth from the center of Ireland reaches the coast. This, of course, has left the kingdom vulnerable and open to outside influences more than anywhere else in Ireland.

Today, Leinster is dotted with active and wealthy farms, industries, universities, convents, and monasteries. The rolling plains and the Wicklow Mountains, as well as the Boyne, Blackwater, Liffey, Slaney, and Nore rivers, define the essence of the geography and heritage of Leinster. Leinster also includes within its borders the fifth province or middle kingdom of *Midhe*, or Meath. It was from this kingdom that, in some legends, Merlin stole by magical means the great standing stones that became Stonehenge in Somerset, England.[88]

Leinster and Meath have a rich spiritual heritage. The Boyne Valley is the apex of the Neolithic passage cairn building culture at Newgrange, Knowth, and Dowth, as well as Uisneach and the Hill of Tara. At the royal and sacred centers of Ireland, at Uisneach and later Tara, the tradition of the *ban feis* between the high king and Ériu was held for over a thousand years. *The Book of Kells* was completed in Leinster. Overall, Leinster's geographic vulnerability has allowed it to be culturally diverse and wealthy and to sustain a powerful spiritual vitality that is very much of this world.

Third Cross-Quarter Holiday: Bealtaine
Date(s) of Fire Festival: April 31–May 2
Traditional Realm: Munster (Irish: *an Mhumhain*)
Matron Deity: Áine/Anu or Mór Mhumhan
Sacred Center: Cnoc Áine (Lough Gur)/Rock of Cashel
Traditional Cultural Roles: Musicians

From Kildare in Leinster, the *óenach* crosses back over the sacred center (Uisneach/Tara) en route to the southwest and the kingdom of Munster for the second most important Celtic holiday to Samhain: Bealtaine, or Beltaine. *Bealtaine* can be translated in several ways. The first part of the word, *beal*, in Irish, means "a mouth or entrance to ford across a river" or a pass of some kind.[89] The second half of Bealtaine comes from an Old Irish word for "fire," or *teine*, which in modern

◇◇◇◇◇◇◇◇◇◇◇◇◇◇◇

88 From Geoffery of Monmouth's works on the legends of King Arthur.

89 P.W. Joyce, *Irish Names of Places*, vol III, 1869. p. 134.

Irish is *tine*. Bealtaine can thus mean something along the lines of "mouth of the fire" or "ford of the fire." With the ancient tradition of the community dancing between two fires at Bealtaine and driving their livestock between them in blessing, the translation of "ford of fire" seems most appropriate. Through the ford of the fire, we enter the summer or bright half of the year, leaving behind the heaviness and darkness of winter.

The sacred center of Munster in the pre-Christian era was at Knockainy Hill (Cnoc Aine) and Lough Gur in County Limerick. Here is where the kings of Munster would have married the Goddess and the land via the *ban feis*. Additionally, the fires of the cross-quarter festivals other than Bealtaine would be lit at Knockainy Hill for distribution in Munster. Later in the Christian era, the center of Munster was moved to Cashel. The matron deity of Munster is Áine, or Anu, whose name alludes to summer via attributes such as "brightness," "splendor," and "radiance." The Irish word for sun is *gréine*. Áine is the heart of the sun as we see in the word *gréine*, and the heart of the "ford of fire" in Bealtaine—the beginning of her rule in her half of the year.

Áine is often seen as analogous with the original Mother Goddess of Ireland, Danu. Áine is the goddess of love, fertility, and light. As the goddess of love, she ensures the fertile continuity of the people, beginning at the feast of Bealtaine, where lovers dance and meet between the great double fires in the "ford of the fire." This is the only fire holiday celebrated with twin fires instead of only one as in the other three cross-quarter holidays. Summer begins at Bealtaine in the Celtic calendar, and Áine rules the summer months with her trinity of light goddesses of Anu/Danu and Gráinne, with a loose relation to Brigid as well.[90] Anu is most closely akin to the spring or Maiden aspect of Áine. Danu is the matronly aspect at the peak of summer (summer solstice/Midsummer) of Áine, while Gráinne is the harvest and wane of Áine's summer.

90 *Gráinne*, a singular ripe grain, is from a similar root as *gréine*, meaning "Sun."

Áine was both a goddess and a faëry queen. She is also known as the "Lady of the Lake"—ruling at Lough Gur, where every seven years, she rides forth from the cave in her sacred hill (or from the cave beneath the lake depending on who is telling the tale). She travels around the lake three to five times before riding off on her summer hunt for the summer god or for a human king to rule with her in the Otherworld. At her sacred sites around the country, but mostly in Munster, Áine's braids are woven out of the rushes (*Juncus spp.*) and twisted into a hoop that will be decorated with flowers. These are worn as crowns during the fire dances of Bealtaine as well as placed on the tops of standing stones in the stone circles around Munster. There are almost one hundred stone circles found in Munster, most of which align with the setting or rising sun for various holidays and feasts throughout the year. *Clocháin*, or beehive huts, are also found all along the coast of Munster in remote locations like Skellig Michael and the Dingle Peninsula.[91]

During the Middle Ages, Munster's sacred center shifted from Lough Gur and Knockainey to the ancient sacred hill of Cashel (and the matron goddess Mór Mhumhan). *Mór Mhumhan* means "the great mother" and the province of Munster (*An Mhumhain*) is named after her. She is also a sovereignty goddess of the province. Her name is synonymous with Anu (and Áine) and she was also known as *Mugain*, thus connecting her as the summer variant of the sovereign goddess of the land with the Morrígu. Thus, we balance out the year: Áine/Anu/Mór Mhumhan as sovereign matron deity at Bealtaine, the beginning of summer and the light half of the year, with the Morrígu as the sovereign matron deity at Samhain, the beginning of winter and the dark half of the year.

Munster is well known for its musicians and artists. Its wild rocky coastlines, mountains, crystal caves, and rolling rich hinterlands—once covered in ancient forests of oak, yew, and ash—is truly an inspiring

91 *Clocháin* is the plural form of *clochán*, usually referring to dry-stacked stone "beehive" huts—but can also mean "steppingstones."

landscape that invites the inner music out of everyone. Fionn and the *Fianna* used to hunt and train across the hills of Munster where their greatest bards learned how to play harp, fiddle, and uilleann pipes from the *sídhe.* Still today, we find the greatest collection of traditional and non-traditional Irish musicians across Ireland in Munster, especially in the towns of Cork, Killarney, Dingle, and Doolin. And some of them certainly learned from the *sídhe.*

The tallest mountains and the most extensive ancient forests in modern-day Ireland are found today in Munster as well. The Shannon River, which plays such a vital role in Irish pre-history and history, also is a dominant feature in the Munster landscape. Pilgrimages to the Holy Land and to *Santiago de Compostella* in Spain left from Dingle. The very land itself is saturated with music—guiding the seeker ever deeper on the path of unfolding the riddles of intuition. The Celtic knots become a guide to the living music of the landscape, the soul, and the twining of the mysteries within and between the sacred sites.

Fourth Cross-Quarter Holiday: Lughnasadh
Date(s) of Fire Festival: July 31–August 2
Traditional Realm: Ulster (Irish: *Ulaidh*)
Matron Deity: Macha
Sacred Center: Emain Macha (Navan Fort)
Traditional Cultural Roles: Warriors

From Bealtaine, the *óenach* crosses back through the sacred center and into the northeast to the kingdom of Ulster. Seeding the sacred fire of the feast of the harvest, or Lughnasadh, was traditionally celebrated here at Navan Fort—though, this sacred center, similar in respect to the cross-quarter feast day, like Dún Ailinne to Kildare, was moved to Tailtin in County Meath during the late Bronze Age or early Iron Age. In Ulster's sacred and secular center, the sovereign goddess of the land, the Macha, is a third of the Morrígna. The Macha rules from her sacred center of Emain Macha or Navan Fort, where the kings of Ulster married the Goddess and the land via *ban feis*. The fires of the cross-quarter holidays, other than Lughnasadh, would be lit from the respective holiday fires and brought to Emain Macha for distribution across Ulster. Just as Brigid represents the "light half" of the dark half of the year (winter), Macha represents the "dark half" of the light half of the year (summer). The harvest festival of Lughnasadh is when the Macha reminds us that winter is coming and that it would be wise in the seasonal time of abundance to store food away for the cold months ahead. While all cross-quarter festivals would have been riddled with games and competitions, Lughnasadh *was* the festival of games, races, mock combat, hurling championship matches, and musical/bardic competitions. Victors would have been awarded golden spears, modeled after Lugh's spear, *Gae Assail*.

The Macha, as the sovereign matron deity of the land and a winter goddess, is often represented by a horse, raven, or crow. She is associated with the land, fertility, kingship, and war. Like her sister the Morrígu, the Macha is fierce and not akin to flowery speeches and beating around the bush. She demands candor. She wants to get to the heart of matters and is a remover of ego, similar to the Hindu goddess Durga. She marks the edge of her territory of Ulster with her brooch, also known as the "Mast of Macha," referring to the heads of people that have been slaughtered in battle.[92] Preparation, strategy, and foresight are critical traits that she instills. Full storerooms are the lifeblood of the tribe in times of need. The Macha is also known for her curse of the Ulstermen that led to the near fall of Ulster to Connacht in *Táin Bó Cúailgne* (Cattle Raid of Cooley) and still plagues the region even into the modern-day Troubles in Northern Ireland.

Ulster is a gorgeous realm. Vast coastlines in Donegal and along the north coast from Derry past the Giants Causeway command the western and northern landscape. The Derryveagh Mountains create an imposing contrast to the rolling hills of the east, where the largest lake in Ireland, Lough Neagh, snugs up against Emain Macha. In the

◇◇◇◇◇◇◇◇◇◇◇◇◇◇

92 *Mast of Macha,* as in mast of acorns, the seeds of the great trees which were the storehouses of Celtic knowledge in the oral tradition, were also symbols of mind and ego. She wore a necklace of the egos of the fallen; In Celtic lore, the head is the house of the soul. See Tom Cowan's *Fire in the Head.*

southwest, at the border with Connacht, the mysterious Lough Erne holds some of Ireland's sweetest and darkest secrets while the Giants Causeway in the north outlines Ireland's geological, cultural, and mythological connection to Scotland. The west of Ulster holds some of Ireland's most remote and intact secrets, waiting for the *seanchaí*, the seeker, the poet, the musician, the seer, or the bard to uncover some timeless secret and bring it into the light of the modern day. After the celebration at Lughnasadh, the high king and the *ollamhs* would return to the sacred center until Samhain when it was time to continue the Wheel of the Year once again. And thus, one turn of the Wheel is complete, and it begins again.

Chapter Four

MORRÍGU AND CONNACHT

"The impact of Celtic riddles is similar to that derived from the Zen koan: initial confusion, resulting in the stretching of mental limits, which in turn increases the elasticity of the imagination."

~ Tom Cowan

The Morrígu came to me in the aftermath of the destructive forces of divorce. She was the second *aisling* to enter my life from *Tír na nÓg*. At the time, I did not know it, but she was inviting me to heal, to liberation, and to greater responsibility as an Irish-Celtic lore keeper, a *seanchaí*. With no money in my pocket, I followed her dream trails, her *aisling*, halfway across the world to Ireland. The Morrígu had been weaving symbols and waking visions scattered across my path. Once on the Emerald Isle, my Irish sister, fellow bard and *seanchaí* Sinéad de Búrke, helped me follow the Morrígu's clues to their source. Having grown up in the Catholic faith, there was not a lot of room for interpretation of the images that came to me in those months of coming apart after divorce. I was not sure how to prepare for the journey or for what would greet me when I arrived. My world was upside-down. Everything I had come to believe about the makeup of the world and the rules of humanity seemed to be thrown to the wind. I was hungry for an understanding of what had happened in my life and why.

The Morrígu, semi-analogous with the Indian goddess Kali, is quite content to lop off the head of one's ego and throw it to her crows. She did that for me in a big way and has continued to nudge me along in my life. The essence of the divine feminine presence associated with the Morrígu is that of cutting directly to the root of any inquiry. She can be like an impatient mother that does not put up with imbecility—she wants the answer, and she wants it now. She can also be like a demanding lover—telling you exactly how she wants it, when, and where. One is better off not arguing with her and completing the task at hand she has solicited. Ultimately, it is in your best long-term interest anyway.

The Morrígu is also often referred to as the *Mórrígan* (*Mór-Ríoghain* in modern Irish) and her name means the "great queen." Via innuendo, her name can also mean the "phantom queen" and her influence was once known in all the Celtic lands, including continental Europe. Currently, she is mostly known in Ireland and emerges through many myths and legends as a "dark mother" or "dark goddess."[93] Truly, she is the winter essence of the original primordial Mother Goddess. The Morrígu's high holy day is the cross-quarter at Samhain, the beginning of the Celtic New Year. Her name bears the title and rank of greatness: *mór* (Old Irish), literally meaning "great." Her abode is in the west and northwest of Ireland in the historic kingdom of Connacht. In Connacht, her sites are centered on the sacred sites at Ráth Cruachan, specifically at Oweynagat (Cave of the Cats), and north to Keshcorran Hill (and the Caves of Kesh), Strand Hill, Carrowmore, and Carrowkeel.

The Morrígu is an aspect of the trinity of the winter, the north, and the dark goddesses of Ireland: the three Morrígna. The classic Celtic symbol of the *triskele* is hers (Figure 10). In all her aspects, she is habitually associated with war and fate, especially with foretelling doom, death, or victory in battle. In this role, she often appears as a crow (*badb* in Irish). She incites warriors to battle and helps bring about victory over their enemies. The Morrígu encourages warriors to perform brave deeds and strike fear into their enemies. In many classic myths and legends, as well as from the Celtic renaissance, she is portrayed washing the bloodstained

◇◇◇◇◇◇◇◇◇◇◇◇◇◇

[93] The Morrígu is possibly found in the UK, but scholars love to debate. She is everywhere.

clothes of those fated to die. She is the sovereignty goddess of Connacht and is still represented in the flag of Connacht in the white half with the black crow (also referred to as a "black eagle"). The arm represents the strength of the warriors of Connacht (classically the O'Connor clan).

Figure 10: Triskele

The Morrígu, as well as her counterparts in the Macha and the Cailleach (Badb), did not get absorbed into the Catholic faith as a saint as did the summer goddesses like Bridget, Áine, and Anu. The Morrígu as a goddess could not be absorbed into and revered in the new Christian faith as she represented the darker, authoritarian power of women and could not be tucked neatly into the Church's box of what a woman should be: subservient and docile. Instead, she was twisted into what the Irish now call the wailing, shrieking, or keening *beansídhe*. The *beansídhe* are portrayed as dark, malevolent spirits of the Celtic Otherworld and often appear as twisted, crippled, old women—who cry out the death of a loved one or family member. As the sovereign goddess of the land, winter, and fierce protector of her people, the Morrígu is a direct portal to the primordial feminine power of the Earth.

The Morrígu's essence travels through iron and moon blood. She has a potent magnetic allure that can drive any warm-blooded man or woman to rut. She wields a strong arm in battle and is emboldened with fierce passion in love. She often bares the Sword of Nuada in the right hand and the shield of Erin in the left.[94] She calls the mists and the crows to cover the

94 *The Sword of Nuada* is also known as the "Sword of Light," one of the jewels gifted from the *Tuatha Dé Danann* to the Irish people. The Shield of Erin may refer to the White Shield of Hu Gadarn, the all-father of the Welsh. See Kenneth Morris' *Book of Three Dragons.*

field of vision of the foe, and she sings incantations to the winds to bend the course of invading vessels. In the caves that belong to the Morrígu, her lobelia flower is constantly overflowing with pure water, especially in the depths of winter. When she rides to battle with her legions of the Faë, trees bend beneath the howling of her winds and the deluge of her rains. And when she makes love, the mountains tremble in ecstasy. She is the queen of Samhain, the summer's end, and is one of the guardians of the great Wheel of the Seasons and all of Ireland.

She calls to her lover, "Come to me, warrior. Come to me and ride the rhythms of the mountains, buried beneath elf clouds and dragon fog. Tremble and shake. Sing your pleasures as you slide up this falling water that is only mine to share with you from my freedom to choose you on this night."

"Then I shall mount your steed, my Lady," says he. "And I will gladly ride until the sun has risen in the east, and then sets in the west, and your rivers run strong with my seed, bringing fertility to the plains below. Let us ride and sing."

The mountains shake with pleasures that only a goddess can know. It is as if her mountain might collapse on itself, but her lover knows that she has done this before. Whether she rides to battle, to love, or to rule with a strong arm, welcoming breast, or open heart, the Morrígu will always be found where passion pounds like the ocean against the sea cliffs in the lands of Erin.

The Goddess Morrígu

In the beginning, there was darkness. And from the darkness ushered forth a sound: a great cacophony of voices like a murder of crows (*badb*) squeezing through a pinhole-sized opening in the void. The black hole became a great mouth raining the song of the *badb* forth like the cry of a newborn child and the gasping last breath of a crone. A spark was kindled times three, summoning a great fire enveloping the blackness. As the fire curled in intricate designs around and within that blackness, the obscure began to coalesce into a cauldron. Laughter filled the darkness and from the flickering light of the swirling flames, the great mouth, the Morrígu, was seen draped in a black cloak scattered with the pinpoint lights of a thousand stars, scrying over the cauldron. She stirred the contents of the cauldron with a spiraled birch wand while drawing pussy willow flowers, hazelnuts, and acorns from the belt of Orion wrapped around her slender waist, and slowly slipped them into the cauldron.

Laughing heartily with the thunder of crows beneath her voice, she sprinkled more hazelnuts across the surface of the boiling cauldron whilst stirring the death of one star and the birth of a new one. The black hole of death became the white hole of the womb of creation.

"Come ye again from the Summerlands, my love," she cried. "Come forth from the void and return, return, return. Take flight! Become life! It is your time! Twist you then through the confines of death beyond death, and braid again your essence through the spiraling, undulating Celtic knots of your heritage. Beneath wing and wind, set your soul afire and ride again across the heaving breasts of *Éire* in her ecstasy of conception and through the birth pains of creation."

Our DNA is a fragment of the cosmic serpent twining betwixt dark matter and atoms—binding them together in the temporal forms in the mystery of life. Our DNA is the Celtic knot of our creation story. There is no end and no beginning—only threshold moments of change where matter and energy change form.[95] The energy current that we know of as life is a continuum. The Celtic heritage is the codex instilled in the First Law of Thermodynamics.

In our human forms, as we are dependent on the cycles of life and the sun, we have created relationships with the predictable patterns of our known universe to prepare ourselves for the threshold moments: birth, conception, marriage, god-consciousness, death—spring, summer, fall, and winter. Life begins with conception in the dark of the womb just as it began in the cauldron of the Morrígu stirring from the darkness. And

95 The first law of thermodynamics implies that matter can neither be created nor destroyed. Through the work of Albert Einstein, we now know that the total amount of energy in a closed system cannot be created nor destroyed—though it can be changed from one form to another as mass and energy are essentially equivalent. This is what Einstein meant when he wrote $E=MC^2$. Mass became another form of energy that had to be included in a thorough thermodynamic treatment of a system. We also know that there are truly no closed systems outside of academia. The universe is a dynamic birth and death of all things changing forms and transferring energy.

so, the Celtic New Year begins when Orion's seed is planted in the womb of the Great Mother, the Morrígu, at Samhain. This also happens to be when Orion arrives on the eastern horizon at sunset in the northern hemisphere. The Celts believe their constellation of origin is Orion, specifically the belt.

The Morrígu calls for her star lover to lay his seed within the warm earth of her womb. Acorns and hazelnuts alike, buried throughout her ripe fields of Connacht, awaiting the warmth of spring, are planted deep by squirrels and other allies of the Winter Dreamer. It is in the dreaming that these lovers call to one another as perhaps you were once called by your beloved.

It can be difficult to hear the call and the dream of the Morrígu if one is completely absorbed in the summer of life or the light spectrum. If everything in life has gone perfectly smoothly, according to plan, and you are most akin to a character in "The Brady Bunch" or "Leave it to Beaver," then perhaps you know this place, but then you probably would not be reading this. If one's world is simply perfect—too warm and comfortable—the soul stagnates and can become complacent. Laziness and apathy set in—leaving the soul starving. Too much effortlessness leaves little room for the subtle to enter—there is no room or willingness to learn.

> *"The dark side of the human reality [is] with no conflict, no challenge, the fire within winks out without the flame. Society stagnates, slipping into slow decline. A conflict, a challenge, is a reason to exist."*
>
> ~ A.G. Riddle

The Morrígu has a way of showing up in most people's lives when they have been broken open by hardships—through the dark nights of the soul. Let us be real: very few people really want suffering, coldness, hunger, or to experience loss or betrayal. Yet, most people experience these to some degree in their lives, even as a culture. We Celts are fiercely willing to defend our freedom. Over the ages, our ancestors have gone through great lengths to avoid the hungry arms of insatiable empires and to sustain our cultural sovereignty. And thus, our ancestors migrated north and west again and again to the cold fringes of the known world to maintain freedom and avoid the sickness of empire states that dominate the complacency of warmer climates.

When we have been broken open by life's hardships, we run to the arms and heart of the Great Mother, often to the Morrígu amongst others. Through the cracks of life's trials and tribulations, the Celts seek out the quiet and loving embrace of the void where all things begin. Many scholars believe that the Morrígu is the original Mother Goddess of the dawn of humanity. I am glad that they think that, if it makes them feel better academically. For us Celts, not bogged down with the need to please the empire of academia, we already know that she is the original Mother without need for references and old scrolls…just like I know my eyes are hazel green without needing an optician's confirmation.

The Morrígu calls to us in our dreams. She calls to the broken warrior to come home. She cries out over those who have fallen in the battles of life. Her crows and ravens circle the carnage of our lives, picking at the remains, leaving only clean, scattered bones to bleach in the sun and return to the earth. She is the great peace that comes with death. She is the sovereign goddess of the free Celts and the ward of the mists that cloak our trail as we disappear into an ancient forest of gnarly oaks and linden. The Morrígu protects us from the ravenous, insatiable appetites of those who would seek to control us and bend us to their will. In her dark, cold mystery, the Morrígu is the ultimate freedom of the divine feminine. Listen for her and the three Morrígna's battle cries in the icy winds of winter, in the cool evenings of autumn, and in the heat of conflict.

I grew up in the house of the summer goddess—with a strong sense of place, family, belonging, abundance, and health. I know the summer and her eternal presence like the back of my hand. Gold resonates in the entirety of my soul due to the gift of place and belonging that my family and heritage bestowed upon me. I do not take this gift lightly. As Irish poet Seamus Heaney so aptly says:

> *"If you have a strong first world and strong set of relationships, then in some part of you, you are always free; you can walk the world because you know where you belong, you have some place to come back to."*[96]

◇◇◇◇◇◇◇◇◇◇◇◇◇◇◇

[96] Seamus Heaney at the Magherafelt Civic Reception, January 1996.

The summer light within me blinded my vision to the rich dark places that exist in the worlds within. As a parable, I recall in 2015, a time when I was leading a group of adventure-seeking twenty-somethings into the primeval cloud forest in Guatemala—long before we had secured the conservation of tens of thousands of acres. One night after sunset, some of us crawled out of our base camp under the dark of the new moon. We brought flashlights but left them in our pockets. We crawled over massive ancient tree roots and past little waterfalls, "seeing" by feeling where we were going with our hands. Our eyes adjusted to the dark of the forest in about twenty minutes once we were away from the campfire. Wonder and magic slowly revealed themselves like partially-transparent silk sliding off the skin of a lover in the depths of night. Phosphorescent life peaked out from the barely-discernable shapes of the forest; slowly at first, until our eyes adjusted. Bioluminescent mushrooms, leaves, and mycelium declared themselves slowly in long threads throughout the forest floor, along trees, and up-hanging vines. All along, this gorgeous biological yet Otherworldly phenomenon was present right in front of our faces, but we could never see it due to the overwhelmingly bright light of flashlights and staring into campfires.

We had been blinded by the light.

Yet, with this new discovery of bioluminescence, we were absolutely in heaven. We covered our faces and bodies with the mycelium until our skin glowed. And we were off in our imaginations—not having to stretch it too far—in the Mayan Otherworld, following the trails of jaguars and screaming with joy at the howler monkeys who had come to observe our *redicularity*.[97] This lasted for several hours, a few minutes, or a couple of years depending on who is sharing the telling. That is neither here nor there, for it truly was timeless...until one of our Mayan guides came into the forest looking for us with a bright flashlight.

Oh! We were blinded! The light hurt our eyes. And guess what? We could not see a thing anymore. After sending him back to base camp once we let him know we were okay, it took another twenty minutes for

[97] Yes, I made this word up. Hail to the wordsmiths who have gone before us! Otherwise, we would still be grunting in caves.

our sight to return. After a few more moments of living light bliss, we chose to head back to camp as our guide was concerned that we would become a jaguar snack.

The Morrígu reminds us of one thing in particular: sometimes the light can blind us. I had been blinded by the light.

It was not until my life was coming apart during divorce that there was room for the deeper light, the living light of bioluminescence, to penetrate my sight and reveal undiscovered worlds. It was not until Rome cut and burned the sacred groves of our Celtic ancestors in Gaul that the Celts recognized the importance of the cloister and the true gift of freedom. My divorce was the shattering of an idea. On one level, my life came apart and granted me the opportunity to reinvent myself. On another level, I experienced the shattering of an imbalanced relationship with the divine that allowed the Morrígu to finally be seen and heard.

She began by taking me apart, piece by piece, deconstructing my beliefs and my idea of the shape of the world. The Morrígu was initiating me to the first order of the Celtic Mysteries: die to be reborn—the circle of life is a continuum. As I crossed the threshold of my unmaking, I found the raw materials within for something greater. To become a refined instrument of the divine in the symphony of life, I had to first find the elements for inner alchemy. Deep into the void I turned, calling to my allies found along the way in life's journey. I found the stones, wood, and ore in sacred caves, streams, and mountains along the quest. These raw materials were in turn fed into the hot fires of the Morrígu. Through the progression of the journey and through the dark of life and the dark of the year—the raw materials I gathered were heated and melted. The Morrígu helped me draw forth the impurities until the resultant pure gold, silver, and copper emerged. Through practice and refinement—through the massive internal pressure of change like the Earth's tectonic movements where fine gems grow—a better man and the *seanchaí* began to emerge through the alchemy of transformation.

And so it is every year in a lesser way. Winter sets in at Samhain and we spend our dark months refining until we have drawn forth the precious gifts of our inner alchemy. Then, and only then, are we ready for Bridgit's flame at Ímbolc. Then, and only then, are we ready for the forge, anvil, and hammer of the divine to shape us into something beautiful, unique, and stronger than ever before. With the aid of the Morrígu, we continue to refine, learn, and be made whole. We become the living craft of the divine—the turning, twisting cosmic serpent, alive in our DNA, coursing ever through the universe.

The Morrígu calls from her high haunts in Connacht. She calls from her Caves of Kesh. She calls from Oweynagat, Carrowkeel, and Carrowmore. The Morrígu calls from the mists in the Twelve Bens of the Connemara. She calls through the pain of betrayal or the guilt of digressions from our true path. The Morrígu calls from the icy dragon winds of winter. She howls on the cliffs of the Atlantic Ocean. She beckons through the Dark Mother and a thousand cultural forms and names from around the world. She rises in our tears and cries for freedom and relief. Through the cold, she cuts through the fluff and demands the refinement of our gold. The Morrígu brings our inner eye to the most effective places in our lives where we should commit energy, intent, and time.

When the Morrígu calls, it is because it is time to look where you do not want to look—to see your blind spots. When she calls, it is time to stand for what you believe in and claim your birthright. It is time to take a stand for the essence of all things Celtic: freedom, loyalty, and the health of the land. The Morrígu calls us home.

At Samhain every year, the Morrígu rides forth from her *sí* (home) near the town of Sligo with her mounted troop of the *sídhe*, searching across the land for those who are ready to come home. And so, I close with the magical writing of one of our forefathers whose *aisling* also brought him home to lands of the Morrígu to witness the annual riding of the *sídhe* from the Caves of Kesh, William B. Yeats. He invokes in this classic poem the essence of the *Slua Sídhe,* the fairy host who travel in the whirling wind as it sweeps through the countryside at Samhain.[98] In front of the host rides Niamh, the fairy maiden who enticed Oisín to spend three hundred years in *Tír na nÓg*:

◇◇◇◇◇◇◇◇◇◇◇◇◇◇

[98] *Slua Sídhe* is the galivanting host of the Faë and the wild winds they create in their wake are called the *Gaoithe Sidhe.*

The Hosting of the Sídhe

The host is riding from Knocknarea
And over the grave of Clooth-na-Bare;
Caoilte tossing his burning hair,
And Niamh calling Away, come away:
Empty your heart of its mortal dream.
The winds awaken, the leaves whirl round,
Our cheeks are pale, our hair is unbound,
Our breasts are heaving, our eyes are agleam,
Our arms are waving, our lips are apart;
And if any gaze on our rushing band,
We come between him and the deed of his hand,
We come between him and the hope of his heart.
The host is rushing 'twixt night and day,
And where is there hope or deed as fair?
Caoilte tossing his burning hair,
And Niamh calling Away, come away.

Offerings Appropriate for the Morrígu

Offerings are often left at the dozens of cairns located on the mountains and hills of counties Roscommon, Leitrim, and Sligo as well as in her caves at Kesh, Oweynagat, Cong, and more; her lakes of Lough Key, Lough Arrow, Lough Allen; in springs/streams of Connacht, Glencar Waterfall; and in the blanket bogs of the Twelve Bens of Connemara (*Na Beanna Beola*). They can be left in her fire at Samhain, the twisted old oak groves of the Connemara, or buried in the earth at Carrowkeel, Strandhill, Carrowmore, and her other favorite haunts. She can be demanding and will make it obvious what the appropriate offering you should bring is—especially if it makes you feel some initial resistance to making the offering due to attachments, either positive or negative. The offering contains a power that supersedes our mortal nature and thus will enact change via the tribute. She will let you know. I suggest listening and following suit—it will bode you well in life and with those that you love. She is fiercely loyal to those who respect her.

Offerings include, but are not limited to: Jewelry (iron, gold, silver, bronze, copper), obsidian, clay votives, goddess figurines, knives/blades, acorns, hazelnuts, hair, bones/teeth (engraved or painted too), stone/crystal, milk and honey, woad powder/paint, rushlights, pleasure/sex, sexual fluids, flowers, spearheads, bronze/gold/silver/copper torc(s)/brooches.

Chapter Five

BRIGID AND LEINSTER

Brigid may be my favorite goddess and saint in the Irish tradition.[99] My family has a powerful connection with her, both as a goddess and as a saint via the Catholic Church. My mother's family has held St. Brigid's Feast Day (or Ímbolc)—on February 1—as sacred since I was a child. My mom's mother used to travel on pilgrimage to Ireland to visit Brigid's sacred center and holy well in Kildare in the historic kingdom of Leinster. She also kept Brigid's crosses and statuary in and around her home. Every spring, the family collects the rushes (*Juncus spp.*) from sacred springs and meadows to create the equally-armed Brigid crosses to hang over doors, give as gifts, and leave as offerings.

The beauty of contemporary Irish culture is the hybridization of traditional beliefs of the indigenous Celtic people with that of the Ionian Church and later the Roman Catholic Church. As we see in the context of Irish history, everyone who invaded Ireland essentially became Celtic through the adoption of cultural traditions, language, and the arts. Brigid is a golden example of the marriage of the ancient traditions with the new or Celtic with Christianity. I can remember my grandmother speaking fondly of Saint Brigid. She would allude to the beauty and power of this Irish saint. Granted, Brigid of Kildare is a saint for all Catholics, but there is something in the fierce Irish pride that claims her as one of our own.

99 The Foleys will kindly remind me that everything is my favorite: every season, flower, aspect of the divine…I stand corrected.

Before going into many details or stories, it is important to share the essence of Brigid from my personal relations. She is the promise of the end of winter. She is the fire of illumination in the dark of winter. She is the kindling of the flame of inspiration that dispels the shadow of lethargy, fear, and feelings of lack. She is family and abundance. She is the energy cracking the seeds we have stored for the winter, both from within (potential) and without (environmental). She is the return of the light in the dark half of the year.

Let me set a scene...Brigid is an ancient goddess of all six of the Celtic nations. Yet, in Ireland, she was most revered. In Ireland, the keepers of Brigid's Mysteries have sustained a continuous lineage for thousands of years, initially as a localized priestess and a druidic order, next as an internationally renowned order of bards, then as the Brigidine Sisters of the Catholic Church. *Solas Bhríde*, or "Brigid's Light," was an eternal flame kept in her sanctuary in Kildare from the Neolithic age all the way to the English attempt at Irish-Celtic cultural genocide via Oliver Cromwell in the sixteenth century. The *Solas Bhríde* was relit by the Brigidine Sisters in 1993 and they have maintained the flame ever since.[100]

On my first visit to Kildare, I had the honor of singing and dancing with the Brigidine Sisters. I was spending an afternoon at Brigid's sacred well south of the village. I was making offerings at the very well that my grandmother used to pilgrimage to when she was still with us. Looking into the water while listening to the mulling of cattle in adjacent fields in the shade of a hawthorn tree, I heard the music of a giggling gaggle of women. I turned to see a group of about thirty women beginning to weave their way among the straight row of standing stones connecting the flowing stream to the sacred well. If you are Catholic, then imagine something like the Stations of the Cross combined with saying the rosary. If you have been initiated into the Hermetic Order of the Golden Dawn or the Masons, imagine the first few tiers of initiation. If that all sounds like mumbo-jumbo to you, imagine a series of standing stones. Each stone represents a tier

◇◇◇◇◇◇◇◇◇◇◇◇◇◇◇

100 See Rita Minehan's book *Rekindling the Flame: A Pilgrimage in the Footsteps of Brigid of Kildare.* I highly suggest this for anyone going on a pilgrimage to Kildare.

of consciousness, perhaps an archetype or a stage of the journey. When one arrives at the first stone, there are certain prayers offered, songs sung, or intentions held. This helps to unwind our density, sense of separateness, and relinquish the grips of time in an alchemical process that is constructive and life-supporting. After each stone or tier is passed, one reaches the perceived goal, the holy well, and meanwhile, has brought themselves completely present.

The Brigidine Sisters were weaving between the stones, offering their prayers and libations to the holy place as I observed from the well. At each stone, they had some sort of activity, either personal or as a group. When the nuns had attained the fifth stone, they gathered in a large circle, holding hands.

One of the Sisters turned to me, smiling, and said, "Would you care to join us?"

Of course, I would! I ran over and took my place in the circle. As an image, visualize Pan and the nymphs, but the Catholic version. We spent the next twenty-five to thirty minutes singing songs, dancing circle dances, and making prayers for justice, peace, and human rights around the world. My grandmother's *aisling* was there with me, shadowing every dance and adding her strength to my singing and prayers. I know that she was dancing in the Otherworld somewhere too, albeit *Tír na nÓg* and the Kingdom of Heaven. It is all one and the same. In the end, when the dancing and prayers were complete, I discovered through introductions that only about ten of the women were Brigidine Sisters. The other women were from a German Catholic order of nuns who had come to Ireland on pilgrimage. Specifically, they had come to Kildare to spend time at all the sacred sites and to study with the Brigidine Sisters. Here is a portion of a traditional song to Brigid that I have relearned and memorized:

Gabhaim molta Bríghde, iníon í le hÉireann.
Iníon le gach tír í, molaimís go léir í.

Translation:

I give praise to Brigid, daughter of Ireland.
Daughter of all lands, let us praise her.

Brigid the Goddess

Brigid is the matron of healing, poetry, and smithcraft—all pragmatic yet inspirational bodies of wisdom that are critical for the survival of a thriving Earth-based community. Brigid is a fire deity, and her name means "exulted" or "high." Frequently depicted with red hair in the arts, Brigid's attributes are light, inspiration, and all skills associated with fire—especially fire that pushes back darkness and fear, for she is the promise of the return of the light half of the year. Although she may not be identified with the physical sun as is Áine, Brigid is the benefactress of inner healing and vital energy, and thus an alchemical derivative of the Sun. Revered in all Celtic countries and over most of Europe, she continues to be present over thousands of years, fulfilling different roles in divergent times under different religious banners. As Saint Brigid of Ireland or Brigid of Kildare, she may be the most powerful female religious figure in Irish history as can be witnessed in many place names and holy places in Ireland to this day. She is known as *Brigitania* in England, *Bride* in Scotland, *Brigandu* in France, and *Ffaid* in Wales. The Irish goddess is also known by the name spellings of *Brighid*, *Bridget*, *Brid*, and more.

Brigid's varying names and aspects reflect her original image as a triple goddess, as do most Irish goddesses. Each of the three aspects of Brigid differ in their gifts that they bestow upon people. The goddess Brigid first worshipped in ancient Ireland was the daughter of the god Dagda and the Morrígu. Originally, each aspect of Brigid was a sister of the other aspects. These three sisters in the form of the triple goddess were called the "three mothers," "three sisters," or just the "goddess Brigid." The ancient triple goddess Brigid does not represent the three chronological stages of a woman's life (maiden, matron, and crone) as in some other traditions. The three sisters or aspects of Brigid are all the same age.

The three aspects of Brigid were distinctive in their attributes and how they related to their craft. The triple aspects of Brigid are the sacred flame keepers of the Fire of the Hearth, Fire of the Forge, and Fire of Inspiration. As the goddess of the Fire of the Hearth, Brigid is the goddess of fertility, family, childbirth, and healing, thus the matron of midwives and herbal medicine. As the goddess of the Fire of the Forge,

Brigid is the matron of crafts—especially metal smithing, weaving, and embroidery—and of justice, law, and order. In this aspect, she was the goddess called upon to bring peculiarity, magic, and long life into the creation of tools, weapons, and plows.[101] The third aspect of Brigid, the keeper of the Fire of Inspiration, was the matron of poetry, song, history, and the protector of all Celtic cultural tradition; thus, the matron of poets and bardic lore.

Brigid the goddess was born at the exact moment of daybreak (think the day star—Venus) and ascended into the sky with the sun with rays of fire beaming from her head. She is the mantle that stitches together the worlds through illumination and inspiration. The goddess Brigid maintains an apple orchard in the Celtic Summerlands wherein her bees would bring their magical nectar back to Earth—the nectar of inspiration. As the goddess of spring and the promise of the return of the light half of the year, she can be seen walking the edge of the twilight with bluebells, shamrocks, and other small flowers appearing at her feet. In her love of the Earth and all things living, she eases into her sacred wells for renewal and rebirth, but first hanging her druid's cloak upon the rays of the Sun. Brigid is the light of summer in the dark of winter at Ímbolc, reminding us that we are halfway through the dark half of the year and the return to summer is nigh at Bealtaine.

Brigid as the Healer

Both a goddess and a saint, Brigid is known as a powerful healer. One of the legends of Brigid revolves around two lepers who appeared at her sacred well at Kildare and asked to be healed. Brigid agreed and instructed them to bathe one another's wounds in the holy water until their skin healed. After some time, the first one was healed. Instead of feeling empathy for the other and continuing, the healed leper felt total revulsion and would not touch their companion or continue bathing

[101] The role of the smith in any land-based tribe was a sacred duty associated with alchemical powers. This is because it involved mastering the primal element of fire and molding the metal derived from earth through skill, knowledge, and strength into a usable tool that supported the community.

their wounds. Brigid quickly realized the healed leper had not truly received the lesson in miracles and caused their leprosy to return and sent them on their way. Brigid then gently placed her cloak around the other leper who was immediately healed and walked away a whole new human being, filled with the light and renewed faith.

Ireland has over 3,000 holy springs and holy wells, and hundreds of them are named after the goddess Brigid. Her primary well is found in Kildare, though her holy well near the Cliffs of Moher in County Clare is a powerful place for healing and release and may receive as many visitors per year as her holy well in Kildare. Water is a portal to the Otherworld. Water is the source of life, and where pure water ushers from the earth, it is truly a miracle like birth and often creates powerful healings for pilgrims. The holy water from springs and wells is thus a sacrament—truly holy water—that when received in grace, faith, and devotion—or from the heart of the *sídhe*—miracles occur.

At her sanctuary in Kildare, Brigid and her priestesses taught people how to harvest, dry, prepare, and use herbs for their medicinal properties while also teaching the lore of the care of livestock and smithcraft. Her sacred center at Kildare was located near an ancient Irish oak (*Quercus robur*) that was sacred to the druids and wisdom keepers before even the Celts' arrival in Ireland. Brigid's shrine is so sacred that weapons were never allowed there. The shrine, like the other ancient sacred centers in Ireland, contained an ancient college of priestesses who came from all over Europe. These young women committed twenty-one to thirty years of training in various arts and lore. After this, many left and married into Celtic families all over Europe. These highly trained women were able to provide the council of the Goddess in a changing world. During their first seven to ten years, they received training in the arts and humanities, memorizing the runes, chants, and lore of the Celtic heritage. The next seven to ten years were spent tending the sacred wells, groves, and hills of Leinster; tending the forges in or around Kildare and Cnoc Ailinne; or promulgating the fire of inspiration, midwifery, and herbal lore. The last seven to ten years were spent teaching those who followed behind them. The priestesses also tended the perpetual flame of the sacred fire of Brigid, *Solas Bhríde*, that had burned for thousands of years. This flame was snuffed out by the English in the sixteenth century, according to Irish legend and to Rita Minehan, a leading member of the Congregation of Brigidine Sisters. The Brigidine Sisters relit the eternal flame of Brigid in 1993.

Brigid helps illuminate our path in the dark labyrinth of life. She fills us with a sense of promise of a return to the light, beauty, and grace, but she also reminds us to feed our ancestral traditions. Her eternal flame is the promise that summer is coming and that the immortals, the divine, are just within reach.

Saint Brigid of Ireland

Brigid of Ireland is one of Ireland's dearest saints, along with Saint Patrick and Saint Columba (Colm Cille), and I would propose perhaps that she is the most important saint to Ireland—even more than Patrick. Saint Brigid is Ireland's sweetheart and incorporates some of the quintessential essences of the goddess Ériu. The basic Irish biography of Brigid establishes her as an early Irish Christian nun, abbess, and foundress of several monasteries of nuns, especially that of Kildare in Ireland. Kildare was her most famous and revered abbey during the dawn of the Celtic Church in Ireland and into the present. Whether there was a historic Brigid, or if she was the combination of the goddess and a historic figure, we may never know—other than on faith alone. Brigid is believed by the Catholics to have been born in AD 451 in Faughart, just north of Dundalk, in County Louth, Ireland, in Leinster. According to legend, her mother was an enslaved Christian Pict who had been baptized by Saint Patrick, and her father was a powerful Irish chieftain.[102]

The chieftain's wife forced him to sell Brigid's mother to a druid when she had become pregnant as she did not wish to have an illegitimate child around. Like Saint Patrick, Brigid also experienced slavery, however, while Saint Patrick was captured, Brigid was born to it. Brigid learned the traditional Irish ways of healing and craft, while her mother continued to instill the new Christian fire in her heart. As she grew older, Brigid performed miracles, including healing, feeding the

[102] Picts are the indigenous people of Scotland.

poor, and giving alms when she could. Brigid was eventually returned as a household servant to her father, where her charitable nature led her to donate many of his belongings to anyone who asked. As she gave more of his wealth away and kept asking him to build her a church, her father eventually was forced to deal with her. After refusing her repeatedly, he one day exploded in anger, whipping off his cloak and shoving it into her hands. He told her, tongue in cheek, to take the cloak and spread it across the land. Wherever the cloak would cover, she could call her own and do with it as she saw fit.

I imagine he thought she would thus have enough space to build a small round house, as you see in the old ringforts of Ireland, and then he would be done with her. Yet, Brigid lifted the cloak and spun it over her head to catch the light of the sun. As she spun the cloak, it became a rainbow shower of color. She sang prayers and incantations as she spun the living rainbow over her head in the sunlight, and when her song was complete, she spread the cloak out across the land. And oh, did it spread. The rainbow cloak kept spreading and spreading across thousands of acres of her father's kingdom. Thus, Brigid legitimately claimed the lands of Kildare from her aghast father.

And so, the Christening and claim of the sacred lands of Kildare into the Christian era were completed by a pagan king in his anger trying to rid himself of his worrisome half-Christian, half-druid, and illegitimate daughter of his slave. So it goes! Lo to the man who forsakes the might of women. And furthermore, women came in droves to her call. First chapels, kitchens, farms, and houses were constructed by Brigid and her followers. Over time, their efforts of charity and grace, while maintaining the eternal flame, *Solas Bhríde,* gave rise to one of the most powerful and sacred centers of Celtic Christianity and eventually the Roman Catholic Church in all of Europe. This legacy was not strained until the Cromwellian years and the Reformation under King Henry VIII of England when the flame was extinguished.

Brigid acts as a bridge between the ancient polytheistic world of our Celtic past with the mostly monotheistic world of our present while still maintaining quintessential essences of her traditions. According to the Faërie lore of Fiona Macleod and the nineteenth-century collections of Scottish Highland legends by Alexander Carmichael,

Brigid was the midwife to Mother Mary at the birth of Christ.[103] She could step through doorways to the Otherworld from Iona, stitching together the Celtic lands of the far north with the Canaan.[104] Brigid baptized Christ in the sacred waters and initiated him into the lore of the *sídhe* and the druids before making her way back to Iona.

Ímbolc: Past, Present & Future

On the calendar, Ímbolc falls exactly between Midwinter and the vernal equinox. Celebrated at the beginning of February (typically February 1 or 4), it is the celebration of the beginning of spring and the light half of the dark half of the year. Ímbolc is the halfway point between Samhain and Bealtaine and is thus the "light half" of the dark half of the year.

Brigid is the matron of Ímbolc, and her important association with the cow (and sheep, specifically the ewe) coupled with its critical necessity in Celtic culture and history relates to the festival of Ímbolc. Remember that cattle (both steer and cows) were the greatest form of wealth to the Celtic people of all Celtic nations, not just in Ireland. Ímbolc is celebrated in response to the birthing of spring from winter via blessings of wealth and the good health of the people at the turning of the year and life. The key components to the Irish holyday include snuffing the hearth fires (and cleaning out the ashes), the lighting of the central sacred fire at Kildare (and later Tara) by the goddess/saint, the relighting of the home hearth from the central fire, and visiting sacred wells. Celebrations include the purification of implements, tools, livestock, and family members with well water and the braiding of the equal-armed Brigid's crosses to bless guests entering the home for the year to come.

To fully grasp the significance of Ímbolc, it is crucial to understand the life-and-death struggle represented by winter in any agrarian society. In a world lit only by fire and snow, cold and ice, this season literally

◇◇◇◇◇◇◇◇◇◇◇◇◇◇

103 Fiona Macleod, *The Washer of the Ford and Other Legendary Moralities*, 1896.

104 Iona, from the hill of *Dùn Í*, or the Hill of Iona, the Hill of the Yews. Fiona Macleod, *The Divine Adventure*, 1903.

holds one in its grip, only relieved with the arrival of spring. Ímbolc is the harbinger and the promise that better times are coming. During the cold months, certain issues become pressing. Is there enough food for both humans and animals? Will illness decimate the tribe, especially in the case of the young, the old, and nursing mothers? And what of the animals whose lives are so crucial to our own? One of the most burning questions would be with the pregnant cows and ewes since their milk is used for drink, for cheese and curds, which might mean the difference between life and death.

By Ímbolc, these animals will have birthed their young and their milk would be flowing. Milk, to the Celts, was sacred food, equivalent to the Christian communion or to the Hindu *prasad*. It was an ideal form of food due to its purity and nourishment. Mother's milk was especially valuable, having curative powers. The cow was symbolic of the sacredness of motherhood, the life force sustained and nourished. The flow of milk is not representative of a passive cow giving milk, but of life versus death—an active mother fighting for the well-being of her children.

Ímbolc, over time and dilution (immigration), has become the contemporary Groundhog Day in the United States, Saint Brigid's Day on the Catholic calendar, and the Feast of the Purification of Mary (Candlemas) for Christianity more broadly. I clearly remember this festival in my parish as a youth. All the candles! The music! The feasting! My favorite songs from mass at this time were called "The Canticle of the Sun" and "Dance in the Darkness."

Dance in the darkness, slow be the pace—
Surrender to the rhythm of redeeming grace.

I remember all the lights being out in the church and deep silence: a processional of women in all white floating toward the altar, one carrying a candle lit high on a brass rod. Music would build and erupt with ecstasy as the dancers flitted wildly about in the dark, churning the buildup into crescendo. Then the dancers would light their candles from the single candle and dance into the audience to light the waiting candles of all those in attendance. And the fire would spread. First, a few were lit, then hundreds, then a thousand. I remember trying hard not to drip wax onto the pews or onto my hands, or other times specifically *trying* to drip the hot wax onto my hands to fuse my fingers together. I still remember how that felt. After mass, we blew out the candles and brought them home to light our altars and hearth.

And traditional, non-Catholic Ímbolc celebrations…oh, I can remember thousands of them! Specifically, I recall the four kings of Ireland bringing Brigid across the lake on a barge of flames with flaming arrows soaring over the water from the Otherworld, and thirteen women in white dancing the spiral dance, calling in the resurgence of the holy fire. Brigid stepping through the fire hoop, spreading her flame amongst the tribe and the wildness of the dance as the inspiration spread with the light.

I too remember the lighting of the great bonfire at Cnoc Ailinne and later at Kildare by the druid keepers in white, green, and grey cloaks.[105] Male druids gathered to illuminate the space as the priestess druids collectively drew the sacred and holy fire from the Otherworld into a firebrand and rammed it into the mountain of wood. It is said that you could see the flame of that fire across all of Ireland, but I would not know as I was always there before it. The fire would sing into the night, sending sparks dancing. Scryers would look into the flames or follow the play of the sparks into the night to read the bodings of that which was to come for the year. Poets, bards, and musicians engaged in deep bouts of skill and lore craft—becoming the very living embodiments of the goddess Brigid. Feasting and merriment spilled over into the valleys, and the riders and runners would come from the four kingdoms of Ireland to light their torches and brands to carry to the other sacred centers of Ireland.

Offerings Appropriate for Brigid

Offerings are often left at the thousands at holy wells and springs all over Ireland but especially in counties of Kildare, Wicklow, and Offaly—in particular, her spring near the town of Kildare on the pilgrims' path and the spring near the Cliffs of Moher in County Clare. Additionally, offerings are left for her in the springs/streams/waterfalls of Leinster, in

◇◇◇◇◇◇◇◇◇◇◇◇◇◇◇

[105] Cnoc Ailinne, or Dún Ailinne, is the ancient sacred center of Leinster, later moved to Kildare. Also, Fionn mac Cumhaill's seat with the Fianna.

the bogs of the Wicklow Mountains, the lakes/springs of Glendalough Reeks, and in her fire at Ímbolc. They are also left in the old-growth Celtic Hardwood Forests of Glendalough, tucked into the bough of an old oak, buried in the earth at Cnoc Ailinne (Knockaulin or Dún Ailinne), and placed on the household hearth. Most importantly, as with any offering, it should truly come from the heart—and truly be a gift, not something that is dropped, lost, or is something that you want to get rid of to clear off your altar. What would you give to the most inspiring person in your life? What would you feed the very fire of your soul that inspires you to live life fully? That is where you should look.

Offerings include but are not limited to: Candles, a well-tended hearth, fire, an equal-armed cross (made with rushes), poems, verses, songs, jewelry (gold, silver, bronze, copper), clay votives, sacred/holy water, stone/crystal, milk & honey & cinnamon, alms to the poor, financial donations to social and environmental justice groups, whiskey, hazelnut tea, coins, hazelnut flatbread, bronze/gold/silver/copper torc(s)/brooches.

Chapter Six

ÁINE AND MUNSTER

"Myths are basic truths twisted into mnemonics, instruction posted from the past, memories waiting to become predictions."

~ Richard Powers

The goddess Áine, sometimes tightly braided in association with the goddesses Anu and even Danu, has been a part of my life since birth. In dreamtime, Áine is my lover and my teacher. She was the first *aisling* to enter my life from *Tír na nÓg* to guide the golden journey of my youth. She often came to me in visions as a teen and in my twenties through the direct light of the sun. She presents herself to me when my eyes are closed while lying on the earth in the sunlight or with my back against a tree. Sometimes, she appears in my mind's eye while I am drinking milk and eating grains or cereal. I see her dancing her radiant warmth in the ripening grain fields of my imagination, intuition, and prescience. Her light holds back the dark and decay of the world and was my primary association with the divine feminine, other than Mother Mary, well into my thirties when life handed me some serious hammering. The heavy experiences in that decade of my life allowed the Morrígu to begin her initiatory work on me in the years of maturation.

While I am ever a student of the Morrígu, I am first and foremost a student and son of Summer—of Áine or Anu. The golden fields of plenty and the fractal light on the edge of a storm that creates rainbows radiate from within the core of my soul—and the effervescent color has only been further augmented by the dark storms that raged through my thirties. Summer is my eternal home. I will always return there within this lifetime and beyond. I am of the Summerlands, *Tír na nÓg,* and I was born from the belly of Summer, the Áine. I grew up in the house of the summer goddess—with a strong sense of place, family, belonging, abundance, and health. I know the Summer and her eternal presence like the back of my hand. Gold resonates in the entirety of my soul due to the gift of place and belonging that my family and heritage bestowed upon me. I do not take this gift lightly.

From my earliest memories, I have been traveling within my mind's eye, imagination, and intuition, between the worlds to what I eventually came to understand was the Celtic Summerlands. I have come to understand the Otherworld as the Summerlands, perhaps partly due to my heritage, or perhaps because the Bright Realm found me. More than anything, *Tír na nÓg* revealed itself to my limited human consciousness in a form that I could understand and digest, and in which my teachers could best prepare me. This is the essence of the mysteries—that which is eternal will ever seek to find the best translation to bring our mortal nature as close to its soul's eternal nature as efficiently as possible. But do not hold on too tightly, because the climate will change, the winds will shift, divine streams will alter course, and the sea will rise and fall, changing the shape of coastlines.

Through the Celtic lens and the blessing of Áine, I have been drawn to the Summerland within my heart-mind to the sacred portals in the landscape of Ireland and beyond. When I was first awakening in my late teens and early twenties, I often found myself in vision; trance induced states and dreams, emerging in consciousness—very visually with my eyes closed—within a low circle of stones surrounded by a ring of beech and oak on the crown of a conical hill. The hill lay on the northern end of a lake fed by four streams pouring in approximately from the cardinal directions. No stream allowed water to drain from the lake. In the center of the lake was a forested island. On the eastern shore of the lake was often a village—sometimes medieval, sometimes pre-historic—sometimes a castle, and sometimes a field of brightly colored tents like one might see at a modern festival.

Once I had risen within the circle of standing stones in this reoccurring vision, I could make any manner of choices about where to proceed with my next steps. I could walk down the steep hill and dive into the lake to journey through the cave tunnels beneath the water. I could visit the oracle in her home on the forested island. I could visit the dry land caves and cairns or other stone circles around the lake. Additionally, I could visit whatever incarnation of the village presented itself on the eastern shore of the lake and typically find the soul of anyone I needed to connect with. Of course, this was well before the advent of smartphones and thus I depended completely on the original inner-net that allows souls to communicate via mycorrhiza, underground springs, and neurological pathways. This has been the primary form of distant communication that has connected humans with humans and humans with nature since the dawn of time. Áine's blessing and the tools of communication that the earth has provided allow us to communicate through the neuro-mycelium network that connects all beings.

The beauty of this world that I have come to know intimately is that this reoccurring vision of the hill, circle of stones, lake, streams, forested island, etc.—where I was brought to hundreds of times in my teens and twenties—is a real place on the planet and it is found in Ireland. It had been calling me for years to come home to the Erin and to Áine's blessed garden. On my first pilgrimage to Ireland at twenty-six years old, I met a selkie woman, Sinéad De Búrca, who guided me on a sound journey into *Tír na nÓg* in the heart of 4,500-year-old *clochán* on the Dingle Peninsula in County Kerry. The gentle waves of her voice over the pulse of the *sídhe* animating her *bodhrán* created a multi-scaled keening.[106] I found myself back in the familiar vision from throughout my life: rising through the stone circle in the ring of beech and oak over the lake with the four streams converging into it. After she brought me back from the journey, I found myself sharing the vision and the years of having the same magical location present itself again and again. Sinéad gathered up some maps and proceeded to say, "Well, lad. Why don't we go there tomorrow and have a look?"

And we did. My life will never be the same and that is part of the reason why we are here together: my hands dancing over paper in the art of wordsmithing and your eyes turning the words into images and feelings in your mind.

106 Traditional Irish frame drum.

She guided me to Lough Gur. What I found therein has humbled me ever since. What I saw seemed to come straight out of ancient mythological tales: an *aisling* guiding a human between the worlds for years until they arrive in the Otherworld or complete the necessary task to balance the harmonies. I am doing that now, here in this book. When we arrived at Lough Gur, with all its geological and human-accented structures, it looked almost exactly as I dreamed and perceived in all the visions. There were a few exceptions, such as where the village stood is now a museum highlighting Lough Gur as one of Ireland's oldest human-inhabited areas with over 6,500 years of known archaeology. Black Castle is the most prominent human habitation that remains on the shores of Lough Gur today. Additionally, the stone circle on top of the conical hill that was surrounded by beech and oaks in the vision had also changed. The stones are almost completely trampled under grass by cattle (though still quite visible), and according to the docent at the museum, the trees were cut down over 100 years ago after many of them were blown over by a wild Atlantic storm. It is a powerful spot with 360-degree views of all of Munster.

At this point in life, I know now that I had remembered Lough Gur. Call it genetic memory or soul memory, it makes no difference to me which angle we look through the lens. The result is the same. I remembered Lough Gur before arriving there in this life or having any interest in Ireland whatsoever, other than knowing my mother's people came from there.

Here at this holy place is where we remember the sun, Áine. Lough Gur is the sacred center of the Kingdom of Munster, the sacred center of the goddess Áine, and the seat of the sacred fire at Bealtaine. My dear friend, guide, and selkie queen Sinéad had brought me to one of the most sacred centers of all of Ireland where, through the mysteries, I had been many times before but never in the current body that I inhabit. She helped me remember the sacred center of Áine—to give it a name and home on the map. She introduced me to Cnoc Áine, Lough Gur, and Cnoc Finnine.

Áine, queen of the Faë, beckons to her human votaries to come home and listen. She sings in her passionate love embrace from the Grange Stone Circle, Cnoc Finnine, Cnoc an Dúin, Cnoc Áine, and all the unremembered names of countless caves, stone circles, cairns, and the remains of 6,500 years of human habitation and votive offerings. Some of Ireland's finest votive offerings from the late Megalithic all the way up to the modern age have been found in Lough Gur.[107] Offerings of weapons, shields, tools, chariots, and more, made of gold, silver, bronze, and iron. Votive offerings of antiquity are still found to this day. There remains a deep Otherworld and divine presence at Lough Gur, enough to make the heart sing and the mind pine for dreamtime amongst standing stones and ancient trees.

The Goddess Áine

The Áine is the lover and benefactor to those who embrace the virility and fertility of summer and are guardians of the bright half of the year. Often, she is depicted with a red or white mare, as a lover, or as pregnant (with the sun as her womb). Her priestesses and priests would have conducted divinations via walking with or tracking a consecrated white or red mare in her ancient oak and ash groves.[108] As a sovereign goddess of the land, Áine is the matron deity of the traditional kingdom of Munster, the southwest of Ireland. Her primary home is at Lough Gur in County Limerick, though she has many sacred sites across Munster and elsewhere in Ireland. She is patient, loving, and kind. She will wait months, years, and lifetimes for a soul to make its way home. She has all the time she needs. She knows you will come when you are ready.

Often depicted as the sun goddess of Ireland and the queen regent at the high holy day of Bealtaine (as well as Midsummer), Áine is the goddess of love and fertility; she maintains sovereignty over grain, crops, and livestock. In Irish, *Áine* means "brightness, glow, joy, radiance" with a strong emphasis also on "splendor, glory, and/or fame"—like the sun. Áine, while a manifestation of brightness, summer, and pleasure, was also the key source of *ímbas* or inspiration to the poets and druids of Munster.

◇◇◇◇◇◇◇◇◇◇◇◇◇◇◇

[107] *Megalithic* comes from the ancient Greek words *megas* (large) and *lithos* (stone).

[108] From *The Agricola* by Tacitus, written in AD 98. He also noted that the priestesses/priests would walk with a cow, goat, or other creature of the forest in addition to a red mare.

Poets, musicians, dancers, playwrights, and writers "shut themselves off from the world by blindfolding themselves or isolating themselves" in darkened rooms, caves, and other hermitages to seek her blessings and *ímbas* via esoteric practices, austerities, and travel into the Summerlands.[109]

And Áine, just as many of the other Irish-Celtic goddesses, comes in triple form: Áine, Fenne, and Gráinne.[110] Fenne is the bright lover at Bealtaine, Áine is the pregnant mother-to-be at Midsummer, and Gráinne is the matron and grain at the harvest at Lughnasadh. Gráinne also intertwines in the mysteries with the Macha and Danu, the ever-present Mother giving birth and nurturing life. Academics love to debate over the various ways these goddesses interrelate. I think they should just go outside, make love with their spouses, dance the Bealtaine fires, and romp naked in the sun for a while. Then they will see their scholarly debate is utterly ridiculous and the names are just various utterances that were likely local pre-historic deities blended.

The most prevalent triple aspect of Celtic divinity found within the context of Áine is her relationship with her two sisters: Gráinne and Fenne. Gráinne is directly associated with the Macha and the harvest. Fenne remains Áine's closer sister and shieldmaiden in the heart of Knockfennel at Lough Gur.[111] Her symbol, and the symbol of the sun on ancient sites, is three concentric circles or three circles stacked on top of one another (See examples in Figure 11). This is often much more artistically depicted on sword hilts, brooches, rings, shields, earrings, and other adornments. The famous "sun shield" created in her honor sometime during the Bronze Age was left as a votive offering in Lough Gur, yet now is on display in the National Museum of Ireland located in Dublin.

◇◇◇◇◇◇◇◇◇◇◇◇◇◇

[109] Manchán Magan, *Listen to the Land Speak,* Gill Books, 2022.

[110] Sometimes the trinity is Áine, Anu, and Danu.

[111] *Fenne,* anglicized as "Finnian," is the Irish *Fionnán*, meaning "little fair one." An appropriate name for the spring aspect of Áine that appears with the beginning of summer, or Bealtaine. Can also refer to the fennel plant *Finéal,* which in Latin (*fenum* or *faenum)* means "hay"; yet another relation through etymology to the grain/solar aspect. Fennel begins to bloom in Ireland during the Moon after Bealtaine—an appropriate edible flower of Áine.

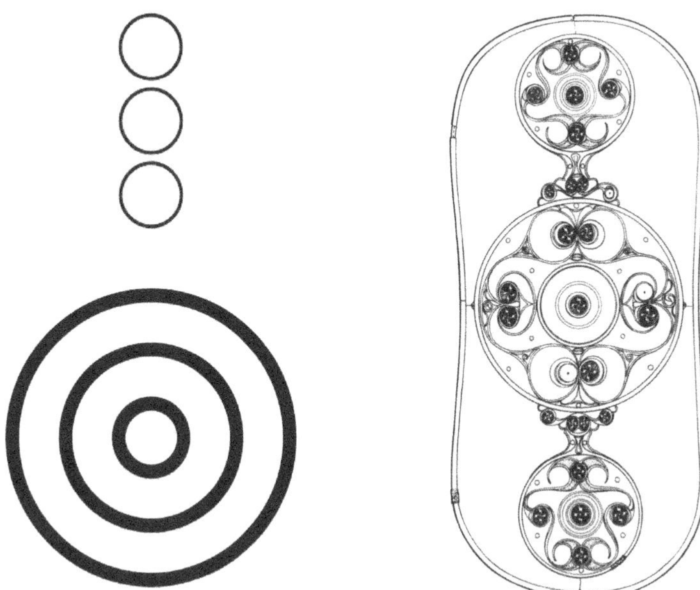

Figure 11: Triple Sun Circles

At the cross-quarter high holy day of Bealtaine, also spelled *Beltáine,* we celebrate the beginning of summer. The root of the Irish word *Bealtaine*, often hotly debated, I find best suited in P.W. Joyce's *Irish Names of Places*, where he states that *béal* is "a mouth" or "entrance to ford" across a river; and, *tine*, or *teine*, transliterates as "fire."[112] Bealtaine is thus roughly means "the fording of the fire" of the threshold between winter and summer, as well as this world and the Summerlands. At this feast, we celebrate the Anu aspect (as Fenne) of Áine, or the lover, the early aspect of summer at its inception. Twin fires were traditionally set at Cnoc Áine to bless all the livestock. The people also danced and continue to dance between the twin fires at Uisneach, Ireland's sacred center. Fires are also still lit or carried to the top of Cnoc Áine to this day. Áine is most directly celebrated at Midsummer when we

112 P.W. Joyce, *Irish Names of Places,* 1869. Also see Niall Ó Dónaill, *Foclóir Gaeilge-Béarla*, 1977.

celebrate the setting of fruit in our orchards from summer's heat and the fattening of grain, vegetables, and livestock.

The other aspect of the summer goddess is the ripening of the grain at Lughnasadh, where Gráinne becomes the Macha while Lugh and Crom battle over the dominion of the harvest. It should also be noted that the triple goddess Brigid plays a key role in the return of the light at Ímbolc, where Brigid, as the embodiment of Áine's sister, Fenne, pushes back the reign of the winter goddesses with her eternal flame at the onset of spring. This takes place as the Macha, an aspect of the winter goddess, claims her seat in the "dark half" of the light half of the year at Lughnasadh with her cool nights bringing the onset of ripening to the harvest.

Áine, in all her aspects, is most associated with love and fecundity, especially with magnetizing people to one another to create things that are larger than life. In this role, she often appears as a red horse, the sun itself, or rays of light pouring from behind clouds or at sunset. She incites lovers and allies to find one another in the vast sea of souls that pass through this world. Áine encourages patience and discernment, yet passion and inspiration grounded in tangible, real-world tasks. In many classic myths and legends as well as from the Celtic renaissance, she is portrayed as a beautiful maiden who leads as a queen regent.[113]

As the sovereignty goddess of Munster in her triple form, she is still represented in the flag of Munster by three golden crowns. Classically, these three crowns represent the historic sub-kingdoms of Munster which are Thomond, Desmond, and Ormund, where Áine, Fenne (Anu), and Gráinne sit respectively as sovereign land goddesses (Figure 12).

In the form of Mór Mumain, Áine was the wife of the Irish sea god, Manannán Mac Lir, a deity who was particularly important for Celtic warriors as well as the key guardian of *Tír na nÓg*. Hence, he was the guardian of the goddess of summer—his wife. They lived at their home at Dunmore Head at the westernmost tip of Ireland in the Kingdom of Munster on the Dingle Peninsula. The fact that this aspect of Áine,

[113] An *aisling* would ask a great boon or task to be fulfilled to help the divine or immortals influence the affairs of humans. Also to increase the amplitude of divine representation here among the mortals to maintain a strong bridge between the worlds.

Mór Mumain, has the title for "great" *(mór)* in it, indicates that the Mór Mumain is the primordial aspect of the Great Mother in her summer goddess form—as the Morrígu is the primordial aspect of the Great Mother in her winter form.

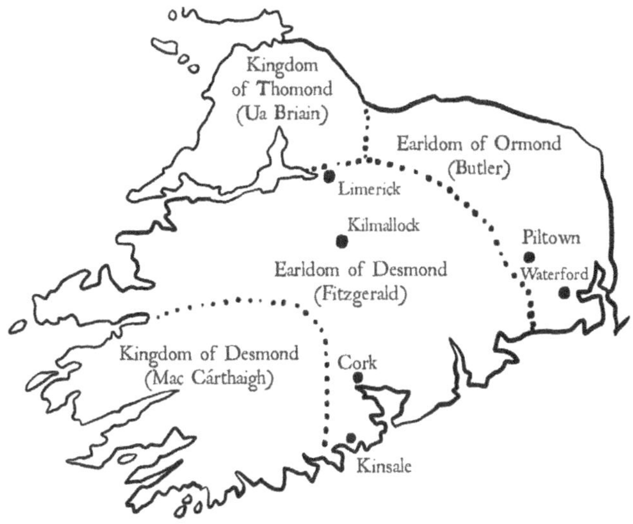

Figure 12: Map of the Sub-Kingdoms of Munster

Áine is the goddess who wards Munster in the southwest of Ireland. Her essence travels through sap, running water, and the warm rays of the Sun. She can have a potent sexual allure when she chooses, but in the mythologies, she has been subjected to the uncontrolled ravings of the masculine that often come with war and conquest. Therefore, she can also represent the resilience of the land and of women rising throughout the dark nights of the soul to sovereignty and healing. Her persona is patient, kind, and downright saucy if desired. In the caves that belong to Áine, she waits to be stirred into her passionate abandon by those who have earned the right or who seek her boons. She rides forth with her legions of the Faë every Midsummer. Some Irish say that every seven years, she rides around Lough Gur and the Irish countryside, spreading allure and desire for life before diving back into the depths of Lough Gur to emerge again later from her sacred caves. She is the queen of Bealtaine, the summer's beginning, and is one of the great guardians of the great Wheel of the Seasons and all of Ireland.

Áine calls to us through visions. She calls her people to come home. The refinement of pure elements from the raw materials gathered in the winter under the Morrígu's tutelage are shaped into intricate tools and art by Brigid. They spring to life between the twin flames of Bealtaine and work to create abundance and rich harvest under the heat of Áine's sun before the Macha brings us around the Wheel of the Year to Samhain and rebirth again. During Áine's reign in the Wheel of the Year, all become fertile, vibrant, whole, and rich. She is the embodiment of action, pleasure, and love. She is the quick growth sprouting from the intricate plans of winter and the planting of seeds after Ímbolc. Áine and the celebration of Bealtaine are the fiery expressions of life and vitality. As the ward of summer, she is pure celebration and the essence of life.

The dark and cold of winter would destroy us through erosion and decay if it were not for the brightness of the summer light to keep it in balance. Life would not be possible without the life-giving sun whose brightness brings all nourishment to fullness. In far-north countries like Ireland, the Sun's life-giving qualities become amplified and critical for life—while perhaps in the regions closer to the equator, the sun can be harsh and cruel. I believe this is why the sun is considered a goddess to the Celtic people as her warmth is life—not like the harsh warrior sun gods of the Mediterranean.

Áine calls from her sweeping landscapes in Munster. She calls from her caves at Knockfennel (Cnoc Finnine) and Knockadoon Hill. She calls from the great stone circles of Lough Gur and all over the west of County Cork and the east of County Kerry. She cries ecstatically to her people to come home to Cnoc Áine, Cnoc Finnine, the Paps of Anu, and from hundreds of holy wells and springs across Ireland. She calls from the dancing light of the sun through mist and clouds draped over mountains, and from her fortress at the edge of the world at Dunmore Head. Áine calls to us through vision, pleasure, and the unencumbered path where the obvious answer is the only answer. Áine calls through languid, humid winds of summer and the rainbow after the storm. She cries in passion at the breaking of her lover's waves, again and again, along the red sandstone cliffs of her earthly limbs where they embrace the Atlantic Ocean. She beckons through the Bright Mother and a thousand names from around the world: Mother Mary, Saraswathi, Venus, Aphrodite, and more.

Áine rises with us in our victories, joys, and deep, true healing. Within the warmth that she provides, she encourages us to trust and let go. She magnetizes our awareness to the abundant places in our lives on the near horizon, or perhaps already found right in front of us in our blind spots. Áine is always gently calling. She will patiently wait until we get all our obstacles out of the way or until we are ready to admit that obstacles are just part of life and that any self-deprecating stories we keep telling about ourselves are simply our own tethers and limitations. She reminds us that it is time to step into our whole, healed selves, and accept our birthright of thriving with abundance, wellness, and kin.

At Bealtaine every year around the first of May, Áine invokes the fertile *sídhe* of the earth and sky to stir the recalcitrance of winter. She stirs the longing for life and restores the fire in our blood that keeps death held back another year—and opens the pathway to birth new life.

Offerings Appropriate for Áine

Offerings are often left at the hundreds of stone circles of counties Kerry and Cork, in her caves at Lough Gur and Dunmore Head, in her lakes (Lough Gur and others), in her springs/streams, in the waterfalls of Kerry. They can be left in the bogs of the McGillycuddy Reeks, in her fires at Bealtaine, in her old-growth Celtic Hardwood Forests of Munster, or buried in the earth at Cnoc Áine, Cnoc Finnine, the Paps of Anu, Cashel, and other favorite haunts. Most importantly, as with any offering, it should truly come from the heart—and truly be a gift, not something that is dropped, lost, or that you want to get rid of to clear off your altar. What offering would you give to the love of your life? That is where you should look.

Offerings include but are not limited to: Jewelry (gold, silver, bronze, copper), chert, rush braids, flower crowns, clay votives, goddess figurines, silk strands, shields (wood, bronze, gold, silver, copper), hair, stone/crystal, milk & honey & cinnamon, woad powder/paint, pleasure/sex, cyprine, seminal fluid, bread, grain, flour, flowers, seeds (native to the region, please), swords, axes, bronze/gold/silver/copper torc(s)/brooches, songs, music, and musical instruments.

∞

Chapter Seven

MACHA AND ULSTER

"It's not what you look at that matters, it's what you see."

~ Henry David Thoreau

The Macha is the goddess that I thought I knew the least about, and through the unfolding mysteries, ended up being the sovereign goddess who I know the most intimately—just not in name.[114] For years, I found myself musing over how the Irish goddesses had all been working with me, calling me, and singing to me since I can remember—except for the Macha. When I finally ascended her mound at Emain Macha in the summer of 2018 for the first time with my wife, Carrie, I felt almost nothing.[115] The day was lovely. The ancient ash, oak, and beech trees were tossing gentle conversations betwixt themselves, with the crows and magpies adding the high notes. Other than that, there was a gentle numbness in the energetic field at Emain Macha, even with all the wind singing and the gorgeous views of the rolling countryside and

114 Martins/Kilmartins/MacGilmartins/Gilmartins of Sligo, Galway, and Roscommon in Connacht, through which my mother's kin lines run, were the descendants of the chiefs of the Barony of Clogher in County Tyrone in Ulster—the heart of the Macha's sovereign domain.

115 *Emain Macha* is the Macha's sacred center in Ulster.

village. Little seemed to be communicated from where I had frequently heard what I understand to be the voice of the Goddess or of other local variants of the sovereign divine feminine.

I was a bit let down initially. It felt like I had just come home from a long international pilgrimage—where my entire soul had awakened in exultation to the majesty of the universe—and then I entered my parent's house in the US in the lower Midwest and was directed to the couch in front of the television to talk about random things of no import. No one asked me what I experienced out there on the journey. Family business as usual. But wait! I have so much to share, and no one seems to be interested in asking about what I have seen and found along the Way...

I sat in the center of the mound at Emain Macha and closed my eyes. I am not sure what I was expecting: bells and whistles, a parade, or a bunch of ancient Celtic warriors to step out from behind the gnarled old oaks and say, "Behold! Our great chief has returned from far away. His ancestors fled this place because they were starving to death. And they were experiencing one of the most vile attempts at first-world genocide in the history of the Western world. All hail!" No, what I found was a deep quiet—a haunting quiet—like the peace of resting your head on the breast of your mother or some other kindred soul whose love goes beyond time, space, and definition.

When I opened my eyes, there at my feet was a cluster of raven feathers. In exchange, I left a fingerful of dried mugwort, some of my hair, a horned coral fossil from the Ohio Valley, and a splash of water from Brigid's well in Kildare. I knew that the feathers would make lovely Macha braids for offerings later or to tie in the mane of the horse that my daughter Aela was working with in equine therapy. At this point, I knew it was also time to leave Emain Macha. The Macha did not seem to have a big medicine for me like I was hoping to find, but instead, the Macha gave me a few feathers that I could pass on to my daughter and her stubborn horse.

It was not until much later that I recognized the beauty and power in the gift the Macha had given me. Her medicine for me was not about ovations, visions, and clear explosive experiences like I have had with the Morrígu, Brigid, Áine, Danu, Mór Mumain, and the Cailleach. The Macha's medicine for me was that some aspect of her *is* my mother. She provides abundance so that I lack for nothing yet does not give too much so I become lazy, complacent, or recalcitrant. She provides strength so I may lean into her when I am weary and lift me up when I have fallen. She provides succor and nurturance so that I am at home in the world and ever nourished by the grace of God, whatever the cultural or gender assignation or name. She encourages confidence and exploration so that the only limits of what I can do in the world are self-created. She instills compassion and empathy, to remember that many people are starving and need to be lifted. More than anything, she is love—the deep love of belonging, place, people, and faith. She reminds me ever to listen to and follow my heart.

No matter what I find in the world, when I return home, there are always chores and piles of hot delicious food fresh from the garden. Coming home to my mother is just like coming home to the Macha. The Macha does not have much interest in grandeur. She never falls for glamor spells. She wants the real deal—clearly and expressively. And do not cross her or make her angry, for then you get to see the wrath of the Macha as her green eyes bulge out, her red hair stands on end, and steam pours out of her ears, nose, and mouth. The Macha is fiercely loyal, sometimes to a fault, and is ever forgiving—until she is not, and then, my friends, it is kind to say, get out of Dodge, get out of Ulster—get out of wherever she is, for the Macha becomes a dragon with a fury to melt steel and stone alike.

If the Morrígu can be semi-analogous with the Indian goddess Kali or Durga, then the Macha can most be associated with the Kali aspect of Parvati.[116] She protects that which needs protecting. She gets straight to the point of things without any tolerance for lollygagging. And if driven to extremes, the Macha will discipline and punish to teach a vital lesson. The children of Ulster are still not fully recovered from a curse, the Irish *géis,* that indirectly keeps the majority of Ulster from joining the Republic of Ireland, and under the direct rule of England, in the United Kingdom.

---

[116] Parvati is the Hindu goddess of fertility, love, beauty, harmony, marriage, children, and devotion as well as divine strength and power. Kali is an aspect of Parvati which destroys evil to protect the innocent.

The Goddess Macha

The Macha is the sovereign goddess of Ulster, the northeast kingdom of Ireland.[117] She is both a winter queen (or dark goddess) and a solar sun goddess (like Áine in her Gráinne form) at the time of the harvest in high summer. She rules from her sacred center at Emain Macha, or Navan Fort, where the kings of Ulster would have married the goddess and the land through a Macha priestess, thus earning the temporal right to rule as in the other kingdoms of Ireland. The Macha, like how Brigid represents the light half (spring) of the dark half (winter) of the year at Ímbolc, represents the dark half (autumn and harvest) of the light half (summer) of the year at the feast of Lughnasadh at the end of July into early August, typically August 1, or the closest Sunday. Macha represents the return of the sun toward winter. She sits at the peak harvest season and reminds us of the importance of planning ahead and strategy. With all the abundance of a harvest, without forethought and planning, a community of people could starve in the heart of winter. Her fierce loyalty and protective nature are the calculated wisdom that creates abundance, guardianship, and resilience.

Like her sister the Morrígu, the Macha is fierce and not akin to flowery speeches and beating around the bush. She wants to get to the heart of matters and is a remover of ego. She marked the edge of her territory of Ulster with her brooch of heads, the "mast of Macha." Her hand, bloodied by battle against the *Fomorians*, is still represented in the red hand in the flag of Ulster. The golden background represents her abundance at the harvest festival and the red cross is a Christian underlayment but can also mean the four quarters of Ireland, as many of her kings in Ulster were also the high Kings of Ireland. The Macha is also known for her curse of the Ulstermen that led to the near fall of Ulster to Connacht in *Táin Bó Cúailgne* (Cattle Raid of Cooley) and even the undermining political situation with the Troubles in Northern Ireland.

Macha means "of the plain" in Old Irish, and she is most often associated with horses, fertility, and battle. On the shores of Lough Neagh, her horses

[117] In the modern day, the historic kingdom of Ulster and six counties are primarily found in Northern Ireland, though counties Donegal, Cavan, and Monaghan remain a part of the Republic of Ireland.

certainly still enjoy the rich fertile plains of central Ulster. These plains are named after her (Mag Macha). She is associated with magpies, ravens, and crows like her sisters the Morrígu and the Cailleach. As you may recall, these sisters of winter and the north are called the three Morrígna. The classic Celtic symbol of the triskele, while typically linked with the Morrígu, is also associated with the Macha and all the Morrígna.

In some parts of Ulster, the Macha was called *Grian Banchure*, the "Sun of Womanfolk," and some of her sacred sites recall this aspect of her naming. In Ulster, her power center is the sacred sites at Emain Macha (specifically at Navan Fort), Mag Macha (Macha's plain), and Ard Macha (Macha's height, today called *Armagh*), though she is truly the sovereign of all Ulster. Other sacred sites of the Macha in her sun (harvest) form are found at Grianán na nAileach and at the holy well or spring at Kilnagreina in County Cork.[118]

The Macha, as well as her counterparts in the Morrígu and the Cailleach, did not get absorbed into the Catholic faith as a saint as did the summer goddesses Brigid and Anu. Nor did she become a beautiful faëry woman in modern Irish lore and legend. When she does appear in modern Irish folklore, she is often betrayed as dark, angry, or corrupted by things within or not within her control, such as the fate of parts of Ulster today. In many ways, the Macha has disappeared into the landscape and has been absorbed into the very fabric of the Irish people—the "fighting Irish" who do not know how to lose—they keep getting back up and fighting for sovereignty, justice, and freedom just like she does. As a sovereign goddess of the land, winter, and a fierce protector of her people, the Macha is the direct source of fierce passion and loyalty that runs hot in the blood and spirit of most Irish people.

◇◇◇◇◇◇◇◇◇◇◇◇◇◇

118 *Grianán na nAileach*, or "Grianan of Aileach" is located in Inishowen, Donegal. Kilnagreine— "The Well of the Fountain of the Sun" is in County Cork. Lady Wilde has this to say about Kilnagreine, also spelled *Kil-na-Greina: "The ritual observed was very strict at the beginning, three draughts of water were taken by the pilgrims, the number of drinks three, the number of rounds on their knees were three, thus making the circuit of the well nine times. After each round the pilgrim laid a stone on the ancient altar in the druid circle, called the well of time sun, and these stones, named in Irish the stones of the sun, are generally pure white, and about the size of a pigeon's egg."*

The Macha in Mythology

The Macha appears in the Mythological Cycle of Ireland on multiple accounts. In these first brief appearances, she is depicted as a priestess or goddess of the old world. In both incarnations, she comes to help settle Ireland and create new temples, arriving first as a daughter of Partholón, and then as the wife of Nemed. In her third incarnation, she arrives in Ireland as one of the *Tuatha Dé Danann* and comes in full battle array to vanquish the *Fomorians* with the other Morrígna. As a member of the tribe of Danu, she is said to have vanquished so many enemies that she wore their heads as a necklace, which is often referred to as the "mast of the Macha." The Macha also helped kill Balor, the king of the *Fomorians*, and thus helped to establish a new order of the sovereign land goddesses, agriculture, and smithcraft in Ireland.

The Macha's fourth incarnation was Macha Mong Ruad (of the "red hair"), daughter of Áed Rúad ("red fire" or "fire lord"—another name for the Dagda). In this incarnation, the Macha was the only woman to ever become high King of Ireland. This did not come without a struggle. Family members tried their best to oust her from her due claim, and so she went to battle and defeated them on several occasions. Several of her cousins from this insurrection escaped the last battle, but she pursued them across Ireland incognito. Some stories say she dressed as a leper, but most say as a lusty woman who ensnared them with amorousness and killed them in the heat of their lust or tied them up and dragged them back to Ulster in bags tied to her horse. The ones she brought home she enslaved, and they were ordered to build the mounds, temple, and palace for her at Emain Macha.

The Macha's fifth incarnation is perhaps the best-known story. She embodies a young, beautiful, red-haired woman who shows up at a simple Ulster farmer's house one day after his first wife died. She takes care of the house, farm, and livestock as if she were his wife. He, of course, falls for her and they marry, and she quickly becomes pregnant. Meanwhile, since she is secretly a sovereign land goddess, she brings much wealth and abundance into his life and to the farm. Thus, his status begins to grow. Her husband, Cruinniuc, goes to the *óenach* of the great feast of Lughnasadh to participate in the games, feasting, revelry, and trade, as well as to pay his annual taxes. The payment of his tribute to the king of Ulster was much higher than any other year, so he was audited. Well, he was questioned on the spot. He told his story of having this amazing wife who was beautiful, strong, fast, and powerful. More so, he spoke of how his fortunes had turned since she had come into his life. After a bit of drinking and boasting, he got out of hand and told some of the king's men that his wife was so fast and strong, she could outrun any of the horses they were racing at the festival.

His boasting was his own downfall as well as that of Macha and Ulster. Of course, the king heard about this fantastical woman from his men and immediately demanded, under penalty of death, that Cruinniuc bring her immediately, at nine months pregnant, to the plains of Emain Macha to race against his horses. She was furious and berated Cruinniuc, but she complied, knowing her husband would have been slain for her failure. She lined up at the starting line with the horses and, at full term, she whipped the horses in the race and then promptly collapsed after crossing the finish line and gave birth to twins.[119] She named the boy *Fír* and the girl *Fial*.[120] For the intensity of the completely disrespectful behavior from the king (and somewhat for her drunken braggart husband), she cursed the men of Ulster to be overcome with weakness—as weak "as a woman in childbirth"—at the time of their greatest need. This weakness would last for five or nine days, and the curse would continue for nine generations. Some people believe this curse still lasts today and thus most of Ulster remains in the hands of the English.

Macha and the Feast of Lughnasadh

The etymology of the word *Lughnasadh* is the combination of Middle Irish words for the god Lugh, and *násad,* which means "an assembly." This feast is not in honor of Lugh as many people surmise, but in the Mythological Cycle, he holds the feast in honor of his foster mother, Tailtiu. Lugh's foster mother was so engaged with evolving with the times (from primordial hunter-gatherer to agriculturalist) during the early Neolithic Age, that she is said to have single-handedly removed many of the ancient oaks from Mag Macha (and across all of Ireland) for farming and grazing. She literally worked herself to death. Lugh

◇◇◇◇◇◇◇◇◇◇◇◇◇◇

119 *Emain* means "twins" in Irish.

120 *Fír* means "true" in Irish. *Fial* means "modest."

wanted to honor her for her self-sacrifice in support of the needs of the *Tuatha Dé Danann*, so he held the first "assembly" to commemorate that with feasting, games, races, and more. Lugh's mother is not named "Macha" according to the Irish archives, but Tailtiu is one and the same as the Macha when we follow the trail of her essence.

The Celtic people of all the Celtic nations, pre-Christianity, believed in reincarnation. The Celts believed, and I will say many of us still do, that the soul, upon leaving the body, passes over to *Tír na nÓg,* rests for a while, and then is reborn again. The Celts want to be here on this gorgeous planet we call home, and we fiercely seek out our freedom to respect that while also stewarding the Earth. Prior to conquest and subjugation, there is little to indicate that the Celts had any aspirations to "leave" the planet as is frequently found in religious beliefs stemming from the Middle East or Asia. In these cultures, the purpose of life is to ascend beyond biology, karma, and "Maya" to ascend to some eternal end game where we somehow maintain our singular autonomy while simultaneously merging with the divine.

The Celts believe that we are already in the perfect garden, especially if we leave it alone and are not too greedy. When we are reborn through the womb of our mother, we are being birthed through a fractal of the womb of the Great Mother. She births us again and again if we are willing to return and continue our soul's work in whatever times we are born into. The Celts believe that we return to renew our vows and to sustain our unique signature in the dynamic symphony of the universe. We are here to balance the harmonies while celebrating life. The divine, whether we are seeing the wholeness of the All or in various fractals of the whole, are concentrations or conglomerations of souls bound by similar frequencies—through who we are, what we serve, and deeds rendered.

The divine feminine that is embodied in the very essence of the mythology, stories, and service of and to the Macha, as with any divine form, transcends the cultural establishment of place with respect to name. The Macha is an incarnation or embodiment of the life current we associate with her: fierceness, loyalty, fertility, abundance, stamina, strategy, passion, and practicality. The ancient Irish-Celtic people divined her name through the luminary fabric of dreams, visions, ecosystems, cultural worldview, diet, soil chemistry, language, and habit. Yet, the Macha is also truly a force of divine consciousness that is beyond time and embodiment. She emerges through the mists of time in her incarnations as seen in Irish mythology. I believe that the Macha was also embodied in the incarnation as Lugh's mother.

Lughnasadh is the final cross-quarter festival in the Celtic year, and most importantly, it is the feast of the harvest. Macha is the harvest as she is also the grain. Macha's son, Fír, is an incarnation of Lugh. Keep in mind that Lugh is a child of two worlds during major climate and cultural shifts on the earth. He is half-*Tuatha Dé Danann* and half-*Fomorian*. His father is Cian of the *Tuatha Dé Danann*, and his mother is Ethniu: daughter of Balor, king of the *Fomorians*. In other words, Lugh is half primordial hunter-gatherer and half agrarian. On the divine plain of existence, Lugh is the hybridization of the primordial earth titan-god consciousness associated with the *Fomorians*, and the illuminated earth and sky-god consciousness of the *Tuatha Dé Danann*. Lugh, incarnated as Fír, is thus born to an exhausted and fierce mother—the Macha.[121]

Now the classic telling is that Lugh's foster mother, Tailtiu, was a *Firbolg* who had been adopted by the *Tuatha Dé Danann*. As a primordial incarnation of the Macha, Tailtiu sought to bridge the changing climate of the world in the transition from the Neolithic Age to the Iron Age brought to Ireland by the *Tuatha Dé Danann*. To sustain the need for more cleared land, Tailtiu overextended herself in the removal of the ancient forests on the central limestone plains of Ireland. Tailtiu died of exhaustion. The two-week feast, or *óenach,* that Lugh hosts at Lughnasadh is in honor of his stepmother, the Macha, as both a funeral feast and the finest wake in the Irish fashion. Lughnasadh is known for athletic competitions, as well as musical, oratorical, and storytelling competitions. Of course, singing and dancing competitions, arts and crafts exhibitions, trading, and festivities of all kinds abounded. The feast of Lughnasadh, most celebrated in Ulster at Emain Macha, was in honor of the labors of the goddess to help the people evolve with the times, but mostly to provide for family and kin.

◇◇◇◇◇◇◇◇◇◇◇◇◇◇

[121] Lugh also became the father of Ulster's great hero Cúchulainn, or perhaps Lugh is the actual incarnation of Cúchulainn himself, who lifts Macha's curse in the *Táin Bó Cúailgne,* thus continuing the soul cycle of the greater harmony they are bound to or serve.

This feast time is depicted as a time that the Lord of Light (Lugh) and the Lord of the Earth (Crom Dubh, possibly an ancient aspect of the Dagda) struggle over dominion of the harvest—literally fighting for the control of the grain or Gráine.[122] There is a practical level to this: the grains must be stored and dried or they will mold and rot in the storehouses over the winter. During Lughnasadh, victors at the games and competitions were believed to be heroes struggling to help Lugh win the grain from Crom Dubh so that the tribe could be fed through the winter. It is easy to see the relationship between the Macha, who in her most prominent form represents sovereignty, abundance, and the harvest, and Tailtiu, who is fostering the growth of a new world and the training of a gifted being—Lugh. Yet, that abundance comes at the expense of the forest and the loss of many of her ancient sacred oak trees and oracle sanctuaries. It could not have been an easy decision, but as the Macha continuously reminds us, we do whatever it takes to be loyal to kin and to the embodiment of our soul's purpose.

At the feast of Lughnasadh, the power of the fertile goddess of the land and abundance is being fought over by two seemingly opposing masculine forces that want to reap the rewards of her harvest. At the Macha's feast of Lughnasadh, we are celebrating the amazing harvest and fertility of the land, and the toil that it takes to grow it with strategic planning, intelligent design, and in honor of the sacred land that yields it. And simultaneously, we celebrate the warning against any power grabs of beauty and abundance.

Lughnasadh in the Hearth of the Twenty-First Century

Lughnasadh is the Celtic fire festival marking high summer and the beginning of the harvest season. Historically, it was widely observed throughout Ireland, Scotland, and the Isle of Mann. Originally, it was held on August 1 or about halfway between the summer solstice and autumn equinox. Over time, the celebration shifted to the Sunday nearest August 1. In Ireland, the feast of Lughnasadh is also called

---

122 Crom Dubh's festival also happens to fall on August 1—the same as Lughnasadh.

"Reek Sunday" due to the annual pilgrimage hike to the top of Croagh Patrick in County Mayo. Mountains in Ireland are often known also as "reeks" or "slieves." Thousands of people from all over Ireland and around the globe make the climb to the top of Croagh Patrick on Lughnasadh to celebrate the cross-quarter holiday with picnics, mass, ceremony, celebration, and more. A small church rests on the top of Croagh Patrick and I was able to attend a mass there with, amazingly enough, a group of Indians from Tamil celebrating the mass in Tamil and Hindi.

Croagh Patrick is considered by many to be the holiest mountain in Ireland. The tradition of pilgrimage to this holy mountain is known to stretch back over 5,000 years from the Megalithic Age to the present day without interruption. Its known religious significance dates to the time of the Neolithic and the pre-Christian Celts who revered this mountain as one of the homes of Lugh. In AD 441, Saint Patrick practiced some potent austerities on the mountain, including fasting for forty days and forty nights. The top of Croagh Patrick, even during high summer at Lughnasadh, is often freezing cold and extremely windy. Supposedly, Patrick's vigilance on the mountain was how he was able to vanquish the old gods of Ireland and banish the "snakes."[123]

More than likely, anyone with a fierce heart, vivacious spirit, clear mind, and willingness to sit in a place like that[124] is going to attract the attention of the divine, warranting some type of boon, *siddhi,*[125] or union with the Irish *sídhe*—the immortals, the *Tuatha Dé Danann*, and in this case, the Macha and Lugh. It seems more likely to me that just like the Irish demonstrated their adaptability and cultural malleability to influx and change across history, Patrick was able to internally alchemize the ancient currents of the land and the traditions of the old gods, the

---

123 "Snakes" meaning the druids.

124 Sound familiar? I believe some aspect of the Macha incarnated in Patrick, or at the very least, he won her and Lugh's favor.

125 *Siddhi* is the Sanskrit word for "spiritual fulfillment or accomplishment." Siddhis can be material, immaterial, paranormal, supernatural, or may otherwise possess magical powers, abilities, and attainments. This is the product of yogic advancement through *sādhanās* such as meditation and yoga.

Tuatha Dé Danann, with the evolutionary and spiritual waves of that which was to come: the Celtic Church.[126]

History shows us that in Ireland, of all places, it was peacefully completed. To become one with the *sídhe* through austerities, perseverance, discipline, and practice is like the yogic attainment of *siddhis*. Thus, based on one's ability to overcome worldly hurdles, we merge with the divine. The key difference between Celtic spirituality with the Vedic practices and Buddhism is that the merging with the *sídhe* allows one to remain embodied more fully here on Earth.

An Invitation

On the feast of Lughnasadh, may you find the top of whatever mountains you are climbing. May your dreams find sustenance in every step you take. May the high summer bring you the spaciousness to give thanks for the abundance and health in your life, and where it is missing, may your kin grant you strength. May you find the wisdom to tuck away some of the abundance of the now for the winters to come. And may your path ever be illuminated in the dark nights and bring you home, again and again to the heart of the mountain within. Blessed be.

> *"Follow your heart, acushla! 'Tis a safer guide than any promise before you knew what it was that you were saying."*
> ~ Conan Doyle

The Macha's Invitation

The Macha's invitation is to be resilient, and at the same time, fiercely loyal. While some aspect of her is intense—and she certainly is a warrioress—she also seems to represent the cooling of a hot temperament or the direction of fierce energy into life-supporting action, even if it means some personal cleanup and potentially dealing with conflict on the way. The Macha is

---

[126] I highly suggest reading *How the Irish Saved Civilization* by Thomas Cahill if you are willing to digest his Abrahamic law superiority complex of pre-Christian Ireland.

autumn. She helps us see the importance of not fearing conflict, but to take care of responsibilities in a practical way. Do not be meek and kowtow to forces arrayed against us. We all have allies if we are willing to call on them. Ultimately, the Macha is inviting us all to healing and peace, not through a complicated and heady approach, for she would rather add your head to her necklace in the obliteration of ego, but instead, by simply giving your time and energy to the tasks at hand in taking care of others. Defending the sacred. Fighting against injustice. Feeding people. Creating abundance. Chopping wood and carrying water.

Do not expect a lot of flash and glam when working with the Macha. She would rather remain invisible most of the time and expects that we will follow suit. If we forget, she will remind us. If we trespass or cause injustice, she is the mighty voice of righteousness that can send a kingdom to its knees for nine generations or more. She also reminds us that as we slip in and out of incarnations, the story may change a little bit. The better we get at fulfilling our soul's purpose here on Earth, the better off everyone will be. I close with the heart of all things Macha, for from an awareness of abundance comes an understanding that others may lack therein. Eventually, on the soul's journey through life or lifetimes, we will wake to see the true spirit behind the evolution of consciousness. The heart of her essence cannot be captured more appropriately that in the words of Sufi master Ibn Arabi:

> *"At the level of the world, there is 'yours and mine.' At the beginning of the spiritual path, 'mine is yours and yours is mine.' On the path itself, there is 'no mine and no yours.' And at the end of the path, there is 'no me and no you.'"*

At Lughnasadh every year, the Macha reminds us of the beauty of something ending and making room for something new to be born.

Offerings Appropriate for the Macha

Offerings are often left in the fields of Ireland or tied to the branches of trees. An apple or a carrot for a horse or cow goes a long way in sharing kindness with the animals we are so intertwined with. Macha braids, made of crow, raven, swan, or duck feathers bound with colorful threads or ribbons are hung from horses' manes or in trees over flowing water (or other places above where energy moves passes quickly, such as wind flowing, people walking, or regular fires burning). She may be demanding in her requests and timing, or she may expect little at all. Such is her nature. She reminds us all of humility on the path to illumination and abundance.

Macha offerings include but are not limited to: Jewelry (iron, gold, silver, bronze, copper), fossils, clay votives, goddess figurines, swords/axes, shields, chariots, horse figurines, acorns, hazelnuts, strands of your hair, mugwort, stone/crystal, milk & honey, woad powder/paint, flowers, poplar leaves, feathers, Macha braids (described above), songs, rapture, ecstasy, and spring/holy well water.

Chapter Eight

IRISH ORIGIN OF THE GRAIL

"The journey is the destination. Finding the answers for yourself, achieving understanding is part of your journey. There are no shortcuts along the path."

~ A.G. Riddle

I can remember a day in my first semester at Thomas More College when I could not find my dorm room key. I was playing college soccer. We had two-a-days at the beginning of the season—where you train and practice at 6:00 a.m. followed by classes at the end of the day. I also had a full load of science classes with labs and mandated college athlete study halls. My days were almost completely regimented. The little bit of free time that I had was during mealtimes where I could mix and mingle with the other students, enjoy a ten-minute cat nap in the sun (if it was nice outside), or play with casual bantering of jokes with some of the other guys on the soccer team.

Well, on this particular day, after enjoying some bantering *and* a short nap in the sun, I made my way back to my room to collect my books for my afternoon classes. I walked all the way across campus, stopping to chat with friends along the way, arrived at my dormitory door, and realized I had lost the dorm room key. It was not in my pocket where I always put it. Keep in mind, I am very habitual and typically always put things either where I found them or in a habitual place in my house or on my person.

I grew a bit worried about the key. I ran back across campus, searching through the now all-but-empty cafeteria to no avail. Then I backtracked to the place where I was having fun with friends after eating and then to my nap spot. No key was to be found. I then backtracked all my conversation places on campus. No key. Next, I sprinted back to the locker room at the gym to see if my key was in my soccer gear.

No key. I was utterly defeated!

Eventually, I wound my way back to my dorm room and figured I could sit outside the door until my roommate came back. I was hoping that he would not have already left to go to classes. I resigned to being super late for class or having to go without my notebooks, lab books, and texts. I made my way slowly back to my room while mentally unwinding any additional places that I might have missed in my backtracking. I could think of no loopholes. Arriving at my room, frustrated and a bit anxious about being late for class, I sat down, leaned my back against the door, and let out a big exhale. Pulling my legs up into my chest, I buried my head into my hands on my knees and felt a sharp pain in my left thigh from my jeans. I stood up and fished my left hand into my pant pocket to see what had hurt me. Lo and behold, there was my dorm room key.

You can imagine the embarrassment and the humor. Here I had spent the last forty minutes running all over campus looking for a key that was in my pocket the entire time. How did I miss it? It seemed so obvious, right? And "right" is the significant word: I was so habitual with my pattern of putting the key in my right pocket that it did not even occur to me that I may have thrown it into my other pocket while my mind was preoccupied with catching up with friends.

I wonder if you could tell a similar story yourself—whether it is about misplacing something as simple as a key, earring, wallet, mobile phone, or hairbrush. Perhaps you have a funnier story of misplacing a car or a scary story of misplacing a person. The essence of this sharing really focuses on the concept that sometimes we misplace or miss something that is right in front of us, or even more so, we do not see a pattern or answer that has obviously been in front of us all along: "hidden in plain sight."

It is amazing how "blind" we can be when our awareness is fixed and the world is determined to look, act, and behave in a certain way. This reason, more than anything else, is why I choose to travel the world and saturate myself in other cultures: it liberates my definitions and preconceptions of how the world looks, acts, and behaves. Our cultural norms will be alien and sometimes offensive to another. Other cultures' norms may shake the very foundation of our beliefs and personal constructs.

The Quest

> *"The wise know that questions have no true answers. Life is made from these wonderings and from the answers that we each and every one are finding for ourselves."*
>
> ~Tad Williams

There is a level of cultural comfort in Ireland that is so familiar to many people from North America, Europe, and Australia. Perhaps that comes from so many of us having not only some heritage originating in Ireland but also a strong sense of personal connection or desire for it. It is comfortable for me as an American to travel to Ireland. It is a fairly affluent, developed country, with liberal politics and a strong sense of tradition. For the most part, the Irish love Americans (do not include the forty-fifth president among that general statement) and make us feel warmly welcome, offering their cultural continuum as a gift in return for our patronage. Because of this level of ease, often we can forget (as visitors) that our worlds, though similar, are significantly different—whether in respect to values, social equanimity, faith, language, or heritage, we are truly a world away.

The journey for many of us home to Ireland is simply checking off a box from our personal bucket list of places to travel in this life and to take some pictures. Perhaps we go deeper into the cultural experience by drinking a Guinness in a dark pub full of Irish farmers, watching some Irish dancing, going to a traditional music session, or hill walking. Perhaps we are called by the ancient ruins from thousands of years of history (and prehistory). Perhaps while in Ireland, we can find out more information about our heritage, where our ancestors once hailed from (and perhaps some relations still reside), and an understanding of who we are. We cannot go wrong with Ireland. It is fun, gorgeous, musical, quirky, rebellious, free, humble, and downright magical. In Ireland, there is an ease of place, belonging, and comfort as mentioned above, which often makes for an amazing trip where everyone gains a few pounds and goes home a little happier and stress-free.

Yet perhaps something deeper is calling you: a dream, a knowing, a riddle, an *aisling*...something rich and often beyond words. Perhaps you cannot quite put your finger on it, but it has something to do with the Celtic essence, Gnostic Mysteries, ancient druidic visions, or the Holy Grail and the Goddess traditions. Likely then, you have already peeled off the conditioning and programming of your upbringing, have rebelled and went slightly feral, and have now found a new relationship with the search for answers, traditions, and a sense of place and belonging in the world. I know this place: where abstractions and obscure symbols unfold into clear answers, while clear definitions of cultural programming have become muddy, clouded puddles that are undefinable and provide no clarity whatsoever.

I wonder if you have found yourself dreaming under an ancient oak or beech of other times, other places, or possible distant futures. Have you found yourself dancing in a meadow under the full moon and noticed that though you were alone, all of creation was humming through your body? I wonder if you have heard the singing underneath the wind in a pine forest and what the song illuminates in you. I wonder if you have heard the sighing of the willow maiden as she reaches her long fingers through her waterfall of hair and tresses down to the glassy-still surface of a lake. I wonder if you have felt your heart burst with anguish or empathy, lavishing oceans of tears on the altar of your soul as you watch your understanding of the world crumble before your very eyes. I wonder if you have embraced and become saturated through every pore of your body by divine ecstasy in the arms of your lover, whether just for one night or after thirty years of marriage. I wonder if you have placed your lips to a standing stone, whispering your soul's secret in truth, knowing that you were really whispering into the ear of a giant who was waiting for your message before awakening. I wonder if you have seen the Celtic knots running through your body, the trees, rivers, and all of life.

Many people know that the veil is thin in Ireland. It is ever so thin—the threshold between this world and the other is ever-present. Yet, that is only the tip of the iceberg or the edge of the mist. If you have felt any of the wonderings that I mentioned above, you are not being called to just visit Ireland and to dabble with crossing over the veil, you are being called to saturate yourself in the deep mists and become an emissary of the Light of Erin, the eternal essence of Kathleen ní Houlihan, the spirit of Ireland. You are being called to follow the riddles and mystery beyond the beyond, to *Tír na nÓg*, to the sweet Summerlands. I would go further to posit that you are also being called to not only go all the way into the mists to disappear or to ascend, but like Fionn mac Cumhaill, to come back to this world with gifts from the other side. I only offer this as an invitation. Wherever you are called and follow the call, the journey is your quest. And I believe that we are all questing for paradise and deep peace. Not in the Otherworld or in the afterlife, but in this one. I believe we all are each a unique embodiment of the sacred heritage of angels, the *sídhe*, and the Great Mystery of Divinity. Our life quest is the emptying and filling of our personal Holy Grail en route to paradise and deep peace.

The Holy Grail in Ireland

I am going to make a few assumptions here. First, I am going to assume that you are familiar with the Holy Grail and its connection with Christ and the Last Supper. Second, I am going to assume that most people know of the Arthurian legends connected to the endless search for the Holy Grail—to return it to Christendom from the infidels and pagan barbarian hordes, etc. Third, I am going to also assume that you have some understanding that in Gnostic traditions, the Grail is also representative of the bloodline of Christ and Mary Magdalene's offspring.[127] And

[127] Gnosticism was the root of Christianity. *Gnôsis* is the Greek word for "knowledge" or "insight." The teachings of Christ called for his followers to become like him. Most prominent in the second and third centuries, and partly of pre-Christian origin, the Gnostic doctrine taught that the world was created and ruled by a lesser divinity, the demiurge, and that Christ was an emissary of the remote supreme divine being, esoteric knowledge (Gnosis) of whom had enabled the redemption of the human spirit through the journey of personal sovereignty. The key is that all people have access directly to the divine and do not require another person to act as a go-between as in the modern church where a priest, deacon, or minister is the controlled central source of access to God.

fourth, I am going to assume that you have an understanding that the Grail is a symbol of the divine feminine. If you do not meet these assumptions, then you have a fine feast of mythological and cultural exploration ahead of you.

Ireland is the origin of the Holy Grail and, it may be its final resting place, though evidence seems to indicate that it was stolen by Merlin and brought to England (more on this later). The origin of the Grail tradition is rooted in the Celtic heritage of the cauldron.[128] The cauldron is a symbol of abundance, wealth, renewal, fertility, and immortality throughout Celtic mythology—from the cauldrons of the Dagda and Cerridwen (Welsh) to the Holy Grail of King Arthur. The cauldron is a symbol of the womb, the void, and creation.[129]

Traditionally for the Celts, the cauldron was symbolically where our soul would cross the gateway after death into the Otherworld and then be born again. With the Christian adoption of the tradition of the cauldron as the Holy Grail, an initiate drinks from the cup of everlasting life—thus reseeding the embodiment of the initiate's promise for everlasting life through the suffering of God incarnate in human flesh: Christ. More than anything, the cauldron and its evolution into the Holy Grail is a powerful symbol or codex to the divine feminine and to the Goddess traditions—long before the hungry war gods that arose in the Middle East and the Mediterranean began ravaging the ancient landscape.

The traditions of the Mother Goddess are older than our cultural memory. The recent upstart of the masculine war gods that arose in earnest in the Middle East and Mediterranean during the Age of Aries largely occurred in parallel with the change of climatic conditions worsening (becoming warmer and drier) in that part of the world. During the time of Christ, most of the Goddess traditions across the globe were already in a steep rate of decline, yet the Goddess-centric cultures were still thriving in the Celtic and Germanic lands in northern Europe, the

◇◇◇◇◇◇◇◇◇◇◇◇◇◇

[128] Alfred Nutt, *Studies on the Legend of the Holy Grail with Especial Reference to the Hypothesis of it Celtic Origin*, 1888.

[129] Matthews, Caitlin & John, *The Encyclopedia of Celtic Wisdom: A Celtic Shaman's Sourcebook*, 2001, p 223.

North Sea, and Asia. In the Gnostic traditions, many guardians of the ancient traditions know that Mary Magdalene, as well as Mother Mary, was a high priestess. Some connection has been made to the Temple of Isis, and strong connections have been made to the Grail-Cauldron traditions of Gaul and the Celtic Isles.[130]

In the Gnostic traditions, the name "Mary" is actually a title for a priestess who bestows grace, power, strength, and healing upon her male counterpart (as in Christ, a king, or sovereign). Recall that the sovereign can only rule through the grace of the Goddess, and thus the "Mary" is a highly trained priestess who bestows this grace upon he who is ruling on behalf of the Goddess and the land. A "Mary" is deeply initiated into Goddess traditions and has prepared her entire life to be in a ruling capacity with her beloved and as a go-between the mysteries, life, the divine, and her people. *Mary* is derivative of *Maria* in Greek, but it is a transliteration of the Hebrew name *Miriam*, where the root of the ancient name in Hebrew and Aramaic means "to be strong" and "beloved." Additionally, the Hebrew noun spelled מור (mor) is spelled identically to the verb מור (mur), meaning "to change"...the title in Irish for a keeper of the cauldron traditions is *Mór* as in *Mór Mhumhan* or *Mor Rígu* (Morrígu). Mary is Mari is Miriam is Mór...a title for a high priestess of the Goddess traditions. Furthermore, in AD 82, when Ptolemy was describing Uisneach, he called it *Raiba*, or *Riba*, similar to Mor *rígu*...Mor *riba*, where *raiba* or *riba* in Hebrew means "kingdom." In Hindi, it means "name of god." So, centered at Uisneach, Ireland, was the Domain of the Marys, or sovereign realm of the Goddess.

The priestess traditions of Isis and of the Grail-Cauldron carried forward the Mysteries of the Goddess into the Christian era and into modern times. Additionally, the Grail-Cauldron and Isis traditions also trained some of their priestesses in the arts of the ancient consort. Priestesses trained in these mysteries were essential embodiments of the Goddess who would marry a sovereign king or chieftain in the ancient rite of *ban feis*. The Celtic people were the protectors of this ancient Grail-Cauldron Mystery and Ireland is the center.

[130] Ireland, Isle of Mann, Scotland, Wales, England, Orkneys, etc.

Figure 13: Star of David

Let us look at the hexagram, usually referred to as *the Star of David* Figure 13). We have volumes of symbolic meaning in such a simple symbol—pictures say a thousand words. This symbol speaks beyond every language in a codified record that would take thousands of years to translate academically. Professors and academics alike have tried. The focus for your soul-eye-lenses I would invite to the important symbology in relation to our correlation with the Irish-Celtic Mysteries. With respect to the Grail-Cauldron Mysteries, we can see that the star is created from two equilateral triangles overlapping. Each point of the star is the same distance from another in relation to a wheel.

When we take apart the star into the two dominant yet individual pieces, we have one triangle that connects the southeast and southwest with its point in the north. This triangle is the symbolic masculine, and similarly, correlates with the erection of the great pyramids in Egypt. And yes, it also represents the male appendage. Whereas the second triangle, based in the northeast and the northwest with its point in the south, represents the symbolic feminine. And what does it look like other than an upside pyramid? It represents a vessel, cauldron, cup, chalice, or grail. It also represents the womb—the place of renewal and creation of life itself. Yet, it is only in the heart, through the sacred marriage of the masculine and feminine—that balance, harmony, and true alchemy can occur—that healthy life can be birthed. Thus, the heart of Christ's teachings, the Grail-Cauldron Mysteries, and the heart of Gnosticism are codified in this symbol. Further, the triangle pointing "up" or north, symbolically and geophysically in the landscape of Ireland, represents the triple aspect of the summer goddess (Fenne, Áine, and Gráinne); and the triangle pointing "down" or south symbolically and geophysically represents the triple aspect of the winter goddess, the three Morrígna (Morrígu, Cailleach, and Macha).

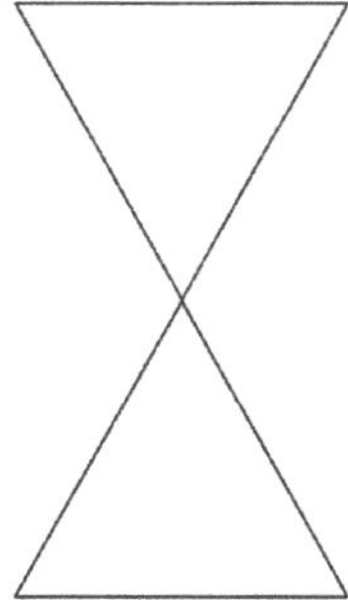

Figure 14: Triangles representing the feminine and the masculine

Feminine: Taking the star apart, we have two equilateral triangles. In the inverted triangle, we have a symbol representing the divine feminine. It looks and feels symbolically like a container. It does not take a lot of imagination to see a womb, vessel, cup, or cauldron. At the very least, it is a funnel that catches something from above and draws it down below. If we can imagine it as a container, it would fill quickly until overflowing.

Masculine: In the classic equilateral triangle, we have a symbol representing the divine masculine. It looks and feels phallic. It does not take a lot of imagination to see the rising symbol of a blade, point, or probe. It is the Stone of Destiny, the *Lia Fáil.* We can easily imagine the forces of the Earth gathering and rising in a spiral fashion within the lower triangle to either fill the tip to point of explosion or to be released through a small space in the universe into another—enabling the seed of all mysteries and creation to come into being—life.

Refer to Figure 8 on Page 69, the map showing where the royal and sacred centers of Ireland are located. Let us play an old-fashioned connect-the-dots game. If we take the more modern sacred center of Tara off the map for a moment and focus on the ancient sacred center of Uisneach, then we can see the relationship of the two triangles mentioned above from the Star of David mapped out across Ireland between the sacred sites. The pathways between the sacred sites were walked in the *óenach* throughout the Wheel of the Year in respect to sacred holidays. The annual pilgrimage, with very little imagination, outlined the classic image of the cauldron (female) and Stone of Destiny (male), and later the hybrid of the two in the Holy Grail across the face of Ireland every year for thousands of years. Uisneach was also one of the most important points in Ireland for rekindling the sacred fires at the cross-quarter holidays—especially at Bealtaine. Imagine being at that ancient celebration right where all the ley lines of Ireland's sacred power centers come together in a perfect balance of light and dark, summer and winter, male and female. I imagine it was saucy.

When I was in college and I could not find the key to my dorm room, it led me on an exciting chase around campus, tracking what I had left behind and could not figure out. The key was in my pocket.

The key is in our pocket. The Holy Grail is Ireland, or at least originated there—layers of the same truth. The map of the sacred sites of Ireland has been available to us for thousands of years. Is this another secret that the Irish have kept so well? Is it another one of these elements of an obvious truth being so ingrained in Irish culture that they, in their humble nature, never speak to it? Many of the Irish subconsciously (or consciously) know that Ireland is the source of the Holy Grail; as Mary Magdalene the sacred consort-queen, or symbolically as the vessel served at the Last Supper. Whether Mary came from Ireland as a youth or came to study with the Goddess Grail-Cauldron tradition colleges—and originally hailed from the Celtic part of southwest France (as many Gnostics believe)—the map of Ireland marks exactly where the Grail (she) originated: Uisneach[131]—the high seat of the druids and home of the Great Rite. And if the

◇◇◇◇◇◇◇◇◇◇◇◇◇◇◇

131 The Grail traditions are very alive around Sligo as well, the oldest inhabited part of Ireland likely where the Mother Goddess traditions were brought when seeking asylum. Mysteries center around Lough Gill, Temple House, Temple House Lake, Hill of Kesh, Knocknashee, Tobercurry, and Carrowkeel amongst others.

Gnostics are correct, then the Mother Mary also hailed from this same tradition, and the "bread of Christ" was born from the "oven" of Mary's womb, and the sacred grain lived on through the children of Mary Magdalene and Jesus.[132]

Figure 15: Sacred Cauldron of Ireland

---

[132] The alchemy of the seed (wheat) being ground into flour and then baked into bread is the seed of the masculine, absorbed into the womb, and thus becoming life.

"X" Marks the Spot

Did you ever imagine that you found a pirate map as a child? How much fun was it to look at the crinkly old paper (even if you baked it with lemon juice yourself) and see the dotted line across the map through all the mountains and swamps, past the slaver's headquarters and the sunken Spanish galleon? Setting out on an adventure to follow the map and see what treasure waited at the end was magical. I imagine that for those seeking the Holy Grail, whether they were Knights of the Round Table (like Ser Perceval), treasure hunters, Crusaders, or pilgrims, the magic potential for discovery at the "X" at the end would have been powerful.[133] Most people would find it an honor to hold one of the most potent symbols of Christianity, albeit a Goddess symbol: the Holy Grail. The Templars, or the Knights of Saint John, purportedly found the Holy Grail, though it seems most likely the Grail's lineage and location had long since been known and they were simply the guardians.[134] We have the map of Ireland and "X" marks the spot of the origin of the Grail and cauldron.

Figure 16: Iota-chi

In case we need further evidence that Ireland is the original seat of the Grail, let us explore the Christian symbols and mysteries as well. The

◇◇◇◇◇◇◇◇◇◇◇◇◇◇

133 Ser Perceval's ancestors are still guarding Temple House in County Sligo, Ireland, as they have for four centuries once the Knights Templar left the estate and were incorporated into the Knights Hospitaller.

134 Stored in Templehouse Lake and warded by the humble Knights Templar Castle at the Temple House estate in County Sligo. See Patrick Benham's book *The Avalonians* to find out more about the Grail Mysteries centered around Glastonbury, England, and the works of Dr. John Goodchild to conceal a mysterious antique vessel in the holy well of St. Bride.

Greek words for Jesus Christ are *Iēsous Christos.* Often, this is also coded in plain sight into Christendom on churches, holy places, and sacred items as the first two letters of both words, which in Greek are "I" (*iota*) for Jesus (*Iēsous*) and "X" (*chi*) for Christ (*Christos*). When they are laid over one another, it creates the symbol *iota-chi* for *Iēsous Christos* Figure 16). When they are laid over one another, it creates the symbol *iota-chi* for *Iēsous Christos.* We can find this symbol all over Christian churches, holy raiment, missals, and more. There it is again, the map of Ireland in respect to the center (Uisneach), the four seasonal centers (Cruachain, Kildare, Cnoc Áine, and Navan Fort), and the high seat of winter (Loughcrew or Malin Head) and summer (Bheara or Rock of Cashel).

Figure 17: Staurogram

Now, if we add in the Christian symbol of the staurogram, built of the Greek symbols *tau* and *rho,* we turn over a little something more (Figure 17). In Greek, *tau* ("T") is an abbreviation for the word for *cross* and has a strong connection to Saint Francis of Assisi.[135] *Rho* ("P") in Greek is the word for "help" and is also the second letter in the Greek word for *Christ.*

Figure 18: Layered iota-chi and staurogram

[135] Saint Francis of Assisi was a late-medieval Christian druid monk from Italy who cared for the earth and for the people of the earth, while "rebuilding the church" from its humble Gnostic roots.

If we add in *tau* and *rho* to *iota-chi*, we end up with yet again another layer of the map of Ireland (Figure 18). This combined symbol now contains the less important arms (relational to the equinoxes) that span into the east towards the Dagda (at Dublin and the Wicklow Mountains) and the Irish Sea (his cauldron) calling for abundance and strength to be received in our receptive left hand (imagine you are on the cross) and in the west calling to Lugh (in the Connemara at Croagh Patrick) for victory and illumination in our giving and healing (or destructive and violent) right hand. Meanwhile, the addition of *rho* allows the energy of the northlands (the Goddess) to cycle back around and touch the sacred site of Tara in east-central Ireland, in Midhe (Meath).

Figure 19: Christian fish symbol

In the early days of Christianity, when Christian initiates were all Gnostic, there was no centralized church organization and people were persecuted for their faith by the Romans. Christians often marked their places of worship and their homes with the symbol of a fish to secretly let one another know where safe houses and places of worship were to be found (Figure 19). This was a derivative of the miracle of the breaking of the loaves and fishes in that only a few loaves and fish could feed the masses.[136] It was also symbolic of the Age of Pisces and the end of the Age of Aries. In addition, Jesus was often referred to as the Fisher King, who called the salt of the earth to be his disciples and follow in his footsteps on the path to the divine. And finally, Jesus was born of a Mary, keeper of the Cauldron-Grail tradition, thus symbolized in the waters of the world that the fish (Jesus) swims in. In the Celtic tradition, the fish, especially the salmon, is a symbol of

136 Luke 9:16—Christian New Testament

initiation and divine knowledge. In Ireland, the salmon is one of the most sacred creatures and has a direct connection to the divine.[137] In Greek, the word for "fish" is *ichthys* (ichthus) which is also an acronym for "*Iēsous Christos Theou hYios Sōtēr*" (literally meaning "Jesus Christ, son of God, savior").[138]

The Hill of Uisneach—The Sacred Center

The sacred center of Ireland is at Uisneach and is the source of the Holy Grail. If we do the same exercise with the root of the word *Uisneach* as we did with *Jesus Christ* above, we find a surprising parallel, and the "X" on the map of Ireland becomes even brighter. *Uisneach* comes from two Irish words. The first is the Irish word for "water," *uisce* (pronounced *ish-ka*). The second word is an erosion of the name of an ancient Irish god of the *Tuatha Dé Danann* named *Nechtan*, which is a probable variant of *Nuada* (or possibly the Dagda).[139] The word or name *Nechtan* also means "to wash-clean" in Irish. He was the god of knowledge and keeper of the archives of the *Tuatha Dé Danann*. Nechtan's home is found at the Síd Nechtain, or the Hill of Carbury, just east of Uisneach. I imagine a daily walk to the sacred pool of the divine feminine was an important part of the stewardship of place. In the parallel of Nechtan and Nuada, we find that Nuada, like Christ, suffered on behalf of his people yet rose again and reclaimed his rightful place at the right hand (or respectfully to Nuada, who literally regained his right hand).[140]

◇◇◇◇◇◇◇◇◇◇◇◇◇◇

[137] Interesting how science and nutrition are logical and objective with respect to omega-3 fatty acids—the polyunsaturated fats responsible for most of the brain and mental health benefits of fish oil.

[138] *Theou* is Greek for "God" and is the botanical name of the genus of the cacao tree, *Theobroma cacao*; *broma* means "fruit," thus, cacao is "the fruit of the gods" in the Mayan tradition.

[139] Some research shows that Nechtan is the son of Nuada.

[140] He lost his hand and thus could no longer be king as he was not whole in body.

At the Hill of Uisneach, there is a sacred well (Nechtan's well)[141] and pool, which also happens to be one of the major source headwaters[142] of the Boyne River. The god Nuada, as Nechtan, was married to the goddess Boann. Nechtan oversaw protecting the sacred pool of water that was at the sacred center of Ireland. Nechtan was thus warded with the stewardship of the Grail-Cauldron traditions from the masculine side. Legend has it that he would go to the sacred pool of water and drink from a special chalice every time the gods needed the wisdom of the beyond and to see into the archives. Most likely, this was in the form of the Great Rite, and it has been obscured over the centuries—what better place to see into the archives than to drink from a goddess? Eventually, Boann supposedly sneaks a drink, and then the sacred pool of water overflows, chasing her down to the sea, thus creating the Boyne River.[143] More likely, the sacred pool overflowed with the pleasure of Boann and Nechtan, thus creating the sacred Boyne River of both of their life waters through ecstasy and union. Nechtan also was likely an incarnation of Fionntán who comes into play at this site more.

After Fionntán's escape from certain doom as the sole remaining male of the Grail-Cauldron lineage—having to pleasure half one-hundred priestesses[144]—he fled to his hermitage in the mountains where he took on many forms to evade pursuit before becoming human again. One of his forms was the salmon residing in the holy pool of water at Uisneach and Connla's Well. Fionntán could not stay away from the priestesses for too long, despite his self-imposed austerities. They had exhausted him. Thus, Fionntán disguised himself initially as a salmon in the sacred pool of the gods.

◇◇◇◇◇◇◇◇◇◇◇◇◇◇

141 Nectan's Well and Connla's Well are often synonymous, though Connla's Well is often believed to be in County Tipperary.

142 Headwaters…Fire in the head…The seat of the Celtic soul lies in the head; in the beginning place.

143 The Boyne River is considered the most sacred river in Ireland. Along its banks are found the Hill of Tara, Newgrange, Knowth, and much more.

144 Remember that *rho* or P in Greek means "help." *Rho* also has a numeric value of 100 in numerology. Fionntán was calling for help.

Through dreams and whisperings braided into the winds, Fionntán as the sacred salmon spread the word across all the Celtic lands that the nine sacrosanct hazelnut trees that guarded the holy pool at Uisneach grew the fruit sustaining the knowledge of the gods (which they did).[145] The salmon residing in the pool ate the hazelnuts on a regular basis and were thus infused with divine wisdom.[146] It was not until the druid Finegas came along, practicing austerities on site for seven years, then catching one of the salmon and preparing it over a fire, that the young lad Fionn mac Cumhaill came along seemingly randomly, albeit with divine guidance. Fionn was asked by Finegas to help cook the fish while he went to gather some herbs and go to the bathroom. Fionn burned his thumb on the hot salmon while cooking it and thus stuck his thumb in his mouth to soothe it. It was fate: he took on the knowledge of the gods because he tasted the salmon first, and Finegas became one of his first advisors and members of the *Fianna*. Perhaps Fionn became the next incarnation of Fionntán—perhaps the true sovereign and protector of the sacred Goddess tradition and of all Ireland—all told in the tales of Fionn and the *Fianna*.[147]

Later in history and the legends, Geoffrey of Monmouth (c. 1100—c. 1155) tells the tale—sourced from more ancient legends—of how King Arthur invaded Ireland to capture the Giants Ring, the largest Megalithic temple in Ireland and all the northern isles. These stones once stood at Uisneach and served as the vessel for the coding of the living Light of Erin, the sacred waters and mysteries of the Holy Grail, and the ancient cauldron of the Goddess. With the help of a Merlin, the stones were lifted from the Hill of Uisneach, the sacred center of Ireland, and transported via magic to their current home in England at Stonehenge. After all of

---

145 The holy pool at Uisneach and/or Connla's Well. I think it depends on if you are looking through the well from Otherworld (Connla's Well in the Summerlands can see into many holy wells and springs in this world—possibly all of them if they are kept pure, tended with reverence, and honored.)

146 Tradition has it that the salmon ate nine of the hazelnuts every day.

147 There are so many delicious versions of the Fionn Cycle tales. Try Ella Young's book *The Tangle-Coated Horse* for one of the best.

their quest for the Holy Grail, the English had finally found it, stolen it, and transported it to their own country.[148] Though as with many things English—stripping the Irish of their natural resources and heritage—it never worked. Ireland is still Ireland. The source of the Holy Grail is still in Ireland. And perhaps she is not dressed in the finery that she was once dressed in, but she remains free, sovereign, and proud.

At the Hill of Uisneach lies the Stone of Divisions, or *Ail na Míreann*, which is the crossing place of all the realms/provinces of Ireland.[149] According to legends, the sovereign Goddess of Ireland, Ériu, resides (or is buried) under the Stone of Divisions. The Irish say that the rocks are her bones; the earth, her flesh; and the rivers, her blood. Either way, Ériu becomes synonymous with Cessair and with the Goddess, guardians of one of the oldest forgotten wisdom teachings on the planet. Ireland is the Holy Grail. The Grail is Ireland. Uisneach is the location of the holy seed and vessel. In Ireland today, if your cup is empty, all you must do is hold it out to the sky and it will fill back up. Ireland is the Grail, constantly filling again and again, no matter how thirsty. Drink deep! *Sláinte!*

Alchemy of the Sacred Vessel of Ireland

Try this meditation and visualization at home, in the forest, or especially at the Hill of Uisneach. Lying down with your head to the north and your back to the earth, ground yourself in the Celtic tree meditation found on page vii in the epilogue. Once you are connected, begin to align with the sacred centers of Ireland respective to the Wheel of the Year. Find the center at Uisneach aligned with your heart. Feel the water flowing out of the sacred pool of the heart and flowing over the landscape of your body, connecting with the streams, rivers, and

148 This has long since been disproven but makes a fine "victim" story. The English did steal the Stone of Destiny from Ireland. It remains under the throne of England.

149 *Ail na Míreann*, also known as the "Cat Stone"—Etymologically, *ail* means "monument" or "stone"; *Mír* relates to *Mor* and *Mary*—marking this again as a place of the Goddess. *Eann* is likely a derivative of *Áine*. An Irish-to-English translation of *Ail na Míreann* is "Monument of the Goddess Áine."

ocean, thus, all waters of the world. Here is a gentle alignment oration (replace the gods with "Christ" and goddesses with "Mother Mary" or "Magdalene" if that is your ticket in):

> *"Nuada at my head in the north—I am the sacrificial god who gives of self so the tribe may thrive and be free. Manannán at my feet in the south—I rise from the mist and mystery beyond time in my union of the sacred marriage with the land. Dagda to my left in the east—I am the ever-giving and abundant God who nourishes and feeds beyond my wants, beyond my fears, from death into life. Lugh to my right and to the west—I am the bright one who brings strength, illumination, and victory to the devout. I call upon the heart of hearts to protect the sacred Grail-Cauldron within the center that it may eternally overflow and nourish the land. Here the Grail is the culmination of the entire Wheel—hidden within the heart—where the divine feminine both sustains and is the Holy Grail. Morrígu and Macha, the northern goddesses of strategy and planning form the sacred vessel between their breasts. Áine and Anu, the southern goddesses of pleasure and abundance form the Stone of Destiny between their breasts. In the sanctuary held between the Stone of Destiny and the Holy Grail, a wellspring of divine ecstasy from the true sovereign within overflows and returns to the sea."*

"When you eat of this bread and drink of this cup, you shall live forever."[150] Welcome to the sweet Summerland. Welcome to *Tír na nÓg*, heaven on earth, the house of the eternal Goddess, and sanctuary of the Holy Grail. Welcome to an ever-deeper layer of Ireland and the secrets that she guards under her thick raiment of mist.

Sic itur ad ast.[151]

150 John 6:51

151 *Sic itur ad ast* translates to "Reach for the stars"; the Latin motto of the Kilmartin and Martin Clan of the Connemara, as seeded by Edward Martyn at Tulira, County Clare.

THE SACRED NATURE OF IRELAND

Chapter Nine

ON THE SACRED NATURE OF IRELAND

"There are locations on earth that exude a powerful aura of both mystery and tragedy. Steeped in rivers of blood and centuries of history, these rare places can haunt the spirit for many years, long after the visitor has returned to his or her place of security in the modern world."

~ Kathleen McGowan

The forests of the world call and I come running. For the past twenty years, I have been conducting botanical inventories, threatened and endangered species surveys, wetland assessments, ecological restoration, and conservation planning around the planet. From the Celtic Broadleaf forests of northern Europe and Bristlecone Pine forests of the American Southwest to the Cloud Forests of Central America and the Rich Cove Forests of the Southern Appalachian Mountains, I have immersed myself in the forests of the world for the purposes of preserving and conserving our natural heritage. And yet, this is only part of the reason why I am called to the forests. I go to the forests because they sing my soul. The forests pull on me like a magnet: come home, Jeremy.

My mother tells me that when I was a child, I was already infatuated with trees—the smells, the texture, the bark, and the cool shade. The best story she tells is of a time when I was about three years old. We were living at the time in Cary, North Carolina, as my father was working with the US EPA in Research Triangle Park. I had a tendency, as many children do, to collect odd assortments of things found in nature. One evening, after a mother and son ramble in the Loblolly pine flats and riparian floodplain of a local park, I professed my love for walnut trees while she tucked me into bed. She of course smiled, turned off the light, and closed the door. I fell asleep dreaming of walnut leaves blowing in the wind and secretly enjoying the aroma of walnuts.

In the morning, my mother was surprised to find that most of my skin was stained a dark charcoal to rich green color. Pulling back the sheets and covers of my twin-sized bed, she found the culprit: I had hulled about a dozen walnuts home with me the day before and snuck them into my bed. Apparently, I loved the smell of the walnuts so much that I wanted to enjoy their aroma all through the night. As far as I know, I have not dragged any field collections with me into my bed since then, but it would be best to ask my wife what she thinks of the matter.

I have always inhabited homes with old trees. Our house in Asheville, North Carolina, is surrounded by over one hundred mature trees including white oak, white pine, Virginia pine, southern red oak, tuliptree, red maple, beech, sourwood, mulberry, hawthorn, American holly, mockernut hickory, wild black cherry, and many more. Haltia Haven, the land and grove that we steward on the Highlands Plateau, is a haven for birch, oak, hickory, eastern hemlock (some are still holding on), beech, maple, and more—all awash in the sound of waterfalls and birdsong. The forest is a haven to return to that washes my heart, body, mind, and soul clean every time I return.

Many of us are drawn to nature in her various expressions. Wetlands, ocean, sea cliffs, mountains, river valleys, old stands of trees, orchards, springs, meadows, and much more. Nature calls us home. She calls on us to remember who we really are outside of the nonsense of the modern world.

May you always find your way home. May you find it in your heart to do what it takes to pick up your weary body and mind and deposit yourself in the heart of the wilds where the water, wind, birds, trees, and medicine of place can infuse your entire being with belonging, health, and true connection. If it is truly in your heart to know the Beyond and the ever-evolving truth of your soul's expression in this temporal moment in time, may you drop all your fancy electronic gadgets and gizmos that have tricked you into thinking you are connected and run home to the wild. Submerge yourself free and clear in the true connection of nature. Come back to the "real world" if you must, but stay if you can, for as long as you can, in the heart of nature. One day, I will not come back. And please do not worry for me, it is my lifelong wish to dissolve into the ancient dream of the forest.

In the traditional Celtic worldview, there is no separation between spirit and matter or between nature and the divine. As the people of the northern forests, the Celts were an intrinsic part of the ecosystem, from language and culture to the stewardship of the land and harvest of food and medicine from forest and field. The first writing of the Celts is built completely around this forest of sound through use of the *ogham*, the tree alphabet.[152]

While there are over 150,000 archaeological sites listed in Ireland, most of which are considered sacred, truly the entire landscape of Ireland is hallowed. Beyond the human-built structures of the megalithic sites, ancient temples, abandoned churches, and abbeys, there are hundreds of thousands of natural habitats and living landscape features. In the deep nature of Ireland, the veil between the eternal and temporal is often extremely thin. It can be difficult to discern whether one is in the Summerlands, in a stage set for a William B. Yeats poem enactment, or in twenty-first-century Ireland. While I can never come close to touching the true expanse of the nature of Ireland with abstract words, at the very least, I can share with you some of the most revered habitats in Ireland with some suggestions of places that I have come to know. Some sites will be obscure and difficult to find, while others are national landmarks of the Republic, Northern Ireland, or even are listed UNESCO World Heritage sites.

---

[152] See Steve Blamires' book *Celtic Tree Mysteries: Secrets of the Tree Ogham;* The *ogham* is believed to have been developed in the fourth century AD.

Chapter Ten

CAVES *UAIMHEANNA*

Most of my life, I have been infatuated with caves, and even as a youth I learned to enter them with respect. I grew up in a karst region in the Ohio River Valley near Cincinnati, filled with countless fossils and thousands of caves of varying sizes and depths.[153] Additionally, my time as a youth in the Boy Scouts of America was of course another great exposure to respectful spelunking. I have been exploring caves from the Guatemalan highlands and the desert Southwest to the Emerald Isle and the Mediterranean Sea ever since.

Caves are an intrinsic part of the human primordial connection with the Earth. When entering a cave, we are being admitted into the Earth, whether to seek shelter from a storm, create a home like our ancestors once did, conduct scientific study, or seek spiritual illumination. Caves mostly form in karst regions due to the softer nature of the substrata. Limestone tends to dissolve in water more rapidly than most other types of stone. Limestone caves are the most common in Ireland. Sandstone and quartzite caves are also common in Ireland, though most of these caves are much smaller and have been formed by seismic activity or oceanic erosion. Within the heart of Ireland and along the coastline, there are thousands of caves to

[153] Karst is a topography formed from the dissolution of soluble rocks such as limestone, dolomite, and gypsum. It is characterized by underground drainage systems with sinkholes and caves.

explore. My favorite caves in Ireland are wild caves along the Wild Atlantic Way, largely untrammeled by the pulsing tourism industry of the Irish west.

Sea caves convey a current of timeless riddles. Resting in the belly of the Earth while hearing the pulse of the sea pounding against sandstone cliffs is enough to reshape my mental landscape into a primordial haven. Some of the entrances to caves along coastal Ireland, especially along the west and north coasts, are closed off by high tides. This, while potentially dangerous to the explorer, can also be extremely exhilarating, and at times, create pressure tubes of air variance within the earth. Compressed air inside a cave due to pulsing tides is a powerful initiation wherever you are in the world. I like to crawl inside narrow passages as the tide is coming up and feel the massive pressure differential of the cave's air pocket compacting and subsiding. It is like laying in the heart of great earthen bellows of the Irish smith Goibniu being powered by the horse of the tides, Aonbharr Mhanannáin.[154] As my friend Angele of the Mesa likes to say, "let the cave breathe you."

The red sandstone sea caves along the edges of Dunmore Head in County Kerry are among my favorites in Ireland. I can spend hours or days walking slowly along the Mór Mhumhan's gorgeous coastline there, darting in and out of caves or sitting for hours inside a grotto listening to Manannán and Mór Mhumhan making love as the sea pulses rhythmically against the sandstone cliffs. Yet, hands down, some of my most powerful experiences have been with the quartzite Caves of Maghera near Ardara in County Donegal. These caves are pulsing with primordial power. Surrounded by gorgeous white quartzite sand and dunes that have formed throughout the Holocene, these gorgeous fissure caves call to the wanderer, the mystic, and the sage in every heart. Most of the caves are accessible when the tide is out, but certainly one should vacate the beach and caves if the tide is coming in. Friends who grew up in the area told us that quite a few people have been pulled out to sea and drowned.

[154] Goibniu was the metalsmith of the *Tuatha Dé Danann* and also associated with hospitality; Aonbharr Mhanannáin was the horse of Manannán Mac Lir who could traverse both land and sea and was swifter than wind-speed.

Having grown up with limestone caves, the draw to Ireland's heartland, as well as almost all of County Clare in the west, has always been strong for me. Caves and sinkholes are everywhere. The Burren in west County Clare is famous for caves, crevices, and underground streams, while the whole of Ireland's karst heartland is like a giant block of limestone-Swiss cheese. In Tulla Parish of central County Clare, near the town of Tulla itself, an entire stream system emerges out of caves in some sections, disappearing underground again in others. We kayaked the streams in the area which allowed us to gently explore the quiet recesses of caverns unfamiliar with human interactions, filled to the brim with deep, cold water. And where the caves and streams opened back up to the Irish sky, ancient beech, oak, and ash hung heavily with mosses and sword ferns, reaching long, stately branches down into the dark of the underworld.

At the center of my love for the Irish underworld are the caves at the Hill of Kesh in County Sligo, and the cave of Oweynagat in County Roscommon. I have shared the tale many times of my repetitive dreaming of Lough Gur long before ever arriving in Ireland in this life, but less so are the dreams that followed. Sinéad helped me navigate them for years. She always knew the places I dreamed of until the Otherworld invited me to the Cave of the Cats.[155] After planning to be in Ireland for four weeks in November and December of 2008, Sinéad and I set off to find Oweynagat at Ráth Cruchain.[156] We spent hours looking for it, and after a few crow courts and a run-in with an elderly druid to point us the way, we were able to slide in beneath the hawthorn and the *ogham* stone to carefully make our way down the rough stone steps into the heart of the cave.

The cave inside is not very wide, and with respect to most caves I have been drawn to, it was also not exceptionally long or deep. Some say that you can see the outline of the goddess Morrígu inside the cave, shaped by the walls themselves. I would not know because I have never taken a

155 Sharon Blackie's description of her first entry into Oweynagat in *If Women Rose Rooted* is powerful and worthy of the read.

156 This was prior to Oweynagat being on the internet anywhere. Now anyone can find it!

light in with me other than in my pocket for emergency reasons. I crawl into the cave and feel my way through the delicious limestone mud at the bottom. Standing, I can just reach out and touch the two walls of the long chamber with my fingers—enough to reassure me that I have not entered the Otherworld entirely.

What happened on that first visit continues to occur in the dozen or so times that I have returned since that winter of 2008. In the heart of the chamber, if you stand still and settle into the darkness, the walls seem to glow with a soft, white, internal light. I do not mean that the walls are host to bioluminescent life or produce light biochemically. The "walls" of the cave literally come to life with an inner light that my eyes can "see" but is not recordable with any devices—cave scrying. This is not an uncommon phenomenon. Science refers to the ability of spelunkers to "see" their own hands or images in the pitch dark of a cave as synesthesia. In Oweynagat, it is almost as if the walls no longer exist. In the dark, it is like the walls of the cave become windows that one can see over vast expanses of the landscape of Ireland, expanses of other landscapes, landscapes of personal memory, or visuals of what could come to pass. Oweynagat, like many ancient strongholds of the Goddess, is an oracle cave. From mythology and history, we know that this cave was an initiation chamber for both the priestess of the Morrígu as well as the kings and queens of Connacht. The cave was a place of power, healing, and of the *sídhe*.

When the walls alight with the tidings of yesterday, today, or tomorrow, the expanse of the cave grows to that of the world. The cave is no longer a container, but a vessel that carries our vision to where we most need to see. From this oracle experience, I was tasked with climbing Sliabh an Iarainn, the mountain where the *Tuatha Dé Danann* landed their floating airships on its summit in Ireland.[157] I was also tasked with sleeping in the Morrígu's caves at the Hill of Kesh for three nights.[158]

Mind you, this was the end of November, and days are extremely short at the latitude of Ireland. When I had left Sinéad and Oweynagat

157 *Sliabh an Iarainn* is sometimes written as "Slieve Anierin" on maps.

158 Unfortunately, this is becoming more difficult due to the internet and recent films that have popularized the site amongst neo-Pagans.

in Roscommon, I headed straight to Lough Allen and found a bed-and-breakfast in the town of Drumshanbo. Though closed for the season, the proprietress was willing to host me for an evening. I was grateful for the hospitality but turned down a proper tea and peat fire to complete the task the vision in Oweynagat had instilled in my heart and mind. As dusk settled over Drumshanbo on the southeast shore of Lough Allen, I set off on foot in the most direct manner that I could up the low mountain. I will say that I have met plenty of blanket bogs in my travels in Ireland, but this was the first time that I was swallowed by one.

As I climbed the mountain in the dark, a heavy mist settled into where I could not see more than ten or fifteen feet in any direction. I kept my eyes on the landscape features so that I could find my way back as I had no flashlight with me. The blanket bog kept trying to suck my boots, and sometimes me, into the wet peat. At times, I skipped from heather tussock to tussock until I reached granite glacial erratic boulders at the top. I could only see about ten feet into the mist at this point as it was pitch dark and no moonlight was strong enough to pierce that Otherworldly mist. I sounded the Eiggeshörn and watched my imagination play out with the dragons in the mist. It was November and cold. I turned around to head back to the bed-and-breakfast. Or so I thought.

I have always wanted to be able to get lost in the wilds or faërie-somewhere. For someone who has good tracking and wilderness skills, it is almost impossible to get lost even in the deepest bush. I can always find my way back to civilization by going down. Follow a waterbody; it will bring me to human settlement eventually. Well, I have never walked in the dark, in a thick mist, and in a blanket bog where everything is saturated by water. There is no flow. The water just sits there in a giant organic sponge the size of a mountain. None of the waypoints I had observed on the way to the top of Slieve an Iarainn revealed themselves on the way back. I spent hours stumbling around in the dark and mist while the ancient ones laughed their hearts out.

"So, you want to get lost in Faërie, do you now?" came the voices of a not-so-forgotten past, "well, here you are, lad. Enjoy your time in the Celtic twilight!"

I must admit that I was extremely excited. *Finally, I am lost,* I thought. Perhaps something interesting will happen and I will find the Good

People. Maybe they will invite me to stay with them in their warm golden halls for hundreds of years and I will return thinking only a night has passed. Oh, let it be so!

I am not sure how many days, years, or hours passed as I stumbled around, soaking wet, through the gorgeous blanket bog of Slieve an Iarainn. What I do know is that I was invited into the golden halls of the *sídhe,* and I never came back ...

Wait...Jeremy. Umm...your tail is getting a little long ...

Oh yes, sorry. After 300 years, the *sídhe* let me ride out on a white horse shod with silver horseshoes...wait. Okay. The pragmatists are reining me in.

After several hours of blundering around in the dark mist with my mind wild with fancies of *sídhe* grandeur (some part of me did indeed reside there for three centuries of remaking in the smithy of Goibniu, the laughing halls of Badb, and the healing hands of Brigid), the mist finally parted. But that did not help. What I saw before me was seemingly impossible. A massive lake, I assumed it was Lough Allen, was spread at my feet. There was not a single point of electric light around the entire lake. The moon hung heavy and full. To my right, the blanket bog ended into a thick forest of native hardwoods and a mixed plantation of conifers. And in the forest, a massive waterfall tumbled over eroded shale cliffs and disappeared into the valley below. I sat there for a while, stunned, drinking in the mystery, beauty, and magic with all my soul.

At some point in the wee hours of the night, I knew that the *sídhe* had released me. I had completed one of the steps presented by the *aisling* in Oweynagat, but not the entire mission. The release of that magical strand due to completion was like the bubble that rises in your sternum before releasing a powerful, cathartic, full-throttle cry. When the invisible silver *sídhe* thread of the *aisling* released within, freeing me to return to the world of humanity, I began using my hands to explore in the broken moonlight downslope along the length of the waterfall until I found the human thread that would take me home: barbed wire. Barbed wire is ever the secular thread back to humanity. I followed the wire until I found a gravel road that led me down the rest of the mountain through a conifer plantation to the R207 and back to the bed-and-breakfast. I promptly took a long shower, stacked my moldering socks on the hot water wall heater, and fell asleep like Rip van Winkle. In the morning, I followed the blue mist of the *aisling* west into County Sligo to find Keshcorran.

Sleeping in the Caves of Kesh can be an uncomfortable experience for the faint of heart, but I was ecstatic when arriving at the Morrígu's caves. Here were the caves of my dreams that came to me before crossing the great pond of the Atlantic from Southern Appalachia. Oweynagat had given me a name, sense of purpose, and a stronger series of *aisling* threads to follow in the weave of the mystery. But the Caves of Kesh was where the Morrígu was waiting for me.

However, she waited two days before revealing to me that I was in the wrong cave. It did not matter. I was so content to listen to the *sídhe* winds, known as *siansán* in Irish, singing through the caves for two days and nights.[159] The view from Cormac Cave's opening was unlike the opening of any cave I had seen up until that point in my life. The openings of all the Caves of Kesh are about halfway up the slope of the Hill of Kesh. Everything below the cave entrances is loose scree covered with bramble and grasses. You can see off into the distance for miles to the ocean, Knocknashee, Templehouse Lough, and the Ox Mountains of the west. My time in the first cave at Kesh gave my heart and mind time to synchronize with all that had come before, yet it could not prepare me for what came thereafter.

On the morning after my second night, I suddenly realized that I needed to move. It was a deep itch in my mind, and the *aisling* moved out of the cave entrance and headed south along the base of the cliffs. I followed the thread. I watched as the *aisling* slowed at each entrance to respective caves. I bowed to each cave as she demonstrated. After it seemed the last cave had been revered, the *aisling* led onward. Slipping on the dew-laden grasses, I stumbled along after her until I came to a cave entrance that not only looked like the shape of a woman but also had a clear, flowing stream running out of the center of it. The stream disappeared almost as soon as it came out of the cave, tricking down into the grass-covered scree.

◇◇◇◇◇◇◇◇◇◇◇◇◇◇◇

159 *Siansán* literally means "the humming winds."

The *aisling* ducked into the cave and I assumed to follow. Immediately, a flock of small birds came shouting out at head level and I almost fell into the stream trying to dodge them. Immediately, I knew this was the place I had been called to by the Morrígu. She had sent the birds to remind me that I needed to ask permission before entering the crevice of the Goddess. And so, I asked, and only the words that were written several hours after the entry into her cave will do any justice:

Sídh ar Crúachâin.[160]

A Bird calls from her window looking west. The lone charioteer smiles as he rides to the stables beyond the sea. The grass on the mount is wet from an afternoon shower. It is here that his golden limbs reach into her chamber...

Trembling in anticipation of his lover's kiss, he has harrowed the fields of the Bird before, but she teases him into fervor.

"Which room am I in? Am I the Black Raven, the Wildgoose, or the Wren on this eve? Which river have I bathed in tonight? Catch me. Catch me. I am gone. I am neither night nor day, Gooseberry or Elder... Catch me. Catch me. I am gone."

"Take me in strong arms. Bend my bow and stretch the strand tight. I cannot release the music of wonder if you do not hold me just so."

"Yes," responds the charioteer, *"And I cannot fire arrows, sweet, sweet Bird if I cannot find the key to the arsenal of your heart. Shall I plunge arrows blindly into the darkness... or will you provide me with a doorway, a light, where my eyes can worship you, my hands can stir you, and my arms can bend you to the ancient music pulsing through our veins?"*

The Bird laughs and throws open her chamber.

"Come then. Catch me. Bend me, but do not break me. If we are to make music, my strings must be strummed lightly... though I beseech you, play the drum of my heart with vigor and abandon, as if this were the last sunrise and sunset.

How many suns have set on that long evening in the Summer Country? How many lives of humans come and gone like the waves on a rocky shore? How many cities fallen to the hammer of time while the charioteer and the Bird made music on the mountain?

---

160 *Sídh ar Crúachain* meaning "Faëry Mound on Small Stack" referring to the Hill of Kesh.

Step out.

Go there, I beseech you. Go there to the place where the moss-enshrouded cliffs are riddled with the pleasures of a goddess—waiting to invite the setting sun to her pleasures. You may find that the Bird and the Charioteer are still making fine music. Music that can shake mountains. Music to stir the loins for lost loves and newly gained passions. Go there, but only if you intend to listen or to become—to become a fragment of the oldest composition of music in the universe.

Go there, but only when you are ready to surrender to the majesty of this ancient harmony."

And so is the story of the beloved ones.

"I stand naked before you. I am wild. I am free. And so are you. Catch me. Catch me if you can. For I may catch you when you start to run... catch you and drag you off to the Summer Country for an eternal afternoon making music with the Faë."

Step up, for the bard Oisín would speak.

"I am a dragon, born of the Rainbow, Ward of the Bridge, Carried here on Birdsong. I have been here a thousand upon a thousand times. Where once I stood in the hall of kings, I now walk alone over windy moors, or I revel in beansídhe song at the hearths of forgotten homes and laugh under the belt of Orion on cold winter nights with the Fianna gathered around me.

I spin and weave under Pegasus and Draco, summer songs that give the Faë a causeway between the worlds, despite the pulse of the tide. I wake sleepers and trees—singing to them to rise from the deep. Dord Fiann has been sounded for the Seven Winds. Friends, it is time to sally forth. Walk onward upon eternal roots. The trees stand tall across countless worlds. Dragon song opens doors and windows that the Light can illuminate the pathway of travelers—of dreamers.

See the song unfolding before us. At times in rote. At times a river but most often, a road between the stars, between the standing stones, between the kingdoms of the heart, and between heaven and earth.

Step down to the circle of stones. The dragon is the heartbeat, lifeblood pulsing drum calling all to dance—to throw down all walls in jubilee. Come! The fire is hot! The Labyrinth's walls are self-created or adapted. Riddles are only there by our own creations or the creation of others if you give them the reigns.

No! Grab the reigns and ride! This is your dragon! Step up from circles of stone. Look to where Oisín sings upon the back of his grey steed.

I live in the Summer Country; this dragon am I. Unveil your dragon—this eternal nature are we. For this tapestry of words would be naught for the temple you hold in the sanctuary of your heart.

Drink shall we from the sacred well of our eternal friendship. Drink! The water is good! Drink…take the Big Dipper in summer and the cache at Orion's belt in winter. Whether we meet at this crossroads of words for pleasure or for tea, comfort, or tears, this is all we have. Here now. Beyond time, what lies before, behind, within us. Let us embrace this moment upon the altar of our souls, for this moment in how we celebrate eternity. If we do not like what we see, let us have a charrette and design anew.

And I ask you, Friend, Lover: Will you remind me that when I have fallen apart, t'is only because I asked for it so that I could design anew? Remind me that I was holding onto too much. And like a human-made lake or pond made to secure water for the future, my dams were bound to fail—to let the waters rush free and true to course; to dash against rock, stone, root, and sand. Remind me that I am whole. Remind me that holding onto life only strangles it. Help me let it all go. Let me cry. Hold me, with love, until I am strong again. That I can stand at the Bridge between the Lord and Lady and say, yes! I am your warrior. I strike with hammer, sword, spear, and arrow. I strike true! Yes! I am your bard. I nurture with chalice, spring, well, and cauldron. I fly true!

And my friend, my beloved One, I shall do the same for you.

Lord and Lady, guide my breath—my words, actions, and deeds. And together we will make lovely music.

I am a dragon, born of the Rainbow, Ward of the Bridge, carried here on Birdsong. I have been here a thousand upon a thousand times. Where once I stood in the hall of kings, I now walk alone over windy moors and revel in beansídhe song at the hearths of forgotten houses and laugh under the belt of Orion on cold winter nights with the Fianna all around me."

Caves will call you when you are ready, yet the worlds will only open if you are ready and the alignment is correct. Always enter with care, respect, and permission. Be sure to let someone know where you are going for safety reasons. And have proper gear, clothing, and equipment for the type of cave you are entering. Enjoy the exploration!

∞

Chapter Eleven

FORESTS, GROVES, AND TREES *FORAISÍ*

Prehistorically, Ireland was covered by ancient forests much like the eastern United States prior to colonization. For both nations, it could once be said that a squirrel could cross the entire landscape without ever touching the earth. It could leap from branch to branch, tree to tree, from the Irish Sea to the Atlantic or from the Atlantic to the Mississippi River respectively.[161] One of the ancient bardic names for Ireland was *Inis na bhfiodhadh* or "Island of the Sacred Trees." It is no wonder then that the Irish language is a derivative of the primordial sounds of the indigenous trees and other plants of Ireland. It is the language of the trees of the northern European hardwood forests, scientifically known as the *Celtic Broadleaf Forest.*[162] Recall that the original written Irish

◇◇◇◇◇◇◇◇◇◇◇◇◇◇

[161] Forest cover in Ireland was reduced massively in various waves throughout pre-history and history. The usual scapegoat is the English plantations and the utilization of the Irish oak forests for constructing the English navy in post-Cromwell years—which, of course, were mostly used to catch Spanish navy cannonballs. Woodlands were also exploited for iron-ore smelting and barrel making.

[162] NatureServe is the authoritative source of delineation of natural communities among biological and ecosystem scientists around the world. Explore further for your area via their website: https://www.natureserve.org/products/explore-natural-communities

alphabet was called the "tree alphabet" and is better known as the *ogham*, which is made up of twenty species of trees.[163] Each species of tree is represented by a symbol directly translatable into a Roman alphabet letter. All twenty letters account for the necessary sounds to construct all words in the Irish language via writing. Therefore, each word is like a small woodland or grove. A poem, song, sentence, or book written in Irish, as well as in Scotch Gaelic and Manx, contains a massive "forest of words." *Ogham* is read from the bottom up, similar to how a tree grows.

Sadly enough, the Republic of Ireland has the second lowest percent cover of forest in all of Europe in the twenty-first century after Iceland.[164] Ireland's once mighty and ancient forests only account for 11.03% of the landscape cover now. And this number is slightly skewed as three-quarters of that 11.03% is planted in a mix of native and non-native conifer plantations which are clearcut approximately every 30 years. Furthermore, of the one-quarter forest cover in Ireland that remains as indigenous Celtic Broadleaf Forest, only a fraction of that forest is ancient woodland. The ancient forests are delineated from other forests if they have had consistent forest cover since the mid-1600s until the present. With this definition of terms, only 0.2% of Ireland's ancient forest remains. Yet where it does still thrive, it is full of timeless song, biodiversity, and wonder.

In my opinion, Ireland's best ancient forests are found in County Kerry and County Clare, especially in the Killarney National Park (KNP) in Kerry. The ancient oak and yew forests of KNP are dreamy, and for the most part, easy to access on foot or bike. Though the ancient beech tree forests mixed in with the native hardwoods are not indigenous to Ireland, they are native to most of the rest of the traditionally Celtic lands and would have played a major role in the Celtic mythos of the trees.[165] The

163 Several of the *ogham* "trees" are shrubs, vines, or perennials.

164 As of August 21, 2011, based on Peter Wyse Jackson's *Ireland's Generous Nature.*

165 Beech trees (*Fagus sylvatica*) were native in parts of the southern UK as well as throughout the European continent and play a vital role in the minds, hearts, and traditional ecological knowledge of the Celts—and still do today. They were brought into Ireland by the Anglo-Norman invaders/settlers in the thirteenth century. Also, more modern *ogham* lists include beech as part of a fifth set of *ogham* known as the *diphthongs*.

ancient forests of KNP, while intertwined with gorgeous lakes and the MacGillycuddy's Reeks, provide a sanctuary for the wanderer to slip out of time and for the botanist or naturalist to explore biodiversity or observe species uncommon in most of the rest of the Republic in the twenty-first century. My favorite forest in KNP is the ancient oak woodland below Ladies View, best known as the *Derrynahierka* Oak Forest.[166] Within this ancient forest are some outstanding rock outcrops, glacial meadows, streams, lakes, and powerful waterfalls tumbling over black, tannin-stained sandstone boulders and bedrock. The quality of the natural energy of the place is exceptional, pure, and calls to the dreamers and bards.

Rainfall in Ireland is substantial enough that most of Ireland could be considered a cloud forest due to mist, cloud cover, and slower precipitation deposition. The indigenous forest community is typically referred to as the Atlantic Temperate Rainforest, a particular subset of the Celtic Broadleaf Forest that received ample precipitation from the Atlantic Gulf Stream.[167] Many of the same species of bryophytes and ferns share Ireland's cloud forest-like habitat with other temperate rainforests and montane cloud forests, including recently-discovered and critically-endangered cloud forest fern, Mouse-ear fern, or *Lellingeria myosuroides.*[168] Though tree species may differ, many of the genera are the same, especially the oaks (*Quercus spp.*), linden (*Tilia spp.*), and ash (*Fraxinus spp.*). For the explorer and botanist who loves cloud forests and temperate rainforests, Ireland's ancient remaining forest gems are a ticket into the primordial heart, mythos, and soul of the free Celt.

There are substantial native Celtic Broadleaf Forest examples across Ireland. One of my favorites is found in Ard's Forest Park in County Donegal. Here, the forest runs along an east-projecting peninsula in the heart of Sheephaven Bay. I have found every tree in the *ogham* growing in the confines of this park. Other outstanding

◇◇◇◇◇◇◇◇◇◇◇◇◇◇

166 *Derrynahierka* in Irish is *Daire na hErka,* named after Saint Darerca of Kerry, Ireland, the sister of Saint Patrick, and mother of several saints and mystics.

167 Dr. Colin Kelleher, Botanist at the National Botanic Gardens in Dublin.

168 Article posted in The Guardian, October 4, 2020: https://www.theguardian.com/environment/2020/oct/04/rarest-fern-europe-discovered-ireland

ancient woodlands can be found in Ireland around Lough Derg in County Clare where the Brian Boru Oak Tree has been growing in Raheen Woods east of Tuamgraney for over 1,000 years. This ancient Irish oak (*Quercus petraea*) is twenty-six feet in circumference at chest height and is found in one of the last surviving sections of Ireland's ancient wild oak forests. The forest at Lough Derg was once known as the great Forest of Suidain[169] of the Sliabh Aughty Mountains.[170] The National Monuments Service of Ireland has listed the tree in its Archaeological Survey as a Ritual Site and Holy Tree. Not too far away, Lough Graney's Raheen oakwood forest consists of forty acres with a more than 100-foot forest canopy. Every inch of the trees provides habitat for a broad range of Celtic Broadleaf Forest species. The oaks and many of the beech trees found there are between 400 and 600 years old. Moss-covered standing stones call any dreamer or poet deeper into the Celtic twilight.

While living and working in Glendree, County Clare, Ireland, in the spring and summer of 2005 on an eighteen-acre biodynamic farm, I had many an opportunity to explore the countryside in much of the west and southwest of Ireland. Meadowsweet Farm was not far from the Maghera Mountain Bogs, and through the bogs to the northeast of the farm was the back "entrance" to the Raheen forest. Kevin, a friend of the farm, lived at the edge of the wood and invited me to come and explore whenever I could. Behind Kevin's house was a long, low stone wall of the style like much of County Clare—dry-stacked, with large gaps between the stones due to the rounded limestone found in the area, covered in mosses and ferns. To enter the forest, I had to climb the wall at a low spot that cattle had knocked over sometime in the last fifteen to 120 years and had never been restacked. There was a place to leave an offering on a large, moss-covered boulder covered with coins, crosses,

◇◇◇◇◇◇◇◇◇◇◇◇◇◇◇

169 McCracken, Eileen. "The Woodlands of Ireland Circa 1600." *Irish Historical Studies* 11, no. 44 (1959): 271-96. Accessed December 21, 2020. http://www.jstor.org/stable/30006457.

170 *Sliabh Eachtaí* in Irish—these glacier-polished mountains stretch from County Galway all the way down through Count Clare almost to Limerick city.

and rosaries. I often would bring a Euro or a Brigid's cross woven from rushes while walking toward the forest.

The Raheen forest is incredible. The ancient trees are dense and diverse, though the predominant species are the Irish oak, and in places, the European beech. I was called to the forest several times during daylight hours, but most frequently, this is where I was drawn when the moon was full. A small outcrop at the top of one of the hills in the forest gave a commanding view of the top of the forest canopy as well as Lough Graney below. I felt a rather strong sense of place here as if I belonged in the forest. Even upon my first entry into the wood, some part of me remembered having been there before. Let us fast forward to the *aisling* that came from the apple orchard at Meadowsweet Farm in Glendree.

She first appeared to me when I was building a small stone "castle" for the children. The dry-stacked stone walls of the castle and faëry kingdom were only about twenty feet from the apple orchard behind the 300-year-old thatched cottage that was our restored home at Meadowsweet. I was stacking some of the finishing pieces on top of the rampart when I saw a woman in a long, white, silky dress, sauntering through the young apple orchard out of the corner of my left eye. Though it was sunny, it was only mid-March, and so seeing a woman wearing only a thin white dress surprised me. I promptly looked up from my work, thinking to see my wife wandering in the cool afternoon air, but the woman was no longer visible to me. At first, I had a feeling she was the spirit of the apple trees, but upon an intuitive spark, realized that she was an *aisling* from the Summerlands come to request my aid in some endeavor.[171] But I soon forgot about her as no direct request was made at that time.

About a month later, I was awakened in my bed by a chilly feeling that I was being hailed from the Otherworld. I looked out the western window of the bedroom through the edges of the thatch and saw a light flashing at me in a repetitive pattern from the top of an old beech tree at the edge of the apple orchard. I could not decipher any code from the flashing, though I did think for a moment in respect to Morse Code.

◇◇◇◇◇◇◇◇◇◇◇◇◇◇

[171] This "intuitive spark" is typically referred to in Ireland as "second sight" and refers to the inner "seeing" into the spirit/Otherworld simultaneously with our normal sight.

But no message seemed apparent other than to get my attention. I did not hesitate for long. When an *aisling* calls, an *aisling* calls, for the heart of wonder is ever fed by discovery and exploration. I suited up for the chilly spring twilight air, popped on my Wellies, and headed out through the orchard to the beech grove. By the time I had gotten to the beech tree, the source of the light was gone. However, a low-hanging limb had a long ribbon tied to it, like when visiting a faëry tree or clootie well. I climbed up the tree and listened for some time. The only thing I heard other than normal sounds of the night was one clear message: *"The key is near."* I went back to bed to catch some sleep before the duties of the biodynamic farm called me.

A few days later, I found myself lucid in a dream. In the dream, the flashing light in the beech woke me again. I stood up from the bed and wandered down the stairs. The wood on the ceiling of the cottage was covered with Celtic knots that seemed to move subtly like bluebells rustling in a gentle breeze. Beneath this wooden masterpiece, I flowed down the stairs, through the kitchen, past the cooling hearth, and out the back door. On the east side of the cottage was a storeroom where we kept firewood and tools. In the dream, I wandered into the storeroom because a gentle white light was emanating from within, similar to the hue of the *aisling* in the apple orchard a month before. When I stepped into the storeroom, the *aisling* greeted me only for a moment.

She pointed at the woodbin and said, "If you want to wake up, you will find the key in here to open the door."

I looked at the wood pile in the bin and then looked back at where she had been standing. Instead of seeing her or the storeroom, I found myself in the ancient forest of Raheen. In front of me was a standing stone with no moss upon it, painted with woad, and bedecked with a flowery Áine crown. Behind the stone, a tall, thin doorway was pressed between the folds of an ancient beech tree. A flash of white light shot out of the doorway inside the beech tree, and I awoke.

I raced downstairs and out the back door like a child on Christmas morning. I ran to the storeroom and started rummaging through the woodbin. I was, of course, not finding anything and was starting to feel that my dream had been a ruse. I slowed down and thought about how I would look for something if it was not a dream. I am methodological and organized. Would not the *aisling* expect me to behave as such on the journey of discovery? I slowed down and began to pull each piece of wood out of the bin and stacked it nicely against the back wall of the storeroom. After having removed about half a chord of wood, I was beginning to see the bottom of the bin and no key yet. With only a few logs left in the bottom, I was starting to despair that I did not share a true dreaming with the *aisling* until my hands found something small and metal in the bottom of the bin mixed in with all the dust, soil, and moldering splinters of wood.

My heart leapt through my chest and out through the top of my crown. I fished the metal object out of the bin and into the light. Then my belly dropped. It was not a key at all. It was a triskele made of silver, with a purple thong ribbon used to tie it to a sea-polished piece of quartzite. At first, I felt disappointment creeping into my waking mind. I took the silver triskele and stone out to the orchard and sat down. I closed my eyes and began to slow down my breath and mind to a deep listening place. In the quiet of the orchard, with a handful of crows cawing at me from the beech trees, I realized that what was in my hand was indeed a key, albeit a symbolic one, and that clearly the *aisling* had shown me where the door was in the dream as well.

Later that day, I headed over to Kevin's cottage and to Raheen wood. Kevin was not home (this, of course, was pre-mobile phone days) and so I parked my car and headed into the forest, leaving a Brigid's cross at the gate in gratitude for helping to shape my dreaming. From the dream, I knew where the standing stone and the beech tree would both be waiting for me.

I wound my way gently through the deep forest, slightly down the slope, and just west of where the outcrop grants the gorgeous view of the canopy and Lough Graney below. I came into the opening under the old trees where the standing stone rests as a quiet sentinel. The alignment revealed in the dream was easy to replicate. I sat down in front of the moss-covered stone and let my mind settle as I stared across the stone to the ancient beech tree. Waiting for the door to appear took hours because it certainly never revealed itself as it had in the dream. What I finally saw was that the door was very tiny, and it was less a door and more of a hole in the skin of the beech tree due to some odd growth or an ancient wound that had healed.

The opening beckoned to me as my mind softened, so I rose and walked forward with the "key" in my hand. The rounded quartzite (I know now that it was most likely from up on the northeast coast of Ireland near Glenariff in County Antrim) with the triskele bound to it by the thong of ribbon fit exactly into the opening. And so, it remains there to this day, with the tree growing promptly around it over the years since. I have not been back in a few years, but I am due to return.

I felt a sense of completion once the key was anchored in the beech. I sat down at the base of the tree and waited for Fionn mac Cumhaill and the *Fianna* to find me, or for the likes of Connla of the Golden Hair, Áine, or some unnamed golden goddess from Mag Mell to convey me away on a white mare or pure crystal ship.[172] While I waited, I read over the incantation of the Golden Lady to Connla in order to best prepare myself:

A land of youth, a land of rest,
A land from sorrow free;
It lies far off in the golden west,
On the verge of the azure sea.

A swift canoe of crystal bright, that never met mortal view
We shall reach the land ere fall of night,
In that strong and swift canoe:
We shall reach the strand of that sunny land from druids and demons free;
The land of rest, in the golden west, on the verge of the azure sea!

A pleasant land of winding vales, bright streams, and verdurous plains,
Where summer, all the live-long year, in changeless splendour reigns;
A peaceful land of calm delight, of everlasting bloom;
Old age and death we never know, no sickness, care, or gloom;
The land of youth, of love and truth,
From pain and sorrow free;
The land of rest, in the golden west, on the verge of the azure sea!

◇◇◇◇◇◇◇◇◇◇◇◇◇◇◇

[172] Mag Mell (modern spelling: Magh Meall, meaning "plain of joy") was a mythical realm achievable through death and/or glory. Another name for the Irish Otherworld, the Summerlands.

There are strange delights for mortal men in that island of the west;
The sun comes down each evening in its lovely vales to rest:
And though far and dim on the ocean's rim it seems to mortal view,
We shall reach its halls ere the evening falls, in my strong and swift canoe;
And ever more that verdant shore our happy home shall be;
The land of rest, in the golden west, on the verge of the azure sea!

It will guard thee, gentle Connla of the flowing golden hair,
It will guard thee from the druids, from the demons of the air;
My crystal boat will guard thee, till we reach that western shore,
Where thou and I in joy and love shall live for evermore:
From the druid's incantation, from his black and deadly snare,
From the withering imprecation of the demon of the air,
It will guard thee, gentle Connla of the flowing golden hair;
My crystal boat will guard thee, till we reach that silver strand,
Where thou shalt reign in endless joy, the king of the Fairy-land![173]

Well, the *Fianna* did not arrive, nor did my golden lady of the *Tuatha Dé Danann*—or at least not that day. What really happened is that I fell asleep under the tree because I had not slept much over the last few nights due to dreaming and scurrying around after the *aisling*.

Yet, in my dreaming, something interesting occurred. I found myself arriving at the front door of a well-endowed plantation home near the shores of Lough Graney. A young butler answered the door and invited me into the sitting room. I was directed to be seated and wait. Looking out the windows of the great house, I could see that the hills around Lough Graney were covered in ancient forest. I heard the clicking of hard shoes in the entrance and turned to see an older gentleman wearing a long grey-white wig that hung past his shoulders in ringlets. I stood to greet him, and our hazel-green eyes met. As soon as our gaze locked, in that instant where all humans measure one another, I saw two things simultaneously. One, the old gentleman was me in another timeline. And two, the standing stone close to me in the forest where

[173] From the *Old Celtic Romances* by P. W. Joyce, LL.D., published in 1879.

I lay dreaming was a new standing stone erected for this gentleman's favorite horse that had recently died.

The moment ended quickly. I was now half awake. I could see the stone at my feet at the same time as I could see the standing stone at Dunmore Head in County Kerry far to the south at the westernmost tip of the Dingle Peninsula. I saw the waves pounding on the headland and at the same time, I could hear Manannán crying over the loss of his horse Énbarr, or Aonbharr Mhanannáin, in the great war of the *Tuatha Dé Danann* with the Milesians. The crying became my own as I woke fully back into this world with the beech tree at my back and the standing stone about twenty feet away from the bottoms of my feet.

Kevin told me later that I had likely had a true dreaming as the lore of Lough Graney is that a gentleman who had lived on the estate of Raheen wood had buried his favorite horse on the hillside near the top in the seventeenth century and had erected a standing stone in commemoration of his proud steed. All I know is that the *aisling* led me true in the stitching of time as she still does, for it is upon the cliffs of Dunmore Head where I married my queen of the stars and earth, the Mór Mumain, and forever this is our home.

Chapter Twelve

MOUNTAINS *SLÉIBHTE*

Mountains call to us across the vast landscape of time and space. Whether they beckon to us with subtle geomagnetic forces or our heart leaps to ascend above the plain of humanity into the beyond, mountains call us home to a sense of freedom and sovereignty. Mountains can also be a wall or great shield to keep marauders at bay and so invoke a sense of protection or possible isolation. All around the world, some of the best-kept traditions, archives, sacred texts, spiritual traditions, and oracles were tucked in the heart of remote mountains. Mountains create sanctuary. Warded by these geologic giants of yesteryear's planetary shifts, rich tapestries of life and traditions have continued to be woven by the masters throughout the ages while temporal human powers and the empires of history have risen and fallen with the tides.

In the last major climate change that brought the average sea level to its current dynamic level, the tradition of my spirit mother's people and the Star Song Oracle holds that the Ancients knew the climate change was coming and the sea levels would rise. The people sent out ships across the planet to find haven to not only continue the thriving of our species, but also to carry the scrolls, codices, and our traditional knowledge to places that would provide sanctuary for traditions to continue and promulgate. Most of the places these ships landed and resettled helped to kindle what we now know as the oldest traditions, cultures, and languages on the planet. These include but are not limited to Hebrew, Tamil, Sanskrit, Egyptian, Greek, Gaelic, Finnish, Basque, Lithuanian, Icelandic, Classic Mayan, Chinese, and Farsi. All these cultures and languages, which still thrive to this day, relate to mountain ranges or single mountains considered sacred, or even as home to their cultural gods.

Part of my work in this world has been to travel to these sacred mountains and leave seed offerings. I am not referring to seeds of plants, but instead to vital catalysts that help weave together the disparate geomorphology of the sacred mountains of the Earth into the beauty of the original Garden. The seed catalysts are most typically crystals. The most important thing, however, is not the type of offering, but the intention of giving in relationship; respect to place and offering the self in service to something greater than will ever be sorted out in our singular, mortal lifetime. In respect, the offering becomes a means of communicating more efficiently in concert with or on behalf of the sacred place, mountain, and culture where the offering is made—like a radio antenna or satellite bouncing and transferring messages and data from one point to another. Seed offerings in holy places also become transponders in our inner landscape—where the Summerlands, the home of our immortal selves, and Middle Earth, our everyday three-dimensional mortal-selves habitat. They are shortcuts in our consciousness to a place of power and reverence.

Ireland is a crucible—a Holy Grail. In general, the heart of Ireland is formed of limestone and the outer fringes and coastline of Ireland are formed of granite, sandstone, quartzite, and shale. This is very generalized of course, but critical to understanding the importance of the mountains in Irish mythology. The Irish were, and arguably remain, very insular, like many indigenous, non-empire nations. The reason for this is partly the very landscape of Ireland itself. The rich heartland of Ireland provided so much for the ancient Irish people that they did not need to go anywhere for their basic necessities, and when basic needs are met, there typically is no reason for conquest, just an occasional cattle raid or hurling match. The outer circumference of Ireland is predominantly mountainous. In many ways, these mountains helped to protect Ireland, and more so provided Ireland with the necessary geomagnetic quality to not only attract the rains from the Atlantic but also to sustain a milder climate than most of the rest of northern Europe.

Mountains are a beginning place. Rains are drawn to mountains like magnets to metal. Clouds form around the mountains and release their heavy moisture to be gathered in mountain streams, blanket bogs, and glacial lakes. As the water coalesces, it becomes bolder, tumbling down the mountains to the fertile plains below. The water becomes rivers, and rivers are the lifeblood of all people and most terrestrial biology. Mountains can symbolically represent the Source—a beginning place of mysteries—cloaked, hidden, but wildly beautiful and worth pursuing and exploring. Naturally, such features in the landscape demand and deserve respect. Purely from a biological and commercial worldview, it is no wonder our ancestors associated the names of gods and spirits with places such as mountains.[174] From a spiritual perspective, ascending the sacred mountain is an act of pilgrimage—of leaving behind the pain and suffering of the world to attain at the very least clarity, if not communion with the divine, or perhaps even a boon or blessing.

Most mountains and hills in Ireland are considered sacred. They all have names. They all have stories. Most of them can be found in the vast archive of Irish mythology. And where that is missing, ask the locals, for there is a story for everything from anyone who has lived there long enough. I have hiked, or hill-walked, many of Ireland's primary sacred mountains, but there are many that still call to me. I can never know when I will have the honor of walking the thin thread of humanity through time in the form of a trail up the sacred breast of the Great Mother's mountains again. And so, I walk the pathway of the Great Mother in my heart and mind every morning as the sun rises, symbolically lighting a candle in honor of the Light of Erin and the Light of the Great Mother who is the Mother of all.

Several mountains speak to me in this time of writing to share about the Emerald Isle. The first mountain is Croagh Patrick in County Mayo in the north of Connemara. Croagh Patrick was the holy mountain of Lugh and Crom Cruach simultaneously, and thus has a direct tie to the great fire holiday of Lughnasadh. One of the original names of Croagh Patrick was *Cruachán Aigle* up until the twelfth century AD, though likely older names

---

174 The art of toponymy: taxonomic study of placenames, based on etymological, historical, cultural, spiritual, and geographical information. See P.W. Joyce's book *The Origin and History of Irish Names of Places* for an Irish context.

that have been forgotten are buried in the archives.[175] Saint Patrick climbed Cruachán Aigle in the year 441 and spent forty days fasting, meditating, and practicing austerities. As a result, he won the boon of the ancient gods—the spirit of the *sídhe*, which helped carry Ireland forward into the Celtic Twilight. To this day, the feast of Lughnasadh is still celebrated at Croagh Patrick as Reek Sunday, where thousands of people make the annual pilgrimage and participate in mass on the top of the mountain.[176]

Croagh Patrick's quartzite geology was discovered to contain twelve veins of quartz running through it in the 1980s. These twelve quartz veins contain vast quantities of gold. One estimate of the amount of gold found in the mountain is over 770,000 tons of ore, pure enough that it would create over 300,000 troy ounces of gold, valued at about $440 million USD in 2021. County Mayo and the Republic of Ireland clearly decided not to allow any mining of the sacred mountain. If there is one mountain that you can fit into your itinerary to climb as a pilgrimage in Ireland, this is the one. The traditional way is to fast from eating before walking and to walk barefoot.

The second mountain that has called my heart and feet many times is *An Earagail*, or Errigal, in Glenveigh National Park in County Donegal. Errigal is the tallest mountain in County Donegal and from the top, one can see all of eternity.[177] The mountain of quartzite is connected culturally via the *Fir Bolgs* to Mount Olympus in Greece, for it is known that the *Fir Bolgs* revered Errigal as they had Mount Olympus before their immigration to Ireland. The entire mountain is an oratory or a place of prayer. Errigal is certainly the source place of the north of Ireland and well worth walking the pilgrims' path to the top to listen, meditate, and pray.

◇◇◇◇◇◇◇◇◇◇◇◇◇◇

[175] *Cruachán Aigle* means "mountain of the eagle" and may refer to the eagle or cloud ships of the *Tuatha Dé Danann* when they first landed in Ireland, but here at Croagh Patrick is where some of them left for the Summerlands to the west, as is so well retold by Tolkien in the exodus of the elves from Middle Earth from the Grey Havens (Mithlond) to the Blessed Realm (Eldamar in Aman).

[176] *Teampall Phádraig*, or "Temple Patrick" is the name of the chapel on top of the mountain.

[177] This is only a slight exaggeration. But ask Saint Brandan the Navigator, Saint Columbkille, or Fionn mac Cumhaill how far they could see.

Perhaps the most breathtaking of all the holy mountains is *Corrán Tuathail*, anglicized as "Carrauntoohil," on the Iveragh Peninsula in County Kerry. This is the tallest mountain in Ireland, and I have yet to climb it without being buried in Otherworldly mist at the top. Certainly, I have seen the top of the mountain on clear days and evenings from Derrynahierka and from between the sentinel stones at the Lissyvigeen Stone Circle, but ever have I been buried in clouds when on the summit.

The meaning of the name has not been entirely revealed from the archives; however, it is known that the Irish word *tuathail* means "something reversed from its proper direction" or to reverse current from its usual path. Certainly, a pilgrimage to the top of Carrauntoohil is at the very least a rigorous hike, but it also is a journey of unwinding a géis. Most pilgrims ascending Carrauntoohil are seeking to let go of some karmic blockage and to create a new inner harmony or right relations with the world, the self, the divine, or other people who constellate in your life. A pilgrimage to the top of Carrauntoohil can help the spiritual seeker reset and recalibrate—to release cords of disease or unhealthy relations. Not everyone will make it to the top of the mountain. There are many dragons and guardian spirits in the landscape along the way. At the top, a steel cross reminds the walker of the personal crosses that we each carry daily. Offerings at the top finalize the release of unwanted *géis*. The Catholic cross on top also serves as a reminder that our pain and suffering can be given over to the divine and potentially released or healed. Look for crystals along the path. The mountain is riddled with rock ice wrapped within the red sandstone.[178]

Additional mountains and large hills that may call the pilgrim of the timeless include the *Dá Chích Anann* (Paps of Anu) in County Kerry to call in fertility or abundance; *Sliabh na mBan* (Slievenamon) in County Tipperary to hail the divine feminine; Kippure at the border of County Wicklow and County Dublin to greet the divine masculine; Strandhill in County Sligo to for strategic clarity; *Binn Ghulbain* (Benbulben) in County Sligo to contact the *sídhe*; *Binn Bhán* (Benbaun) in County Galway for hyper-clear clarity; Slieve League in County Donegal for reclaiming lucid dreams; and *Sliabh an Iarainn* (Slieve Anierin) in

---

178 *Rock ice* is quartz.

County Leitrim to recall creative prowess. Certainly, there is a wealth of knowledge and mythology behind all these mountains, as well as many more mountains and hills, so get out and explore.

My telling of the mountain *aislingí* is simple and subtle like many stories of life, yet within it is contained the seed of the mobility of time and the mystery of the braiding of the immortal with the mortal.

In June of 2014, while guiding one of my first groups in Ireland, the crystal caves of Sleigh Head called me home for the first time. While this is not a telling of a cave, it is important to note that the cave was in the heart of Mór Mumain's breast, or Sliabh an Iolair (Mount Eagle). In this cave, many pilgrims have been exchanging crystals for decades—one goes in, one comes out. While meditating in the cave, I kept seeing a white dragon, long and thin, rising from the top of Carrantouhill, arching over the Dingle Bay, and spiraling down into the top of Sliabh an Iolair. I was drawn to leave a crystal from Minas Gerais in Brazil as a seed. In exchange, one of the native Irish crystals loose on the floor of the cave volunteered to come with me. All that night, I kept dreaming of the massive white dragon spirit that was swimming back and forth through the two mountains and seemingly through the earth and under Dingle Bay.

The clear crystal came home with me and lived in my sanctuary for several years until it very clearly reminded me, before debarking to India in the early winter of 2017, that it was time to travel with me. At that time in my life, I had spent the last four years of pilgrimage entirely in metaphoric northlands: Ireland, Scotland, Finland, Sweden, Denmark, and Norway. Via winter scrying in the hearth, the fire of the equatorial lands called me to the sacred mountain of Shiva to rekindle my inner flame in India. Carrie and I set off to spend a month in Tiruvannamalai in the state of Tamil Nadu in India. Carrie was going for a training while I was on a pilgrimage to Arunachala—the sacred mountain where light in the form of the *jyotir*, spanning all realms and worlds, returned home to be housed in the earth after a dark age, long since passed.[179]

◇◇◇◇◇◇◇◇◇◇◇◇◇◇

[179] *Jyotir*—Dispeller of darkness, bringer of the truth, and bearer of the light. Refers to the transcendent pure light of Shiva that spans infinitely through all layers of consciousness. Arunachala Hill is the concrete form of the Universal Lord.

I spent over a month living in relation to the mountain via walking to the sacred sites, temples, shrines, and caves for meditation and prayer. The ashrams and ancient temples around the mountain called to me as well. In these sanctuaries, I could participate in *pujas* and chant with hundreds, sometimes thousands of people. Yet, it was always the mountain and the wild *saddhus* that drew my heart and soul like a raincloud to its summit. I spent time in the market cultivating friendships with several of the shopkeepers and *chai wallahs* (tea vendors) as well as with Carrie and my host Saravanan. All of whom helped me to understand and be respectful of the local traditions—which, in many ways, is an upside-down version of what we are used to in the West. We celebrated the feast of *Pongal* through village games, adorning cattle with garlands, and singing to our hearts' content. A week later, I was able to join in the barefoot pilgrimage around the circumference of Arunachala under the full moon.

All of this was a beautiful and wonderful cultural experience, but what is most important to note is that my time at the base of the mountain was only preparation for a deeper prayer to rekindle the sacred transcendent fire within. I knew that Arunachala was calling me to come sit on the top—at the source seed of the *jyotir* here on Earth—to dance in the light of Shiva for several days and rekindle my own heart fire.

In the last week of our time in India, when the full moon was waning toward a new moon, I began my preparations to ascend the mountain for a *puja*. I spent a day in the market gathering all the flowers, garlands, ghee, ghee lamps, incense, and everything else that Saravanan had shared with me that I would need, or I had observed while in temple or participating in *ashram pujas*. I just needed enough water to sustain myself for the hike up and back. No food was necessary except for a few mangos for the *saddhus* at the top of the mountain. A thin blanket and sarong would be sufficient for clothing and bedding. I was going to the mountain to let go and listen in respect to those who had been there before and those who would come after, not to pamper myself with modern camping comforts.

I spent a few nights on the side of the mountain just short of the top, listening to *saddhus* chanting, singing, and living their day-to-day service to the mountain, as well as to Shiva and Parvati. This time also allowed for the adjustment of my biorhythms with the geomagnetism of the peak of Arunachala. I attracted a dog friend on the way to the top of the mountain who ended up being a particularly good friend for the journey. He kept all the monkeys at bay. They seemed mostly interested in my clothing since I had no food. One young male was determined to wear my sarong as a dress, but my four-legged dog friend would not allow it.

After the second night, I rose early before dawn and walked barefoot to the pinnacle of Arunachala. The top of the mountain was entirely black with ghee and oil that has been burned there for thousands of years. My feet became slimy and greasy with the thick goodness. I offered the mangos to the *saddhus* who seemed very curious as to what I was doing there. In one word, I said *"puja"* and they all nodded and began to help me arrange the flowers, incense, and red sand which I brought from Sedona where I had left part of my fire in my early twenties. Chanting, singing, and the oiling of my *mala* with sandalwood oil was the second order of action to elevate my consciousness or bridge the conscious and unconscious. I am not sure what happened other than I obtained an exceptionally high state of lucidity, gave almost all my jewelry away to the *saddhus*, and ended up with a dark suntan. I felt a divine presence and a lot of light, but no dancing Shiva—just a lot of light and some dark cloud formation around the top of Arunachala.

I should note that Saravanan had told me that it had not rained on Arunachala or in Tiruvannamalai in over nine months and that the rainy season had passed, so they were not only not expecting rain, but the entire region was in a serious drought. When I had completed the *puja* with the *saddhus*, the entire mountain was blanketed in clouds. Being that I spend most of my time on cloud-covered mountains, I did not think anything of it initially. While packing up the minimal accouterments from my sleeping area, I found a small silk bag inside my pack. Inside the bag was the crystal from Sliabh an Iolair.

I had to laugh. Here was a crystal from one of the wettest, coolest, cloudiest countries on the Earth on the top of a sacred mountain in one of the driest, hottest, clear-skied countries on the Earth. I knew that I would leave it as a gift but was not sure where to place it as I had already closed the *puja.*

I completed packing my things and began the journey down the mountain. As soon as the trail from my camp tied into the main pilgrim path, I smiled. An ancient, twisted pine tree, the sacred tree of the goddess Áine of Ireland, grew miraculously on the side of the mountain right by the path between two massive boulders. I set my things down, gave the last of my water to the tree, to my dog friend, and to myself, and began to see what I had come to India for. I saw wholeness. I saw the beauty of the rich water and earth energy of Mother Ireland and at the same time the strength of fire, austerities, and the rock energy of Mother India. I could see the colors and elements swirling together in my heart and mind. I was momentarily the *jyotir* of Arunachala, or at the very least was sitting within it—like a shower of pure white light both descending and ascending simultaneously.

It was so beautiful that I began to weep. I wept for all the suffering and pain of the world and yet I also wept for love, ecstasy, and pleasure. I wept for all the times when my prayers felt hollow and empty. I wept for all the times that my prayers rang true. I cried for my spirit mother, my blood mother, my daughter, and for all people who do not have kin in this world to welcome them when they come home from afar. I wept for drought, and I wept for over-saturation and flooding.

While I wept, I placed the Irish crystal into a bough of the twisted pine. It fit perfectly into a tight little dark corner, like a cave, where it would not likely be seen by those passing by. Sometimes I wonder if it is still there today, but it matters not. The seed was planted and sprouted immediately, growing in the Otherworld, creating a bridge between Ireland and India in my heart, mind, and through the great mystery of the wormholes braiding our three-dimensional reality. As soon as I took my hand from the crystal and the pine tree, it started to rain. I laughed. I laughed so hard my belly ached and I could hardly stand. I laughed at the beauty and mystery of life! Ireland had truly come to India with me.

Walking down the mountain was a little more difficult since I had not eaten anything for a few days. My dog friend persisted in following me down the mountain. The light of Shiva was certainly strong in my eyes and heart for every pilgrim seeking the heights as they passed gave me a respectful bow, and I, in-kind, bowed to them. India is beautifully respectful to those truly in the pursuit of spiritual illumination—and that is a gift. Eventually, my dog friend and I parted ways as he was only my *vahana*—a guardian and way-shower to the heights of Arunachala.[180]

The story does not end here, however. On the way down the mountain, I met a stone carver who had spent his life in devotion to Arunachala and carved pieces of beauty from the stone. These stone carvers are all over the foot of Arunachala and are happy to sell you about anything, especially objects not made from the mountain but imported from Pakistan or Rajasthan. But this stone carver had grown on me every time I had passed him for the past month. His eyes were beautiful and humble. His works were unique and made from his family's small quarry near the base of the mountain. He took me to meet his family and show me his workshop. I was drawn to his distinctive works. I bought a few *lingams* from him for offerings, but what drew me the most was his carving of the Great Mother holding the Christ child. I purchased this from him for enough to send all his children to school for the next year for it was truly a talisman. The Great Mother sculpture, of course, was gifted to my blood mother. All but one of the *lingams* went to friends upon return to the States. The other *lingam* went back to Ireland the next summer and into the cave at Sliabh an Iolair. And yet, the story still does not end here.

Two months later, I was hiking the pilgrim's path to the top of Croagh Patrick with a small group traveling along the Wild Atlantic Way in pursuit of riddles, beauty, and freedom. I made it to the top of the mountain well ahead of everyone else. I was sitting in the clouds, freezing from my own hiking sweat in the cold winds of Crom, when I heard strange chanting coming from inside of *Teampall Phádraig*. I walked around to the west side of the white stone chapel where the oak doors were closed to the wind. I was surprisingly able to nudge the door open. It had been locked every other time I had been to the top of Croagh Patrick. Inside was the most amazing and unexpected thing I could imagine. Catholic Indians were having mass and singing in Tamil, the native tongue of Tiruvannamalai. I immediately began

---

180 *Vahana* literally means an "animal vehicle" in Sanskrit and is typically an animal or mythical entity. In Irish, *An Bheitheánach* (Bahana) means the "place of the birch trees"—the beginning place of purity.

to weep with the beauty of the mysteries of life. I do not care what camp you associate with: Catholic, Anglican, Presbyterian, some other form of Christianity, Pagan, Hindu, or whatever—a miracle is a miracle. Everything else is simply a human-falsified form of inclusion or exclusion that simply has no bearing on the heart of true mysteries. Blessed are the mysteries!

I was invited to stay for the mass, which of course I could understand little, but I could follow the ceremony because all masses follow the same ritual sequence in whatever language. We sang, we prayed, and we raised our hearts and minds to the Almighty in its millions of forms, no form, and beyond. We shared the sacrament of the Holy Eucharist. We shared hugs and smiles, and my sweet sister in spirit, Tina, joined us right at the end after she had also claimed the top of Croagh Patrick. Truly on that afternoon, the Ancient Mysteries were alive and well. *Erin go Bragh!*

Chapter Thirteen

HOLY SPRINGS AND WELLS *TOIBREACHA BEANNAITHE*

""Whatever you believe and whatever god you pray to, a place where clean water rises from the earth is someway sacred."

~ Charles Frazier

Ireland has thousands of holy springs and holy wells. A survey in the 1960s claimed that Ireland has over 3,000 holy wells or springs that are officially acknowledged as holy sites and that, to this day, the Irish still revere them. Springs and wells are honored through seasonal pilgrimage at the cross-quarter holydays, on Sundays after church, or any time that someone hungers to pray to the Source for healing, peace, or simply because it is what we are called to do. Holy springs and wells are gateways to the Otherworld, for at these sacred locations, pure water ushers forth from the other side. We can literally and symbolically receive one of the most blessed sacraments from the earth and heaven simultaneously—water. We receive grace, purity, and illumination. Even in the modern day, pilgrims at sacred wells and springs in Ireland see visions of saints, ascended masters, ancestors, and the *sídhe*.

Since the beginning of human habitation, springs and wells in Ireland have been revered as the source not only of life via clean water but also the source of what the Irish call *ímbas fiosaíochta* or *ímbas*: "the light that illumines." Bridget Haggerty, in her article *The Holy Wells of Ireland*, opens the heart of *ímbas*, or *iomas*, beautifully with respect to the type of illumination, saying that it means *"the insight and wisdom that comes from a supernatural encounter, rather than the knowledge acquired through conventional study."*[181] To clarify the slight difference between the two, note that *ímbas fiosaíochta* is the seeker's practice of austerities or reception of sacraments that induce a trance or high state of consciousness where the seeker receives answers, teases out riddles, or seeks prophecy.[182] No amount of academia or learning can ever replace the power of *ímbas*. Drinking or bathing in the sacred waters of holy springs and wells provides a direct source to draw the illumination of the *sídhe* within, to find healing, invoke inspiration, and activate *ímbas fiosaíochta*.[183] Living water heightens the power of divination and is often attributed to the cure of specific or general diseases.

Some springs and wells in Ireland have fallen into disrepair, though most are still revered and honored. Some springs, such as Saint Brigid's Well in Kildare, are not only revered but are administered to and prayed with every day by the modern priestess of Brigid—the Brigidine Sisters of Kildare. This comes as a reflection of what was common practice by local tradition keepers throughout time: keepers and guardians of the sacred wells and springs all over Ireland and over much of the world, administering to the overflow of pure life from the Otherworld. Even after the spread of Abrahamic traditions through most of the Western world, seekers, mystics, and prophets always went to the Source to receive illumination and quench their deeper thirst for the divine. In the New Testament, Jesus encounters women guardians of holy wells and springs from whom he would receive a drink of the "living water" as part of his own *ímbas fiosaíochta* along the pilgrim's path of illumination.

Irish holy wells are known to be direct sources of the Great Mother in her myriad of forms and are honored as such. Many of the holy wells and springs are attributed to Ireland's darling, Saint Brigid, though many are attributed to other saints, such as Patrick or his sister Darerca, and a

---

181 www.irishcultureandcustoms.com/ALandmks/HolyWells.html. Accessed 12/24/2020.

182 *Ímbas fiosaíochta* also has a modern Irish variant of *ímbas forosnai*.

183 Celtic texts differentiate between normal poetry, which is only a matter of learned skill, and "inspired" poetry, which is seen as a gift from the gods or God.

host of other saints or even ancient goddesses. While it can be difficult in most cases to track the original naming of holy wells and springs to pre-Christian goddesses and *sídhe*, one does not need to spend a lot of time at the source of holy water to see that the spiritual lineage is true and pure back to the beginning. Thus is the nature of anything that comes from a true Source: a name is a way of association via a verbal mnemonic. A name connects the sanctuary of place with a familiar home within our consciousness. Humans have been renaming holy places since the dawn of time to better associate in a respectful (or at times, subversive) manner.[184] Learn the names and polish the lens, but ever I invite you to the place that is the true Source—and it is always on the move, alive and shimmering through the infinite unfoldment of time, here now.

When you go to the holy springs and wells, look first to see if there are known pilgrim paths, rituals, and practices along the way. Honor and respect them. Some Irish believe the power of healing and access to *ímbas fiosaíochta* is most potent if completed on the Pattern Day of the matron or patron saint associated with the holy well or spring.[185] If you cannot find a tradition specific to a holy well or spring, then do your best to arrive empty of thoughts and distractions. Quiet the mind and heart or come crying and wailing so that you can make room within for *ímbas fiosaíochta* in the holy water to illuminate your entire being. Bring a coin or weave a Brigid's cross to leave in the little alcoves that are typically found near the human entryway to a holy spring or well. Leave a rosary made of stones from a place sacred to you or your family. Bring a crystal to leave in the water and offer a prayer or share a song that brings you home within and in reverence around. Remove your shoes.

Approach with respect. Sometimes this is easy to do as the trees around the inner sanctuary may be covered with ribbons, rags of clothing, and other religious or non-religious charms of the prayers of those

184 Subversive in respect to the conquest and destruction of that which has gone before, instead of the absorption, integration, and hybridized alchemy that is the way of the peaceful.

185 A Pattern Day in Irish Roman Catholicism refers to the devotions that take place on the feast day of the patron saint—celebrated on or the nearest the Sunday of their feast day, also called "Pattern Sunday."

who have gone before you.[186] Some wells, like Saint Brigid's Well at Liscannor in County Clare near the Cliffs of Moher, have a human-created inner sanctuary that is literally covered with prayers for the sick and the deceased. Light a candle for those who have come before or leave a memorial prayer card for one of your fallen kin. Pray that their illumination in the Summerlands, or heaven, whatever your beliefs, can aid you and your living kin in times of turmoil or share your gratitude for the groundwork your ancestors completed in their lives so that yours could be easier. Offer a prayer and tie it to a tree. Most of all, enjoy the living water of Ireland while inviting in the living Light of Erin and beyond via *ímbas fiosaíochta*.

Holy springs and wells within which I have a direct relationship begin here at my home in the Southern Appalachian Mountains. For over twenty years now, I have been tending a spring on the Highlands Plateau in the Cullasaja Gorge that I was taught was named "Moses Rock." I was introduced to the spring in the summer of 2001 and have been helping to clean it, tend to it, as well as drinking this water as my primary source since then. Cleaning out leaves from the source as well as clearing sediment out of the pipe a few times a year is part of the tenure, but mostly the relationship is that of spirit and body chemistry. This water is my body and blood. This pure water helps maintain my health as well as my strong sense of connection to the Highlands Plateau and the ancient forests that still abound there.

I entered a new relationship with a spring recently at Haltia Haven on the Highlands Plateau as well. I had the intuition that there was a holy spring on the land but had not been able to find it during the summer months due to thick foliage. With the onset of Samhain and winter, I was able to slowly track the contours of the land more easily by foot and with my eyes, revealing where a spring would most likely be located. It was not until after I dreamed of a celestite-lined cave with a crystal-clear stream running through it, combined with reading Sharon Blackie's chapter on holy wells and water in her book *If Women Rose*

[186] Ribbons, rags, and whatnot tied to Faëry and well trees are called "clooties" which is an anglicized Scottish term which literally means "a strip of cloth." This practice is believed to drive illness into the cloth that is left behind.

Rooted, that I realized that I knew exactly where the spring at Haltia Haven was. Carrie and I found the gorgeous sparkling stream gushing forth from granite and the roots of an old birch tree the next weekend. The spring is the *Tobar na mBandia*, or the "holy spring of the Goddess," named in honor of all the springs back home in Ireland and the sacred presence of the sacred land.

In Ireland, there are many wells within which I have found a powerful *ímbas fiosaíochta*. In County Kildare, Saint Brigid's Well has been a pilgrimage destination for my family for several generations, beginning with my grandmother who was the first one who could afford to go home on pilgrimage after retirement. This well is perhaps one of the best-attended wells in Ireland that I have been to, as it is tended by the Brigidine Sisters and several non-denominational or multi-faith organizations dedicated to promoting the light of environmental and social justice in the world under Brigid's banner. I defer to the chapter on Brigid for more depth on this holy well.

The second well that bubbled forward in my heart is on the opposite coast of Ireland in County Clare near the Cliffs of Moher. This well is also called "Saint Brigid's Well." It is of special import to me personally, as some of my distant Kilmartin kin are buried in the cemetery there behind Considine's Bar. This holy well is potent and can be emotionally heavy at times. There is a clear pilgrim's path and practice illustrated upon entrance to the outer sanctuary. It can be particularly potent if you say the rosary. Even if you are not a Catholic, following the trajectory of the path and prayers is a respectful and quieting way to prepare yourself for entry to the inner sanctum.

I have entered this inner sanctuary many times now and it never ceases to affect me in the same way. The inner sanctum is a white hallway-like chamber that is covered with thousands of prayers to the sick and the dead. Even the ceiling is covered. It is emotionally heavy. Any empath worth their salt, or even an intellectual, will most likely feel, or at the very least conceive of the heaviness and pain that resides in this entryway to Otherworld warded by Brigid. Most people who have taken the pilgrim's path to Saint Brigid's Well in Liscannor with me typically feel shocked by the deep grief therein. The entryway to this holy spring is a gate initially to the outright suffering of humanity. People come here seeking the boons of the divine for healing and release.

It weighs down on you, this blanket of suffering. If you are willing to pray therein, perhaps reflect on the suffering of humanity as well as the tragedy of the feminine. Linger for a moment and look to the faces of those who you never knew and will never know. Perhaps leave a little of your own suffering there via tears, memorial cards, photos, jewelry, or whatever moves true and clear from your heart.

But persist, I implore you. Go further. Go further until you arrive at the waterfall pouring out of the earth. Listen to the song of the Great Mother as she dances in the refracted light of the inner sanctuary. Leave the suffering behind, for the Great Mother can transmute it all. She may not turn water into wine here at Brigid's Well, but the true seeker may turn pain and suffering into medicine—the heart of inspiration: *ímbas fiosaíochta*. And that is far better than wine. Remember those who have gone before you and perhaps some of the suffering they endured so that you could be where you are today. Perhaps invite the blessing of Brigid to encourage endurance, humility, and respect so that you can do your part to create a better here and now, promulgating a gorgeous future for all our relations. And, at the very least, be a good arm and heart for someone else who is in a time of grief to lean on, for truly then are you channeling the living Light of Erin.

Another holy well, just a few hours north of Saint Brigid's Well across the Burren and still in County Clare, is Danu's Well.[187] Personally, the holy well has been a powerful place of healing and transformation over the years and is only second to Kildare's Saint Brigid Well with respect to my own relationship to its sacred waters. The crystal-clear water flows straight out of the limestone bedrock within a beautifully crafted chapel-like sanctuary protecting a shallow baptismal pool in the center. The water is so alive and full of light. Local parishes still use the water for baptisms, and I would be the first to tell you that it is the water for healing the aching heart. There is a little alcove over which the water comes into the chamber where you can light a candle or leave an offering.

One more well has called me to be of service to and build a relationship with over the past three years. I have been unable to find a name for the

◇◇◇◇◇◇◇◇◇◇◇◇◇◇

187 Danu's Well is also known as the *Mother Mary Well* or *Cregg Holy Well.*

well in the archives yet, and hope to surface one before another edition of this book in the future. It is simply known as the "Holy Well" and is found in the Lough Avalla Farm Loop in the heart of the Burren in County Clare. This "holy well" is truly a holy spring. The water comes gushing out of the limestone mountain in several source places and is surrounded by clootie trees, mostly willow and hazel, covered in the prayers of pilgrims. The water from this well is the purest water I have tasted in all of Ireland. The water is so rich with the dissolved limestone and calcium in the Burren that it tastes to me like cold milk.

My telling of the spring's *aislingí* is going to diverge a little from Ireland, or so it will seem, for it takes us back to my early years of awakening in my late teens. A series of dreams and waking visions on the top of an eastern hemlock in my parents' neighbor's yard in Cincinnati that began in my nineteenth summer had me packing all my things and moving to Flagstaff, Arizona. I was magnetized to communicate and meditate on the landscape around Sedona as well as the Ponderosa pine forests of the San Francisco Peaks, but more so I was being called by Delfina to come and study with her in her apothecary and in the Way of the Circle. Though I was in college at the time, the classwork came easily to me, so I spent most of my time in communion with the red rocks, mesas, mountains, and springs of the region. Exploration involved the almost complete deprogramming of my upbringing, while also finding myself outside of time with respect to nature and sometimes with a community of like-minded seekers and dreamers. Several small miracles happened in relation to springs in this region during these formative years of my life.

I had a sweetheart and friend, Sunwater, who also was my spiritual counterpart in the quest of our late teens and early twenties. Sunwater and I were very strongly connected intuitively and psychically. I had moved to Flagstaff and lost track of her back in Ohio for about six months, but a friend told me she had moved to a town near Sedona a few weeks before. My friends and I were traveling down to Sedona from Flagstaff for a hike and picnic on a mesa in the Boynton Canyon. On the way, we stopped at a beautiful spring to gather drinking water. While I was drinking the water, I saw an image of Sunwater in my mind's eye. I kept drinking the water, and as I was doing so, I allowed my thoughts to merge with the water to the Source and to flow downstream to her. In my mind, I showed her where we were going and roughly what time we would arrive.

Now mind the time. This is 1996. There were no mobile phones or smart devices of any sort. We did not have car phones. If you wanted to talk to someone in three-dimensional reality, you had to either call them on a landline or go find them. I had not spoken with Sunwater in almost half a year. All I can say is that it worked. The communication through the spring to Source and on to Sunwater had worked. She arrived at the parking area ten minutes after we did and caught up with us, barefoot, on the trail to our mesa picnic destination. I embraced her in a colorful hug. She smiled up at me and said that she was sorry for being late! She had gone to the wrong trailhead initially and had to backtrack. I love that woman with all my heart to this day and ever am I grateful for the lessons that she and her kin taught me along the way.

The other miraculous experience that I had with a holy spring was in Boynton Canyon itself one autumn after completing a vision quest. For three nights I had sat on the top of Kachina Mesa for the vision quest and was making my way back to civilization when I realized that not only was I completely out of water in the heart of a desert afternoon, but also even a young buck in his late teens has limits when it comes to bodily needs. I was out of water, extremely lightheaded from the vision quest fasting, and extremely dehydrated. My legs were becoming wobbly. I looked like a drunken version of Jim Morrison stumbling through the high desert if anyone would have witnessed me, but I was alone and deep in the canyon. I knew that I had to keep moving to get out of the desert, but the more I walked and stumbled, the more water I was using up in my sweat that evaporated as soon as it left my pores.

Hallucinations came on stronger as time passed, and the sun continued to rise higher in the sky. I watched heat dragons and snakes curl around barrel and prickly pear cacti, as well as around the occasional juniper and sagebrush. It felt like the entire desert was drifting under me like a slow-moving rainbow river. I knew I needed to find shade as soon as possible to rest for a while. I needed to wait for the sun to drop on the horizon before I could continue. I remembered the lore of the First Nations people in the area. They tell of a dragon that lives in Boynton Canyon, and at this point in the journey, I reached out for guidance as I stumbled and waded my way through what seemed to be the actual living, moving dragon of the landscape itself. I prayed to the spirit of the canyon to show me the clearest way to shade and water.

Perhaps within a few minutes or few hours—it is hard to say when you are between the worlds—I saw a lizard run across my path through all the hallucinations of the rainbow serpent sliding through the canyon. I am quite sure that the lizard existed in the same reality as my body, as if in answer to my prayer, so I followed it. I lost track of the lizard after about five wobbly steps. I sat down to cry, but I had no water to provide the material necessary for tears. Instead, I dry heaved what little moisture was left in my stomach onto the hot earth. I was certain that I was going to die there when suddenly, another lizard of a slightly different color ran across my hand and headed up the slope of the canyon to my right. I leapt up after it and followed for a way until I lost this one, too. I was catching on. All I had to do was wait and the next lizard would reveal itself and show me where to go.

Likely, I looked like a madman, not too far from a starving arctic fox chasing a vole through deep drifts of freshly fallen snow at Midwinter in the Arctic. But instead, I was the desert fox delirious for my next meal to stay alive. I followed lizards for what seemed an eternity in a seemingly random pattern across the landscape until I had forgotten the entire universe apart from "find lizard, follow lizard, and wait for another lizard," until they stopped appearing altogether. I took in my surroundings. The lizards had led me up the canyon scree to the base of the cliffs. I was still in the brunt of the sun's afternoon rays, and surely there would be no water this far up from the canyon floor.

Just as I was considering what it would be like to die of dehydration, I looked behind me at the base of the canyon wall. There was a dark gap in the red stone. I struggled up the scree slope just a bit further to see if the gap might be a cave. No cave presented itself properly, but my heart leapt with joy. It was a rock shelter—a big one. And inside, not only was it cool and shady, but it also contained a prehistoric cliff dwelling. I dragged myself over the eroding walls and collapsed onto the cliff dwelling floor. I was so dehydrated my vision swam and the world was spinning. I certainly could not see straight. I promptly fell asleep.

What I woke to after that dreamless sleep changed my world experience for the rest of my life. The sun was setting over the opposite rim of the canyon. The inside of the cave was illuminated by crimson-gold light and the dwellings seemed alive with dancing shadows. The back of the rock shelter was illuminated by the play of light and shadow.

At the point in the shelter where the massive basalt roof came together with the older layer of sandstone floor, a small tree was growing. A dark streak that seemed almost like a smoke stain on the shelter roof trailed down to the tree. I crawled over to the tree to see if it had any leaves that may be edible when lo and behold, the tree revealed that its roots were storing about a gallon and a half of spring water seeping down through the dark stain in the roof. The roots were covered in moss and the water was so still it was like a black mirror in the fading sunlight.

I put my lips to the surface of the water and drank. I put my face through the surface of the water to cool my burned skin and I drank. I lay there on the floor and drank. I drank until all the water was gone. Then, I fell asleep.

When I awoke, the moon was out and the canyon below was alive with coyotes on the hunt. I turned to the tree and saw that the pool was full of water again. This time, I drank the water slower. This time, I could see the Source lines filling my body, much as I had seen them in the spring in Oak Creek Canyon weeks before when I called to Sunwater. I gave thanks for water and for life. I rested. I gave thanks for water and the earth and drank more. I rested. All through the night, I drank the water slowly enough that the level never changed again. All through the night, the spring restored my entire body. I drank gallons of water. I never urinated until I hiked out the next morning with the sun rising.

As I said earlier, I have never been the same. Every drop of fresh water is precious. Without water, there is no life. Without springs to school the seeker, there is no respect for that which sustains us. Without a respectful relationship with the divine, there is no respect for that which births us again and again. It is my sincerest hope that you are in right relations with your source of water, for it is a symbol of the Source and your ticket home to the Great Mother when you pass over. May you be truly thirsty at some point in your life that even in the beauty of abundant water everywhere, you may appreciate the gift of life that water bestows. Drink deep!

Chapter Fourteen

LAKES AND LAKE EDGES *LOCHANNA*

As an ecologist, it is effortless to understand the relationship of "edge places," or where two or more natural communities converge. Ecologists define edge places as ecotones. An ecotone is a place where energy and nutrients become concentrated, allowing for a greater diversity of species as well as a higher density of organisms. Great examples of landscape-level ecotones are at the mouths of rivers, where meadows meet forests, and where swiftly falling mountain streams transition into slow-moving valley rivers. Life thrives in abundance in these places of transition, where the raw elements of earth, water, and sky converge. Even fire can play a role where hot springs emerge from the earth, or lava flows meet the sea.

Ecotones are places where worlds overlap. The etymology of the word *ecotone* is beautiful. "Eco" comes from the Greek word *oiko* which means "house," and "tone," comes from the Greek word *tónos* which means "stretching, tightening, exertion, pitch of the voice, or accent in a syllable." So truly, *ecotone*, on a basic level, means "house of tension," or "house of music." When visiting ecotones, the song of life is amplified multifold. Birds sing as they gather insects, seeds, or fruits in abundance. Seals squeal as they chase penguins and fish who are thriving off the microbiological life teeming around the surge of available resources. Whales sing as they scoop up millions of krill. Even humans flock to ecotones where mountains meet valleys, where rivers converge, or where geological fault lines create a transition from one geological substratum to another.

In Ireland, some of my favorite ecotones to explore are where Celtic Broadleaf Forests meet blanket bogs, where rush-laden valley bottoms meet cliffs or lakes, where freshwater streams merge with the sea, where the sea meets the earth, and where lakes meet the earth and sky. Something magical unfolds in these edge places. A mystery of life flowers where organisms that are typically only found in water interact with organisms that typically inhabit the earth, sky, forest, and or any combination thereof. The song, or *tónos*, of these combined "houses," or *oikos*, certainly arises from the excitement of convergence. An ecotone is a place of great exchange—a sacred crossroads of biology. As humans, when we meet at a crossroads literally or metaphorically, we make choices about the direction we are heading, exchange gifts, participate in trade, and interchange knowledge. It is no surprise then that an ecotone is also a place where the sacred meets the secular. An ecotone is a place of wonder—a cauldron of imagination, intuition, and inspiration.

The Shinto tradition of Japan has many correlations in mythology and faith to the Irish-Celtic mythos with respect to sacred enclosures, sanctuaries, and houses for Spirit. The sacred center of many Shinto shrines is a veiled mirror. The mirror is a symbol of pure creation from the heart of alchemy. A mirror requires fire to forge particles of the earth into a water-like surface that reflects the sky. To enter a sacred Shinto shrine, only the most devout and trained priests or priestesses may look upon the mirror or tend to it. Most other devotes and acolytes can only cross as many thresholds after the first torii gate as they are initiated to cross. I personally find the rigorous taboos of meeting and crossing the thresholds in the Shinto tradition quite intriguing. I can see the importance of an island culture with a massive population to create a system of entry that screens out those who are not properly prepared. Ireland would likely be in the same boat as Japan if it were not for the potato famine checking the population explosion of the eighteenth and nineteenth centuries.

The beauty of Ireland is thus: there are so few people with respect to the size of the country that there is still room to disappear into or be found within the sacred nature of all things. One can step through the veil of consciousness, or that created by the *sídhe*, just about anywhere in the Irish countryside. One can have an entire mountain, stone circle, forest, cairn, or lake all to themselves for enough time to slip through the worlds. One veil is enough. One mist, like a torii gate, delineates the boundary between the worlds. In the ecotone of spirit and nature, the simplicity of access to the divine and immortal in Ireland is gracefully laid before us like a swan swimming on a glassy lake.

In the Celtic traditions, the edge place where a lake (*loch* in Irish, typically written as "lough") meets earth meets sky in sacred trinity is like a holy well or spring, a door between the worlds. Swans, geese, rushes, and alders stand as guardians on the threshold between the worlds. Willow, ash, and elder lean over the water's edge, reaching for their reflection in the Summerlands just on the other side of the mirrored surface of the water. Walk quietly to the water's edge, there by the shore of the lake. Perhaps you will scare a bullfrog into leaping into the water, or perhaps your presence will send a *sídhe,* disguised as a frog, hurtling to safety into the Otherworld.

Kneel on the lake edge and look within. You will perhaps see into another world with life teeming in the ecotone of earth, sky, and water. You will see life that can only exist on the other side, or like the frog, that can dwell in both. Furthermore, the sky and your reflection appear below you if the light is just so. And yet your reflection is not you; it is another you, looking back at yourself. A reflection is a simple reminder that light bends back on itself. Light is energy in motion away from a source as perceived by the beholder. Yet, when we behold a reflection of self in water, it can reveal what we are walking toward in the multiverse. Listen to the song of your edge place, there by the lake, and see what is being shown to you.

Many of the tales in Irish mythology provide us with windows into the multifold reality of the ecotone lake edges. In the tale of *Oidheadh Chloinne Lir* (the Fate of the Children of Lir), the four children of the ancient Irish god of the sea are turned into swans by their jealous stepmother.[188] After giving her the boot, Lir spends his twilight years at the edge of Lough Derravaragh, in County Westmeath, listening to their songs while they patiently waited out the 900-year term of their *géis*. Frequently, visions of the *sídhe* or ancient gods are seen near a water edge—where the vision will disappear if one enters the water, or vice

---

188 Swans are Celtic guardians of innocence and water, while also being couriers of the Sun. Many priestesses and goddesses, as well as some men/gods, could transform into swans in times of need in Celtic, Scandinavian, and Finno-Ugric traditions.

versa, will not appear until the water has been entered. This is reflected in the legend of Cúchulainn of Ulster when he meets the Morrígu washing his clothing or armor, foretelling his death. Sometimes, the *sídhe* cannot leave the body of water they are connected to or can only leave when the water they are connected to disappears, as in the legend of the White Lady at Lough Gur. As *Bean Fhionn* (or *beanfionn*), the White Lady, Áine rides forth from her bright city under the lake every seven years to claim a lover and draw them into Summerlands.

Some of the strongest experiences I have had with lake edges have been with Lough Arrow at the border of Sligo and Roscommon counties for time-bending; Lough Key in County Roscommon for world hopping; *Lough Bhaile na hInse*[189] in County Galway for ancestral dreaming; Lough Grainey in County Clare for purification; Lough Derg in counties Clare, Galway, and Tipperary for calling in highest vision; Glendalough Upper Lake in County Donegal for primordial purification and innocence; as well as Lough Leane, Muckross Lake, and Upper Lake near Killarney in County Kerry for Deep Peace and Beauty. I have been especially mesmerized by Upper Lake for the variation in habitat that occurs around it, from the ancient oak forest of Derrynahierka and wet sedge meadows to red quartzite cliffs and bracken savannahs.[190] The *sídhe* are particularly strong around and within Upper Lake and easy to connect with when approached with respect.

My telling here would be empty without a referral to the power of Lough Gur. Lough Gur was originally a circular lake belonging to Fer Fí, leader of the *Tuatha Dé Danann* and brother of Áine. For six years, Áine called me through dreams, trance, and drumming to come home to the land of my mother's kin. Sometimes she appeared as the golden goddess Gráinne while I was giving thanks for food. Sometimes she appeared as the green-gold goddess Fenne. Though most frequently, she appeared in all her golden glory as Áine, the *aisling* lover calling me home to her side at Lough Gur.

In my late teens and early twenties, I kept seeing the same vision of a sacred mountain above a small lake fed by four streams with no stream exiting the lake. I found myself in this vision frequently, entering via

◇◇◇◇◇◇◇◇◇◇◇◇◇◇

189 *Lough Bhaile na hInse* is anglicized to "Lough Ballynahinch."

190 *Lough Uachtarach* is the Irish name for Upper Lake.

trance, journeying, and dreams. I had no idea what the recurring vision meant. At the time, I had no association with the place, with Irish goddess names, or even with Ireland. It did not even seem possible to me that it may be a real place on the planet. Whoever saw a lake with streams going in and no water flowing out? Ode to the karst!

On the drum journey to *Tír na nÓg* led by Sinéad de Burke in June of 2003, I was brought back to the same vision-place of the sacred mountain, streams, and lake that obviously only existed in my inner landscape of the soul. After the journey, which was held in a *clochán* on the Dingle Peninsula, I shared the recurring vision with Sinéad. She offered to escort me to the very place of my vision the next day, which was a few hours away in County Limerick. She helped me bridge the vision with real physical space. The inner realm had bridged with the outer. More of this story can be read in the chapter I have transcribed on Áine, for the dance now is with the lakes.

Whenever I would find myself in the vision-landscape of what I now know as Lough Gur, I had several choices for interacting with the vision-version of the landscape. Sometimes I stayed on top of Knockfennell in the stone and tree circle.[191] Typically, I would descend the *cnoc* to the path at the foot of the hill, allowing me to circumambulate the lake like Áine, or the fourteenth-century lord of Munster and poet Gearóid Iarla—also a disciple, devotee, or votary of the goddess Áine.[192] Two

◇◇◇◇◇◇◇◇◇◇◇◇◇◇◇

191 *Knockfennell* in Irish is "Cnoc Finéil," with a "cnoc" being a hill—Hill of the Goddess Fenne, or "Hill of the Little Fair One."

192 Gearóid Iarla (Gerald FitzGerald) was the third Earl of Desmond, Lord of Munster, and Chief Justice for Ireland in 1367 following the Statutes of Kilkenny. He lived from 1338 to 1398 and as well as dabbling in Celtic magic, he composed verse in both Irish and French. As a reward for his service to the *sídhe* and Áine, he did not die but lives beneath the waters of Lough Gur in the Summerlands. In some stories, he is the one who rides out every seven years around the lake margin on his white horse, shod with silver shoes. According to this variant of the legend, when the silver shoes wear out, he will regain his mortal form and restore the glory of the Desmonds. A votary is a person who makes vows of service and dedication to religious service or a god/goddess, derived from the Latin *votivus* meaning "a promise or vow."

choices presented themselves to me once reaching the lake shore. If I walked to the left or clockwise, it took me either to the 6,000-year-old village on the eastern shore of the lake where I could meet with crucial kin and allies. If I turned to the right or counterclockwise, the path would take me to the foot of Knockfennell where votive offerings have been made for over six millennia beneath the cave of Fenne, across from Áine's cave (also known as the "Red Cellar Cave") on Knockadoon.

If I continued straight at the bottom of Knockfennell, I would arrive at the lakeshore. I would dive into the lake and swim out to the forested Garrett Island—not to Knockadoon Hill where Áine's seat on earth, *Suideachan Bean-tige*, is present.[193] Her stone seat is reminiscent of the Hag's Chair (the Cailleach) at the Loughcrew cairns in County Meath.[194] The forested island in my visions always contained a simple cottage in the round, with a thatch roof hidden by a thick canopy of deciduous trees. Inside the cottage, I would find an elderly version of Áine, or sometimes a hybrid of Áine and *An Cailleach Bhéara*. Most of the time, she appeared as my teacher and spirit mother, Delfina. She would be mixing herbs from her apothecary and invite me in to sit by the hearth. Once Delfina had a good cup of tea in my belly and had checked in on why I was there, she would lead me out to the lakeshore and dive in. I was intuited to follow—like Arthur following Merlin through shapeshifting. Instead of coming back to the surface, she would dive deep until we found whatever cave entrance at the lake bottom was most appropriate for the lesson of the day with respect to the purpose of my arrival. Over the years, we got to the point where she would just wave at me when I arrived on the island. Then Delfina would call out the name of the cave entrance under the water and I would go explore on my own.

While swimming between the worlds and in and out of passageways, she helped map out the new neuropathways in my mind as well as

◇◇◇◇◇◇◇◇◇◇◇◇◇◇

193 Knockadoon Hill was once an island in the center of Lough Gur, though arguably it still is due to the nature of the wetlands that connect Knockadoon Hill with the rest of the shoreline around the lake.

194 Located at Sliabh na Caillí (anglicized as "*Slieve na Calliagh*") or the "mountains of the Cailleach."

the geomagnetic pathways threading this world together with *Tír na nÓg*, which has multiple access points at Lugh Gur. I was retrained and calibrated as many of us are by our teachers, guides, and mentors. "She" was Delfina, Áine, Gráinne, Fenne, Cailleach, and many other *aislingí*. Yet really, "she" was a rotating combination of all of them and simultaneously none of them. She was an emissary of the Great Mother, the Mór Mumain, calling her wayward son home to Ireland. Once I had come home to Ireland for the first time and made the pilgrimage to Lough Gur with Sinéad, then "she" was able to train me at a faster rate. I continue to visit the lake in my dreams, visions, and bodily pilgrimages to Áine's sanctuary. She helped me stitch together the worlds more clearly for the highest and best of all beings. *Slàinte Mhaith!* I pray that since you are reading this, she is calling you home to her heart as well—if she has not already. May the illumination of the pathway around the mystery of the lake of your life ever bring you closer to the completion of your part in the reinoculation of heaven on earth—*on earth as it is in heaven*.

Tabhair neamh dóibh![195]

[195] *Tabhair neamh dóibh* is a phrase meaning "give them heaven" in Irish. Thanks, Sam "Fergus" Brett!

Chapter Fifteen

ISLANDS
OILEÁIN

Islands are a magnet for mysteries. The imagination can run wild, dreaming of mist-enshrouded havens populated with holy people, mystics, or immortals in utopian bliss untouched by the blemishes of humanity or time. Islands covered with flowers and fruits all year round, where the sun always shines, and inhabitants are ever youthful and beautiful. Islands invoke images of places difficult to get to, or vice versa, places difficult to get away from. Most frequently, in the Irish worldview, an island is something to be revered and holds secrets from outside of time. Islands are places where the ancient ones still reside, where sacred texts were illuminated, or where a relic or talisman was protected from the corruption of the rise and fall of empires and nations. In W. B. Yeats' reproduction of Gerald Griffin's poem about the island of Hy Brasil off the west coast of Ireland, we get a slight glimpse of the Irish love of the mystery of an island:

"On the ocean that hollows the rocks where ye dwell,
A shadowy land has appear'd, as they tell;
Men thought it a region of sunshine and rest,
And they call'd it 'O Brazil—the Isle of the Blest.'

From year unto year, on the ocean's blue rim,
The beautiful spectre show'd lovely and dim;

The golden clouds curtain'd the deep where it lay,
And look'd like an Eden, away, far away."[196]

Ireland is an island. Ireland is and has been the sanctuary for most of the Celtic archives for thousands of years. Certainly, other islands have also been havens for Celtic traditions, such as Anglesey, Iona, the Orkneys, and the Isle of Mann, to name but a few. Yet, there is something special about the island of Erin—every raiding culture that came to Ireland eventually became Irish—the Vikings, the Anglo-Normans, and yes, even many of the English plantation owners in the post-Cromwell era. And those that did not adapt and adopt the essence of the local Irish-Celtic customs eventually left. During the Dark Ages, when all was collapsing in Europe in the centuries after the fall of Rome, Ireland was a literary sanctuary that re-illuminated the darkness of the Western world through literacy and the Light.[197]

Up until the Viking era, beginning in the tenth century *anno Domini,* off the coast of Ireland were many island havens that traditionally housed druidic colleges and after the fifth century, were inhabited by Celtic-Christian communities and monasteries. Islands provided both protection from the outside world as well as the essential cloister for transpersonal service to the divine. Additionally, in the heart of Ireland, many enclaves, churches, monasteries, and dwellings were built on small islands in lakes across the whole of Ireland for the same purpose: to obtain security and cloister. In many lakes, when islands were all occupied, human-made islands called *crannógs* were built for over 5,000 years and were continuously inhabited until the early eighteenth century.

◇◇◇◇◇◇◇◇◇◇◇◇◇◇

[196] W.B. Yeats' publication entitled *Fairy and Folk Tales of the Irish Peasantry* was published in 1888 and contained his rendition of Irish playwright and poet Gerald Griffin's poem on Hy Brasil. Gerald lived from 1804–1840. Hy Brasil has been a part of the Irish heritage of enchanted isles for thousands of years, long before the settlement of the country Brasil. It is said that Irish fisherfolk found the island in a thick fog and broke the spell of the veil between the worlds by lighting a fire on the shore. May we all find the Isle of the Blessed so easily!

[197] See Thomas Cahill's book *How the Irish Saved Civilization* to dive deeper.

Various scholars, archivists, and seekers will debate their entire lives as to where the heart and gateway to Avalon, *Tír na nÓg*, or the Blessed Realm traditionally resides. That is not a riddle I seek to pursue. Avalon is like Atlantis; it existed in many places and no place at all. Avalon is like Connla's Well—ushering forth from many of Ireland's sacred wells. Access points are as numerous as stars in the universe and axons in a healthy brain. Fortunately, the Irish worldview largely remains intact. The veil is thin in all places, even in the urban, and the Blessed Realm can be found just across a thin veil created by the *sídhe*. *Tír na nÓg* is accessed by parting the veil. Mist can be a veil. Thoughts can be a veil. Beliefs can be a veil. Unhealthy relationships can be a veil. Geomorphological objects such as mountains, caves, or springs can be a veil. Water or fire can be a veil. All we must do as practitioners and pilgrims is find the key that allows us to cross over, whether literally, metaphorically, symbolically, consciously, or even unconsciously.

In the Abrahamic traditions, once the world was created and the original people were thriving in the garden, they could "see" and had access to knowledge. Yet, as soon as they "sinned," eating the fruit of knowledge, they were cast out of the Blessed Realm and have ever been trying to get back in the great pursuit of Paradise. In the Irish-Celtic worldview, the Blessed Realm, *Tír na nÓg,* is next to and parallel with our own. Because of "sin," we are unable to see the Blessed Realm or even access the entire palette of entry places. The root of the word "sin" comes from the Proto-Germanic, Old English word *synn*, which means "moral wrongdoing, injury, mischief, enmity, feud, guilt, crime, offense against God, or misdeed." If we look at the core of what "sin" refers to, it involves any choice that we make that creates a denser veil between us and the divine—like karma in the Hindu tradition. The more misdeeds or sins that we choose to live with, the denser the veil between our world and the Summerlands will be, and thus further the pilgrimage or austerities to pass through the veil and into the Blessed Realm. If we stumble off our path, we may find ourselves blinded or caught up in the hedges originally intended to help us along the way by defining the parameters of the dance of life.

Islands provide entrances to the Blessed Realm. To reach an island, one must deeply commit to the completion of the journey. The effort to set forth on a journey to an island is symbolically the most akin to preparing for a journey to the Otherworld where, at times, one must wrestle for the fate of their own or another person's soul—to bring illumination into the dark. Inside each of us, in our DNA and in our learned behaviors passed down through familiar ties and culturally for generations, is a rich archive waiting to be illuminated—to usher us away from the consciousness of the Dark Ages into the Blessed Realm of heaven on earth.[198] The journey of passing through the veil can relinquish suffering and redirect our pathway in life to fullness in alignment with the divine.

My personal connection with Ireland's islands, beyond the isle of Erin herself, is a mixed bag of lake and coastal islands. In the section on lakes and lake edges, I have already introduced my relationship with Garrett Island and Knockadoon Hill at Lough Gur, but I set those again here as a reminder of the beauty and power of those islands. At Lough Gur, before getting to Áine's cave on the foot of Knockadoon, there also is a lovely example of a crannog—one of the human-created island havens found in many of Ireland's lakes.

In the heart of Lough Derg in County Clare lays *Inis Cealtra*, the Holy Island. To get to this island, you will need your own boat. If you do not have any friends with canoes or kayaks in the area, you can head up to Mount Shannon and hire a local boatperson to haul you across or hire your own boat entirely. It is worth the effort both on a calm, sunny day, or a blustery, rainy day. Each weather type will reveal distinctive experiences on Inis Cealtra. On the island stands an intact round tower, a derelict monastic settlement, a holy well, and loads more to discover.[199] If it is sunny, bring a picnic and enjoy dreaming of a simpler time; living on the island as a druid or Celtic monk. If it is rainy and windy, bring something solid from the modern world to hold onto. The rain and mist can bend our personal relationship with time and send you teetering into the Otherworld.

At Lough Key (*Loch Cé* in Irish) in County Roscommon, the sailor's dream of discovery awaits. Hire a boat, or better yet, bring your own.

198 From the Age of Pisces to the Age of Aquarius—The Age of Aries is found from 2000 BC to AD 1, the Age of Pisces is AD 1 to AD 2000, the Age of Aquarius is AD 2000 to AD 4000, etc.

199 Do not drink from this well unless you have a really good filter.

The lake is dotted with magical islands awaiting the dreamer. Travel to the small Castle Island that contains the remains of McDermott's thirteenth-century castle during the twilight hours to watch the *sídhe* play along the ramparts and the towers or listen to the *beansídhe* playing in the windows. Navigate over to Trinity Island to wander through the ghosts of seventh to seventeenth-century mendicants chanting, or to release political or heart entanglements as did Fair Úna and Strong Thomas.[200] They were not allowed to marry in the early seventeenth century yet were buried there together in eternal love. Steer your vessel to Drummond Island to wander for hours in ruins and ancient Celtic Broadleaf Forest co-dominated by beech, oak, and ash, and see if the sleeping maidens drag you into their dream world. Quietly dock on the shore of Hogs Island and tiptoe amongst the massive ferns and trees, but cover your ears, for the laughter of the giants there can dissolve your bones. See if you can find the wise woman of the lake spinning tales on her loom from beech and oak leaves. Or just row out to the center of the lake, lay down in the boat, and close your eyes for a long nap until you feel the boat bump into an island or the lake shore. See where the *bandia* wants you to explore.

The last lake island I will share is the unnamed island in the center of Doon Lough in County Donegal. This island contains a large solarium or sun temple called a *grianán*, like the Grianán of Aileach further north in County Donegal, built in the fifth century of this era. Both sun temples are built of stone and were constructed for large ritual gatherings as well as secular meetings and are frequently associated with Áine or Gráinne.[201] Many *grianáin* can be found in west County Cork and County Kerry. The sun temple at Doon Lough is called Doon Fort, or Dun Fort, which redundantly means "Fort Fort." This can be said with tongue in cheek, especially when adepts know that it was not built as a fort at all but as a temple, an oratory, and a place of high council, though it may have been used as a fort at times due to its stout construction and protection by the lough. To get to the island, traditionally, you must go

◇◇◇◇◇◇◇◇◇◇◇◇◇◇◇

200 Douglas Hyde, *Love Songs of Connacht*. M.H. Gill & Son, Ltd., 1905. The tale of Úna Bhán (or Úna McDermott) and Thomas Costelloe (or Strong Thomas).

201 These temples were perhaps the site of the local *óenach*.

see the local boatman, a retired gnome about 200 years old in a small hobbit hovel in a hill. Unfortunately, and as far as I know, he does not care to row anymore. I choose to make the pilgrimage in the oldest way possible: strip and swim. In the center, after circumambulating the island, I found the breeze of Manannán and the rays of Áine a delicious respite and invitation to witness the high council of the earth, sun, and ancestors while skyclad. The High Council of the Light of Erin meets in the *grianán* at Midsummer and on other sunny days where decisions with respect to the Harmonies are required. Their timeless song on the island and in the *grianán* ever implores us as living emissaries of the Light of Erin to continue to shape a gorgeous and thriving future for generations to come.

Most of my experiences with coastal islands in Ireland are from along the west and northwest coasts. Some of the most glowing experiences I have had with time bending and stepping through the veil have been with Skellig Michael off the tip of the Iveragh Peninsula in County Kerry. While this island has entered pop culture due to the *Star Wars* and Jedi takeover in the twentieth century, this island has long since been a hotbed of luminary thinkers and mystics. Ancient druidic orders and early Christian monasteries found their homes on the sharp peaks of Skellig Michael. This island, home to many endangered species, is protected as a UNESCO World Heritage Site.

Another set of islands off the west coast of Ireland that calls to the heart of any true sailor of spirit are the Aran Islands. Here, one can bike around the main island of Inishmore and at holydays, experience some of the most intact traditional Irish religious customs in all of Ireland. I harvested my first sea salt crystals at Inishmore—a beautiful and ancient tradition that requires little effort except for loads of patience and some good sun.[202] Inishmore is also home to a beautiful *clochán* that may be thousands of years old, as well as the prehistoric fort of Dún Aonghasa at the edge of a 100-meter cliff over the Atlantic Sea.[203] Other islands off the coast of Ireland that sing my soul include Tory Island off the coast

◇◇◇◇◇◇◇◇◇◇◇◇◇◇◇

202 Inishmore is *Inis Mór* in Irish meaning "Great Island."

203 Excavations at the site of Dún Aonghasa indicate that the first construction goes back to 1100 BC.

of Donegal, home to Balor and stronghold of the *Fomorians*; and, the Isle of Mann in the heart of the Irish Sea.[204] It is with the Isle of Mann that my personal mystery herein unfolds.

In the years between 1998 and 2013, my *aislingí* were calling me again and again to come home to Ireland via the dreams to complete certain tasks and pilgrimages. I spent nearly a month each year in Ireland, apart from 2005 when I lived at Meadowsweet Farm in Glendree, County Clare, for more than six months . Both when I traveled to and lived in Ireland, I was able to follow the *aislingí* and dreams with a lot of guidance from Sinéad and other *seanchaí* as to where in the Irish landscape I was most likely being shown to attend. In the winter of 2012, I began to have another reoccurring dream, though this dream only returned a few times. Yet, the dream was delivered enough times that I followed it. In this dream, the *aisling* was a man who seemed to dwell in the liminal space between the Blessed Realm, the mist, and the human world. He was the guardian of what was disclosed in the dreams as the "Valley of Kings."

In the dream, I found myself walking up the center of a narrow valley between two heather-covered hills. As I walked along the stream in the center toward the head of the valley, I was greeted by this *aisling* man. He was another version of me in some ways—from a time a little rougher and when the spirit and physical world were a little closer together. In the repeated dream, he would embrace me in a warm, cloak-enshrouded hug and, like a gatekeeper, turn and direct me further up the valley bottom. As I walked further up the valley, on the top of the ridgelines on both sides was a string of cairns. On the top of each cairn was a man or woman standing still as a statue, dressed in full armor or uniform from various periods in history beginning in the Bronze Age all the way up to the twentieth century. Each figure was holding a long spear or lance nearly three meters tall, and just below the spearhead, a meter-long white or sky-blue banner rippled in the twilight breeze. As I walked up the valley, there was an understanding that in the dream, this was a valley of some of my ancestors. Each of the figures standing on their respective cairns was the spirit of the one who was interred therein.

◇◇◇◇◇◇◇◇◇◇◇◇◇◇

[204] "Tory Island" in Irish is *Oileán Thoraí* or, historically, *Oileán Thúr Rí.*

As I grew close to the head of the valley, I found a large standing stone covered in Norse runes, Celtic *ogham*, and Pictish spirals. Several times, when I arrived at this point in the vision or dream, the standing stone was a petrified tree. Once it was a living oak tree. And still another time, it was simply a large tree trunk erected upon the location. I would circumambulate the standing stone, tree, or log three times and then continue up the valley. Not far beyond this guardian, I could see the source of the valley's thick mist. A glacier was surging down the valley at the same rate that the thermal heat of a hot spring or small lava pool was emerging from a large, low cavern. Most of the time, it appeared as a hot spring, but a couple of times, it was clearly magma coming forth from the cave. I would breathe in the resultant thick mist through my nostrils. Sometimes I woke up at this point, but frequently, the mist would transport me to other places on the earth, like when I was working with the caverns beneath Lough Gur with Áine and Delfina.

In Indian philosophy, *samskara* are mental impressions and personal characteristics that develop over time, congealing deep inside a person's disposition. These impressions are personified by previous life actions, experiences, choices, intentions, discipline, practice, perception, and more. In this reoccurring dream in the "Valley of Kings," I recognized that my neuropathways were being reorganized by fire and ice, via dream pathworking, to further shape me into an instrument of deep peace while also honoring the memories of heritage. The reshaping and training of the pathways, neuropathways, or *samskara*, is an ancient art of any initiate on the journey to becoming an "adept". Training most frequently comes via a gifted teacher, mentor, or sacred place. In Western Mystery Traditions, one's *samskara* is retrained through pathworkings, dreaming, and selfless service amongst other techniques.

Tracking this "Valley of Kings" on the planet seemed like it would be a little easier due to the particularity of the cave of fire and ice. I figured the location would be in Iceland or Svalbard, but after diving into John Michell's book on the art of finding sanctuaries in the Celtic north, I was guided to the sacred center of the Isle of Mann in the heart of the Irish Sea.[205] His description and map of the *Sanctuary of*

[205] Michell, John. *The Sacred Center: The Ancient Art of Locating Sanctuaries.* 1994.

the Kings of Mann were uncanny. The Isle of Mann is the sacred center or omphalos of the Celtic Isles and has always been known as a place of enchantment. According to Celtic legends and the account of Joseph Train, Mann was the center of Druid Mysteries.[206] The chief *ollamh* resided there at the druidic college nestled in the sacred center of the island. Celtic rulers from all over the isles and continental Europe sent their children to this druidic college for education. Manannán Mac Lir is the patron deity of Mann, hence its name, and perhaps the source of Mann's enchanted nature.

After leading my first group on pilgrimage in Ireland in 2013, I flew to the Isle of Mann to explore the possibility of the sacred center being the same or similar to the landscape of the "Valley of Kings" that I had been dreaming and visioning from the previous year. After dodging motorcycles warming up for the Isle of Mann's annual Tourist Trophy Races, finding no room in the inns (and a bout of food poisoning from some of the worst Indian food I had ever had), I found myself sleeping in the Meayll Hill Stone Circle overlooking the Port of Erin.[207] A stone circle during all the race mayhem certainly felt like the safest place for me to sleep since there was no room in the inns, though I certainly could not have planned for the food poisoning.

The only people I knew from the Isle of Mann were my friend Phil's family, and they were all in Manchester, so there was nowhere for me to go to escape the body-centric intensity of the food poisoning. Instead, I went within. I wove a series of Brigid's crosses from the rushes outside of the stone circle to help me return to this reality if I went too far into the Otherworld, and I laid down on the wet, cold ground in the center of the stone circle. Not exactly what my mother would have suggested, being as sick as I was, but I was being guided through the clarity of suffering. And blessed was that guidance, for I did not sleep the entire night. My body was racked with pain. I was transported on the back of the pain and

206 Train, Joseph. *A Historical Account and Statistical Survey of the Isle of Mann.* 1845

207 The Tourist Trophy Races are annual races of thousands of motorcycles in an amazing—and often deadly—road race around the Isle of Mann. Meayll Hill Stone Circle (Honey Hill Stone Circle) is at the southern end of the Isle of Mann, just outside the village of Cregneash.

suffering to the Blessed Realm by a white mist-like dragon-river-ship. My entire body, including all my internal organs, was scrubbed clean by this giant white sea dragon, like the one that I saw dancing from Carrauntoohil to Sliabh an Iolair years later.[208] It was a baptism from the inside out by a pure white fire, much like the Indian *jyotir*, that ate away thick, complex layers of my own veil, healing generations of pain and suffering. The *aisling* had called me home.

The next day, rising with a hyper-clarity on life and purpose, I continued along the pilgrims' path to the Sanctuary of the Kings at Mann's geological and sacred center. I followed the mythological route called the Royal Road, now renamed the *Millennium Way*, as described in the writing of John Michell. The Royal Road on Mann is, according to the Celtic legend of King Orry, a mirrored image of the Milky Way and thus a sacred road that is approached from the south, walking toward the Pole Star and simultaneously the central sanctuary.

I walked into this landscape, half in a dream, half in a shadow of the modern world. The valley appeared as it had in the dreams with a few exceptions. The cairns did not have ancient kings and queens standing at attention on the ridgelines. Also, the heart of the valley sanctuary where the ice and fire came together was buried by a reservoir built in 1992 by the British. I am not sure if, like my visions, there was ever a standing stone or tree there in antiquity when the druidic college was still active, or even later when it was replaced by the church of Saint Abban of Kildare. It is hard to say due to the reservoir and lake covering up the sacred site. I am not sure it makes sense geologically that a cave would have existed at the valley's head either since the geology of the heart of Mann is sandstone. Also, in the modern world, the head of the valley was filled with a gorgeous Celtic Broadleaf Forest, dominated by oaks and beech, while surrounded by mixed-age conifer plantations.

Whether the images I saw in the original vision were largely symbolic in the context of the landscape or spoke to an earlier time, I am not sure. Perhaps someone else will share some clues with me that they find along the way. However, I did find myself once again in a waking dream

[208] Both mountains are found in County Kerry, Ireland, but divided by the Dingle Bay.

that provided some lovely clues in the riddle of time and connection with the Otherworld. Mostly what I found was Deep Peace along the pilgrims' road. I was internally bathed of my own weaknesses, faults, transgressions, and beliefs that kept me from seeing through some of the veils in the modern world. Yet most of all, what I found on this gorgeous and painful pilgrimage to the Isle of Mann was the beauty and simplicity of the journey through the mist to the heart of another enchanted island. I found another gate to the Summerlands that recalibrated my understanding of the relationship between the devout, the divine, and points of entry along the multi-generational path of my Irish ancestry and beyond.

Chapter Sixteen

SEA CLIFFS AND BEACHES
AILLTE MARA AGUS TRÁNNA

"Walking all the day near tall towers where falcons build their nests

Silver winged they fly, they know the call of freedom in their breasts

Saw Black Head against the sky

Between the rocks that run down to the sea

Living on your western shore, saw summer sunsets, asked for more

I stood by your Atlantic Sea and sang a song for Ireland."

~ Phil Colclough, *Song for Ireland*

Of all the sacred nature of Ireland, I cannot begin to even bring justice to the power and majesty of the sea in relationship with the Celtic spirit. I will do my best to honor the spell that the sea holds over the Irish people, both those who still call Ireland home and those of us whose ancestors have emigrated. The sea is not only an infinite source of mystery, but also provides the Irish people with nourishment, respite, protection, and mystery. Ireland's isolation has guarded its gorgeous mysteries and culture. As a source of protection, the sea has buffered Ireland from many marauders of the world. And when raiders and invaders did make it to Ireland, they were absorbed by the generous heart of Ireland in some way or another. They all eventually became Irish or left.

The sea can also present a deep sense of sadness for many of the Irish—creating a wide gulf between the Irish who have stayed home and those who have emigrated to the USA, Canada, Australia, and beyond. Almost 70 million people around the world claimed Irish heritage in 2021. Only 6 million people are residents of Ireland. The sea is a symbol of the loss of many of Erin's children, and it is still felt across the country. Everyone in Ireland has family in the US, Canada, or Australia. And for those of us born abroad, coming home to Ireland can be a powerfully cathartic experience. Yet, without a love for the mother country, as the Irish know deep in their hearts on both sides of the pond, one cannot even imagine the deep pain the rending in the fabric of family and community emigration has created in recent centuries.[209] The people of Ireland and all of Erin's children around the world know that pain to some extent. Amanda Foley said it so profoundly while in the Connemara in 2021:

> *"I can hardly believe the level of suffering people must have been subject to in order to justify leaving the beauty of Ireland."*

And I concur. Every time I stand on the Atlantic coast of the United States, I can feel the pull of my mother country across the waves to the east. Sometimes I can even imagine that I see Ireland drifting in and out of the clouds on the horizon like some mystical and blessed island I can only get to via the Grey Havens. When I am on the opposite shore, especially along the cliffs and beaches of the Dingle Peninsula looking west, I feel a similar pulling. The Isle of the Blessed is somewhere in between. If only I could follow the straight path of the *sídhe* we could get there. Without the straight path, a crystal ship, a horse with silver hooves, or a torc of gold, the Blessed Realm seems to have slipped away, or perhaps it has been swallowed up by the rift valley along the Mid-Atlantic Ridge out near the Azores.[210] Either way, the Irish are literally

[209] "The pond" is how many Irish refer to the Atlantic Ocean. It makes one's relatives seem less far away, perhaps.

[210] The island of the Flores, the furthest west of the Azores, is one of the birthing places of the *sídhe* and an Isle of the Blessed.

drifting further and further apart. The sea continues to fill with the tears of Lir as his children try to find their way in this modern world, often so far from home. I pray that this book and all the works I do will help provide a bridge across this rift between the worlds, bringing true healing to the Irish heart, and inspiring the Celtic spirit in all people who long for home.

All along the Irish coastline, one can easily get lost in time. Better yet, one can be found by the simple magic of a tidepool filled with undulating seaweed or kelp. Time can disappear and all manners of connection can present themselves as tiny treasures only the sea can deliver. Ancient fossils reveal themselves along sea cliffs, while more recently deceased mollusk relatives are found washed upon along strands or nestled among protected pockets in rocks as the tide recedes. Salt crystals gather in low places along rocky coasts, waiting for the dwarf in you to discover the treasure trove. Seals bob up and down in the waves watching you or sun themselves on rocks after a feast beneath the waves. Seabirds soar overhead, or underneath, calling in gratitude to the sea. Waves break over stones, cliffs, sand, and mud—singing a tireless song that erodes at the hardened heart. *Come home,* says the sea, *come home and remember.*

Some of the most outstanding geological features in Ireland in relationship with the sea are the sea cliffs in the west and north of Ireland. The Cliffs of Moher, which have become exceedingly popular in my lifetime, are enough to take the breath away. To lay at the edge of the world and look down a sheer shale and sandstone cliff over 700 feet to sea below is humbling—where razorbills and Atlantic puffins nest in the thousands. The red sandstone cliffs and scattered islands of Dunmore Head are dreamy, inviting the poet to turn to stone so that they never miss a moment at the edge of the sea. The granite cliffs of Malin Head in the far north of Ireland call to the mythologist and wind monger, while some of the highest sea cliffs in Europe can be found at Slieve League in Donegal and beckon, "unfold your wings…be free."

Beaches, or *strands* as they are called in Ireland in English, can be absolutely gorgeous, especially if you are blessed with a bit of Áine magic and the sun comes out to play. You may have an entire beach to yourself. My wife and I are madly in love with Maghera Strand in County Donegal, while over the years, Glassilaun Beach in County

Galway has continuously been a magnet for magic, beauty, and the upliftment of the weary soul. The unique geology of the Giants Causeway in County Antrim is an astounding place to play during dinner hours in the summer until dark. You may have most of the place to yourself, thus making it easier to imagine the giants of another age bickering over the North Channel. Inch Beach in County Kerry is a lovely place for a pitstop with over three miles of flat sand for running, hurling, or some cold body surfing. In County Clare, Fanore Beach in the Burren calls to the wild at heart to dance the night away or exchange gifts with the travelers. On Inishmore in the Aran islands, the beaches at Killeany Bay and especially Portdeha are particularly dreamy. Any poet looking for inspiration after a doldrum should make their way to Portdeha strand. Lay down in the tall sea grass amongst the dunes. Take a short nap or sleep like Rip van Winkle until the *sídhe* come out to play. Drift between the worlds within the song of the sea in the background until, like the great bard and *Finnian* Oisín, you choose to return hundreds of years later from the Isle of the Blessed to help those in need.

What would be a telling of Ireland without a tale of the sea? It would be a nest empty of life, waiting for the return of those who had forgotten. And what would a tale of the sea around Ireland be without selkies? That, my friend, would be a sad day. And so, let us begin my tale of the selkies of the Blasket Islands.

My favorite place on the Earth is Dunmore Head in County Kerry. I have shared plenty of tales of this rocky headland in other sections of this book. It is appropriate, for I have spent a lot of time there walking, sitting, listening, crying, singing, and playing. I have been visiting Dunmore Head since I first discovered it in the summer of 2003 by a recommendation from a dear friend. I visited Dunmore Head at least monthly when living in Ireland in 2005. For those first few years, I pined to see the selkies—or at least to see the seals. Yet, everyone told me that there were no longer any seals at Dunmore Head or even in the Blasket Islands. People had not seen them there for decades.

When visiting Dunmore Head, I frequently walk all the way out to the headland where the cliffs meet the sea. On low tides, I can sometimes make it across to the razorback sandstone that is typically separated from the rest of Ireland by the sea. I go there to listen. I go there to pray. I go there to practice qigong. I go there to watch water flowing over stone. Yet, mostly I go there to empty myself of myself. Sometimes the emptying comes in the form of laughter, sometimes deep sobbing tears, and other times through deep silence as I listen to the throb of the sea making love to the cliffs. It never ceases to spellbind me, and I never want to leave, even during the stormiest of gales. Perhaps one day I will have a home there and we can walk together to listen to the song of the sea.

In the summer of 2015, while leading a group of women, mostly from New York City, around the southwest of Ireland for a week, my *aislingí* led me home to Dunmore Head.[211] It was a windy and rainy day out on the headland. I wrapped myself in my handspun wool cloak on the cliffs and closed my eyes. The misty rain gathered in little droplets around my eyelashes. I fluttered them to enrich the gray colors of sea and sky. I looked out into the mist that obscured the Blasket Islands. I thought of my family. I thought of my Irish grandmother, Margaret, and the fiercely beautiful life that she lived. I thought of my mother with respect to her continuation of that heritage. I thought of Ireland and realized that my mother was a derivative of the Great Mother and that I could not truly tease apart my own ancestry from the living heritage and heart of Ireland herself.

I began to sing a few lines from Mary Black's arrangement of *Song for Ireland* over the scream of the howling winds, the raging waves breaking on the cliffs below me, and the waves pounding to my left on the hollow cliffs riddled with caves.[212] The booming report of the hollow headland resonated in my chest, almost as if I were singing inside a large reverberation chamber. My lips pooled with accumulated mist that dripped down inside my cloak, sending chills down my spine. As I opened my voice to harmonize with the sea and mountain, my eyes settled closed. My heart swelled with pure joy and simultaneously with the pain of the Atlantic rift between the Irish. I sang and I cried for the gratitude of the life my mother and father had created for me. I held onto

◇◇◇◇◇◇◇◇◇◇◇◇◇◇

211 A week alone would not be enough just to spend at Dunmore Head in my opinion but thank you, Janna Zarchin!

212 "Song for Ireland" was written at Dunmore Head by Phil Colclough and quoted at the beginning of this chapter.

the thread of the song long enough to sustain it through my own gale of chest-wracked sobs as it coursed through the density of my humanity.

I kept singing, lost yet found in the rich tapestry of storms, those within and without. As I sang, I found that my voice was beginning to change in pitch. I watched as the song lilted out into a slow Irish air that was formulating itself through the natural evolution in the circuitry of the song. It grew in sound and structure until it coincided with the guiding current behind all the raw elements at play. There no longer was a "me" separate from Dunmore Head or the sea. The song poured like a waterfall out of the mouth, chest, heart, and body of what I typically identify with, but I was not in control. Nothing was in control. The song, the sea, and the cliffs simply were.

I opened my eyes to take it all in, and what lay before me was complete bliss. Imagine being blind your whole life and then finally receiving the gift of sight for the first time. Every detail and every bit of color became hyper-clear. Down to my left, where the sea drummed on hollow cliffs, floated five selkie heads watching me sing. Four were dark brown and one was white with faint gray spots. The song kept flowering in my heart and poured down the side of the cliffs toward them. The selkies seemed as transfixed as I was; there where the worlds of earth, sky, and sea came together as one. I sang, and as they watched, an entirely new level of the beauty and majesty of life arose through the song. I am not sure if I have ever cried that hard in my entire life. They were not tears of pain or suffering, they were tears of beauty, gratitude, grace, and innocence. No matter what these seal people experienced with me, I know that they gave me the gift of the illuminated heart. They gave me the gift of healing generations of Irish rift. They awoke innocence in my chest once again. The selkies welcomed me home.

Now I know that when I returned to the world of humanity that what I saw at Dunmore Head was a small pod of seals. I know that if they are selkies, they certainly did not need to leave their skins behind for me to find, for I am already bound in marriage to the Mór Mumain. The miracle is that a seemingly lost species has returned to Dunmore Head. I know that almost every time I have returned since, no matter what the weather, the pod comes back to visit. I have never had quite the cathartic experience as I did in the summer of 2015, but what I have shared is the beauty of the selkies with many friends since. I have seen the selkies bring out the song in tears in many a stout heart there at Dunmore Head. I know that if all that occurred in recent times is that a new pod of seals has settled at the Head or in the Blasket Islands, then that is miracle enough. Yet, what I genuinely believe is that the selkies have returned and they are helping to build a bridge between Ireland and all her children around the world. The selkies have swum through the tears of Lir over the loss of his children, across the Mid-Atlantic rift, and delivered the living Light of Erin into the hearts and souls of all who are ready to come home.

Fáilte go hÉirinn!

THE SHAPE OF IRELAND

Chapter Seventeen

IRELAND'S GREAT MEGALITHIC AGE

"The Earth gives us life and we are all drawn back, at certain times, to this potent source of our beginnings for a sense of nurture and completion. Those places where this sense of connectedness is strongest are the sites we term sacred. And, although our lives have evolved a long way from those of our Neolithic ancestors, we are still touched, however unconsciously, by the same earth energies and the same miracle of life. This sense of the divine is reflected in every age, from the ancient cairns of prehistory to the great cathedrals of today."

~ Cary Meehan

When we gaze across the landscape of Ireland together, I find that traveling partners are most often impressed by the vast array and diversity of ancient sacred sites for such a small country. Everywhere we look, we find stone circles, *rátha* (or ring forts), cairns (or barrows), standing stones, dolmens (or passage tombs), holy wells, abandoned churches/monasteries, faëry trees, groves of ancient trees, and more. The question I often hear is, "Why are these sites abandoned?"

It is a good question. Yet, if we review the previous chapters on the Historic and Mythological Cycles of Ireland, and especially to climate change and the immigrations/conquests of Ireland, a story begins to reveal itself: the ebb and flow of human power across Ireland has been consistent. Specifically, changes in political and financial power have historically affected which "sacred" sites are revered and which sites are abandoned to the erosive fingers of time. Despite the historic shift of sacred site importance, there are two things that are unique to Ireland with respect to most Western countries. One, most sites of antiquity, be they secular or sacred, are still held in high regard, rarely disturbed, and often have been protected or even restored over the centuries. More times than naught, ancient sites were still revered up until recent history or are still honored in contemporary Irish culture today. Second, most sacred sites—especially those which played pivotal roles in the evolution of Celtic polity, culture, music, arts, and mysticism—were either regenerated, built upon, augmented, or adapted to suit the needs of whatever political and religious powers happened to reign over (and with) Ireland at any given period of its rich history.

Most sites of antiquity were abandoned more likely due to socio-economic and political changes rather than changes in beliefs and traditions. What remains to this day, however, is the perennial essence of Ireland: her sacred infrastructure. The bones of Ireland, manifest in geology and augmented by sacred structures from the Megalithic Age all the way to contemporary times, are ever beacons of spirit in the darkness of humanity's suffering. Erin is ever calling and waiting for the deep listener to hear her mysteries and perhaps become an emissary of her light. Her invitation is to translate the emanations into tangible wisdom, medicine, poetry, law, architecture, music, and a thousand other channels for people to derive true sustenance.

Many of the sites of antiquity in Ireland, especially early Iron Age sites, may sustain dreamy Otherworld fantasies for the visitor while also imparting a sense of loss and sadness or soulful bliss and a sense of ease. This, of course, is a remarkably similar experience to the evocative summoning of the often-illusive Faë. The Faë communicate from *Tír na nÓg* and often use the ancient sites as a pathway for communication. For most people, the Faë remain "unseen" remnants of our purported imagination or intuition. Recent perspective shifts led me to understand that we are the "unseen." We are the little drops in the ocean of time, flitting about on our brief visits to ancient places, sitting at the edge of time's ministrations. The Faë—often fixed in respect to some physical location—are observing humans in a way that only a mountain, standing stone, river, or ancient tree could if they had eyes: with mild fascination at something that exists barely within the blink of the eye in geologic time. These beings are ancient. For perspective, the timescale of any of those observing us as humans reminds me of the way I may observe a mist descend from a mountain into a valley, a cloud form into a fantastical creature for a moment, the wind tousle beech leaves before a storm, or ants build a seasonal mound one grain at a time.

Despite the odds arrayed against them, some of the ancient Irish were inspired to create massive megalithic structures of stone for sacred and secular purposes during the Megalithic Age and the Neolithic Age. In Ireland, there are thousands of ancient megalithic sites. According to estimates by Irish antiquarian Jack Roberts, there are tens of thousands of stone circles in Ireland—and that is just stone circles.[213] The archaeological record shows us that the first megaliths were likely erected 8,000 YBP. Furthermore, somewhere between 6,000 YBP and 2,000 years YBP, thousands upon thousands of mysterious megalithic structures were built across the landscape of Ireland in a huge range of styles. From around 7,000 YBP to about 3,000 YBP, Ireland seems to have undergone a golden age that lasted for over four millennia. No fortifications and an apparent lack of aggressive materials remain (such as weapons), alluding to an extraordinary culture that appears to have pondered the great mysteries of life, like the Minoan civilization in the Aegean Sea, and was averse to war. It is in this golden era that many of the patterns of sacred reciprocity between sacred sites across Ireland and people seems to have flowered, seeding the patterns that ensued into the Iron Age and the present. Many of these ancient sites held calendric significance and were places of annual pilgrimage.

[213] Jack Roberts, *The Sacred Mythological Centres of Ireland*, Bandia Publishing, 2016; Jack Roberts, *The Sun Circles of Ireland*. Bandia Publishing, 2013.

Megaliths

Most of the megaliths were erected by the Neolithic people, including dolmens, court cairns, passage cairns, stone circles, standing stone rows, and *clochán*. Most archaeologists refer to dolmens and cairns as "tombs" because they have found some cremated bone remains left inside of them. Yet, as with any sacred temple, this is only one level of truth, like pyramids in both the Old and New World and the great churches and cathedrals of Christianity. Imagine a people or race in the future looking back at our historic and modern churches surrounded by graveyards; it would be easy to assume that these churches are tombs. Lo and behold, churches are so much more than places of interment of the dead. Churches are living temples for the celebration of life, community, healing, rites of passage, marriage, illumination, and rebirth/regeneration.

And as many churches are aligned with celestial events, the ancient megaliths sustain a powerful alignment with various solar, lunar, and astronomical events. Newgrange, one of the most well-known passage cairns in Ireland, is found at the UNESCO World Heritage Site of *Brú na Bóinne*, the sacred valley of the Boyne River, in County Meath, Ireland. The alignment at Newgrange is with the sunrise at Midwinter. When the sun rises on the horizon at the winter solstice, it sends a long shaft of light into the innermost recess, illuminating a stone basin within.

There are more than 60,000 megalithic sites across Ireland. The Irish have a way of respecting that which is of sacred antiquity in a way that most other Western cultures have neglected. There are many exceptions of course, but Ireland is alive and well in her people's healthy reverence of the ancient landscape, even if it is from a distance.

There is a pattern to the distribution of megaliths across the landscape with respect to the four traditional kingdoms and their sovereign goddesses. In Connacht, where the Morrígu holds sway, a large concentration of passage cairns are located. In the kingdom of Ulster, located in the northeast where the Macha reigns supreme, court cairns and dolmens are the dominant megaliths in the landscape. In the kingdom of Leinster in the southeast, where Brigid's fire is still sustained by the Brigidine Sisters, passage and chamber cairns (including Newgrange) dominate along with stone circles near the Wicklow Mountains. And finally, the kingdom of Munster, where the goddess

Áine holds sway in the southwest, hosts the largest concentration of standing stone circles anywhere in the world.

When we are invited to enter one of the ancient temples of Ireland, the invitation comes from an aspect of the sovereign goddess of that region. Each of the primary sites also sustains the key attributes of the primordial current that each of the goddesses transmit. The often-northwest-facing entries of passage cairns of the Morrígu are akin to her sacred caves and the cauldron of renewal, speaking to the going within of winter and the cycle of womb rebirth. The dolmens and court cairns of the Macha also speak to the northern aspect of the goddess, the passages are again warding openings between the worlds, and ask us to prepare ourselves for what is coming. In the spring, under the auspices of winter, we emerge with Brigid's fire in our hearts from the underworld of the chamber cairns and embrace the open-air stone circles of Anu/Danu/Áine in the southwest at the beginning of summer.

As you will recall, each of the four kingdoms sustained its own sacred center: Cruachain Aí in Connacht, Emain Macha in Ulster, Kildare/Dún Ailinne in Leinster, and Lough Gur (and Cnoc Áine) in Munster. Uisneach and Tara, as well as multiple other sites, were also crucial sacred centers. The druids and royalty of Ireland would process a cyclic ceremonial journey throughout the year to these ancient *óenach* assembly sites, the places of the tutelary gods and goddesses.

The megaliths in Ireland are portals through which the primordial energy of the Earth flows and the associated aspects of our human consciousness blossom. Though some of the megalithic sites have been disturbed, degraded with time, or are "off-line" for various reasons, most of the Irish sites are still very much alive and connect regionally, nationally, internationally, and throughout the universe to other portals and sacred sites. Our bodies carry coding within our DNA that is adapted or can be acclimated to access the multidimensional realms behind and within the megaliths. Doorways therein open and invite us into the timeless Otherworld where miracles unfold, the space-time continuum bends, and timeline jumping is as easy as playing hopscotch. In such a state, deep healings can flower or awareness of hidden giants in our inner landscape can be revealed—whether they are an apparent ally or foe. More often than not, the megalith portals stimulate the evolution of our own inner riddle in the pursuit of paradise.

Stone Circles

Ireland is abundant with stone circles. Some stone circles have as few as five or seven stones, while others may have sixty or more.[214] Stone circles are most concentrated in the southwest in western County Cork, but they are found all over the country. The only other place in the world that has close to as many stone circles as the southwest of Ireland is in the northeast of Scotland on the same lay line between the islands. Here are some of my favorite stone circles in Ireland that still sing with ancient wordless riddles.

Uragh Stone Circle[215]*—County Cork*

Located in the west of County Cork on a small hillock above a lake and surrounded by mountains, this classic five-stone circle with a massive alignment stone has become one of my favorite access points to *Tír na nÓg*. I have been a part of ceremonies warding this gateway since 2005. This stone circle and the nearby Ardgroom Stone Circle are often associated with Áine, while the entire peninsula that houses both stone circles and hundreds more is associated with *An Chailleach Bhéara*, an aspect of the winter goddesses.

Beltany Stone Circle—County Donegal

Beltany is one of the largest stone circles in Ireland with a diameter of 145 feet and 64 standing stones. This stone circle is associated with Bealtaine and has several alignment stones outside the circle as well. This stone circle is a gorgeous place to watch the sunset and the rising of the full moon. The Otherworld presence here is rich and tangible. You may be the only

---

214 The vast majority of stone circles in Ireland and Scotland have an odd number of stones.

215 Patrick Weston Joyce, in his 1870 publication of *Irish Local Names Explained,* says that *Uragh* means "place of the yews," however, if we look at the *ogham* and the Irish vowels, we know that *ur* means "heather," not "yew." Therefore, *Uragh* likely means "place of the heather."

human visiting the stone circle, but you will not be alone. The *sídhe* presence themselves boldly in the forests and hedges that line the pathway entering the stone circle. Beltany Stone Circle is an easy stone circle through which to traverse the realms and for grounded ascension practices with the intent of returning to the Earth to relieve the suffering of others.

***Drombeg Stone Circle**—County Cork*

Drombeg may be one of the most picturesque stone circles in Ireland. Because of that, this is also the most visited stone circle in all of Ireland. I have never had the place to myself other than after dark. Despite this, the site is extremely alive and conducive to inner travel, connection, and healing. The alignment of the site is with the sunset on the winter solstice. The sun sets in the cleavage between two distant hills, and the light illuminates the altar stone in conjunction with the two guardian stones seen here in the picture at the right. I participated in a gorgeous Midsummer *céilí* and all-night Irish chanting; a singing amongst the stones and under the stars in the summer of 2022.

***Grange Stone Circle**—County Limerick*

This stone circle is located at Lough Gur, one of the oldest inhabited places in Ireland, and aligns with the sunrise at Bealtaine, Midsummer, and Lughnasadh. This stone circle is one that I dreamed for many years before ever visiting Ireland in my body. While often in a pastoral setting with cattle ranging through the circle, this may be one of the wildest *sídhe* stone circles in Ireland. Some of my travel companions over the years have braved sleeping solo in the stone circle.

***Kilmartin Lower Stone Circle**—County Cork*

This small, seven-stone circle with a large alignment stone is found on ancestral lands in the west of County Cork. The initiation ceremony that was held for me at this stone circle greatly increased my personal bandwidth for the multiverse and enabled access to several other cultural traditions that had been latent in my being for years. Finding this stone circle also helped to ground in a personal *Belios*, or world tree with respect to my matrilineal line. Nearby, a classic Iron Age ráth is also located with a *souterrain*—an underground passageway for food storage and escape while under attack. Kilmartin Lower ever calls me home to listen yet again.

Cairns

While there are many cairn styles, they are typically divided into two groups: passage cairns and court cairns. Court cairns are remarkably like many of the megaliths in the Mediterranean from classic Minoan Culture (Crete, Malta, and southern Aegean islands), in having multiple large assembly "rooms." Passage cairns tend to be either cruciform or linear paths to one central inner "room." Again, many archaeologists love to refer to these powerful subterranean temples as "tombs," but they were and remain living temples. Cairns are also known as *barrows* in Wales and Scotland. The design view of a passage cairn appears from above as a long tunnel of standing stones entering the center of a mound with a large room within, or if it is a cruciform layout, it will have a large room within surrounded by three side rooms. Most cairns only have one passage.

Court cairns are a group of monuments constructed for much larger ritual or social gatherings than the inner sanctum design of a passage cairn. There are over 400 court cairns in Ireland, and they are almost all found north of a line between Galway Bay and Dublin—in the northern half of the country. Archaeologists attempt to classify monuments by size, style, and type, but court cairns manage to defy easy organization. In general, there are three types: single, double, and central. Most of them are in a fair state of disrepair more so than passage cairns.

***Loughcrew**—County Meath*

The passage cairn group at Loughcrew is associated with the Cailleach, the goddess of winter who reigns over the feast of Midwinter at the winter solstice. Her throne, the "Hag's Chair," is found here at Loughcrew. Post-Christian Ireland turned the Cailleach into a twisted, old, witchy hag. Cailleach means "hooded one." In reverence, she is the queen of winter, a creator, weather, and an ancestor deity.

***Creevykeel**—County Sligo*

The huge central court cairn at Creevykeel near Cliffoney in County Sligo is one of the largest court cairns in Ireland. This massive monument was built around 5,500 years ago during the Neolithic. The old name for Creevykeel is *Caiseal an Bhaoisgin*, the Fort of Bhaoisgin, Bhaoisgin being a holy well near the cairn. The chamber and court open to the east; the ground is falling away gently towards the sea, so the monument is facing up a gradual slope. A narrow passage, which would have been roofed originally, leads into the massive inner court which can easily hold 100 people.

Dolmens

Dolmens may be some of my favorite megalithic structures in Ireland and around the world. These structures were once also covered by stone and earth like a cairn, but are much older, and so either the material was carried off by later inhabitants or simply weathered away over thousands of years. Now that the dolmens are exposed to the atmosphere, the essential magic of a dolmen becomes so much more tangible with a sunny disposition. Dolmens are portals. They align most frequently with stars or constellations versus the more frequent solar and lunar alignments of most cairns and stone circles.

There are about 190 dolmens in Ireland, and they are the most clearly recognizable type of megalithic monument. Dolmens are known by many different names: Cromleachs, Giants Graves, Leabas, Diarmuid and Gráinne beds, portals, and stone tables. Dolmens generally have an entrance feature, the "portal," though this is often closed by a blocking stone. The most characteristic feature is a massive roof stone or slab, usually weighing many tons and inclined at an angle with the highest part over the entrance.

***Poulnabrone**—County Clare*

The Poulnabrone is easily the most famous of the dolmens in Ireland. Lying in the heart of the Burren in the west of County Clare, it sits high on the karst landscape with broad sweeping views of the glacier-sculpted mountains. Though it is hard to find time alone here, when that time is found, this place is certainly a portal to the Irish-Celtic Otherworld, *Tír na nÓg*.

***Kilclooney Dolmen**—County Donegal*

The dolmen at Kilclooney in County Donegal dates from circa 3500 BC. This dolmen is often found without suggestions of time wrapped around it and rarely are there any other human visitors. Enough space within the dolmen to comfortably fit three can be found in a relaxed, seated fashion. The currents of earth energy moving through this portal are potent and have a strong telluric presence.

***Ballykeel Dolmen**—County Armagh*

Ballykeel Dolmen is found at the foot of the western flank of Slieve Gullion above a tributary of the Forkhill River in County Armagh. It stands dramatically at the southern end of a long court cairn. Most of the cairn has gone, but two parallel lines of carefully set stones defining the edges are still visible. The surrounding mountains and forest truly enhance the quality of the energy present at this dolmen, inviting those who enter respectfully to be immersed in timeless mystery.

Clochán (Beehive Huts)

I had never heard of a *clochán* or a beehive hut until the first time I traveled home to Ireland in 2003, and yet they play such a crucial role in not only bridging the work as an emissary of the living Light of Erin but also for the ancient acolytes of the druidic orders and the Celtic Christian monks. *Clocháin* provide a crossroads outside time for those who are willing to look and practice the austerities to bring one closer to the divine.[216] A *clochán* is a dry-stacked stone hut with a corbelled roof. Most commonly, they are found in southwestern Ireland along the Atlantic seaboard in Munster. The beehive huts may be some of the oldest human-made structures in Ireland, with some of them believed to be over 5,000 years old.

[216] *Clocháin* is the plural of *clochán.*

Tradition holds that these clusters of beehive huts along the southwest coast of Ireland were once satellite druidic "colleges," or places of study, where a *Filí* along with bards and students would cloister to focus on their craft.[217] While this is difficult to know for certain, it can be sensed in these clusters. When the wild Christian monks first began to settle in Ireland in the fifth century AD, they gravitated to the remote, austere, and cloistered nature of the abandoned beehive clusters to be at one with the Light of Christ, the sea, and the wilds of nature.

In 2003, I met a selkie in one of the beehive huts. We exchanged stories and myths and listened to the ages pass like early winter winds over the surface of the *clochán*. She took me on a journey through the worlds and across the veils gently, to the Otherworld I now know as *Tír na nÓg*. In exchange, I invited her to cross the veil with me on the back of the great rainbow dragon into the Otherworld that the Latin American *curanderas* know as *la época de los mitos*—the multiverse world where past, present, and future interweave like strands of a great tapestry. It was a gorgeous exchange. We have been friends ever since, as she has helped to transmit the living Light of Erin from her home in the west of Ireland for her entire life to the world. Blessed be the sweet selkie-lass!

Recently, the beehive huts have taken a whole life of their own as the creators of the third generation of *Star Wars* finally realized that the original Jedi were the druids of Ireland. Originally, scenes were filmed on the sacred druidic dragon isle and Christian monastery of Skellig Michael. This island served as a major center for Christian illumination of the New Testament (such as in *The Book of Kells*). It was sacked several times by Viking raids and finally abandoned. What is most important here is the reentry of ancient druidic and Celtic Christian centers into modern mythological beings: the Jedi. Unfortunately, the set team damaged some of the area, so the remainder of the film had to be shot on a fabricated replica on the Dingle Peninsula.

---

217 *Filí* means "seer" or "one who sees"; an aspect of the druid as a magi, lawgiver, ecologist, healer, judge, astrologer, counselor, and/or poet.

***Skellig Michael**—County Kerry*

After traveling by boat across the open Atlantic Ocean, one first passes the island of Little Skellig covered with thousands of birds and seals. Ascending eight-hundred hand-hewn stone stairs to the top of Skellig Michael, we find one of the most preserved clusters of beehive huts anywhere in Ireland. It is easy to see and feel why the directors of *Star Wars* saw fit to call this the original home of the Jedi Order. When sitting inside the huts, the sense of eternal harmony and universal balance is tangible...even with the ghosts of Vikings hacking their way through the cloister. Skellig Michael and Little Skellig are extensions of the mountains of Kerry. 7,000 years ago, when Doggerland was still above sea level, one would have been simply standing on top of a long mountain chain connected to the whole of Ireland when standing in this cluster of beehive huts. The essential raw nature of the dragon line that runs through Skellig Michael is potent if you can give yourself enough time to slow down to its rhythms.

***Dingle Beehive Huts**—County Kerry*

The Dingle Peninsula in the west of County Kerry has numerous beehive hut clusters. Many of them are exceedingly popular tourist destinations and can be accessed easily from the Dingle circle road. However, the selkie showed me where several clusters are that one can avoid time and humans altogether. What a gift it is to be able to rest in ceremony and deep listening inside a 5,000-year-old sanctuary for knowledge and spirit. Magic happens here.

Rátha & Ring Forts

Technically, *rátha,* also known as "ring forts," which are circular fortified settlements mostly built during the Bronze Age up to about the year AD 1000, fall under a different class than the megaliths. Ring forts come in many sizes and may be made of stone or earth. Most are made of earth. A *ráth* would have been marked by a circular rampart (a bank and ditch), often with a wooden palisade along the top of the rampart. Both stone and earthen ring forts would generally have had at least one building inside and typically were for everyday living in the wilds of Ireland. They served to protect the human inhabitants and livestock during times of trouble or raiding.

I include the *rátha* as part of this section on megaliths not because they are large earthworks (or stone) of the Neolithic Age, but because most *rátha* have been completely reclaimed by the Faë and have powerfully transformative energies. Many *rátha* are now forested with ancient trees. An excellent example of a reconstructed classic Iron Age ring fort or *ráth* can be found at the Craggaunowen living history museum in south central County Clare. Honestly, I prefer the wild ones out in the forest, in an old farmer's field, or in the heart of the Burren. They are so alive!

Ballyallaban Ring Fort (An Ráth)—*County Clare*

An Ráth is easily the most potent and alive *ráth* that I have found yet in Ireland. Whether it is the ring of ancient beech trees that line the ancient ramparts that one can climb to the canopy or the grove of fairy hawthorns tucked within the shade at the center of the circle, this circle sings with life. I find myself coming back again and again and always discover more. It has been closed for public access for over five years now as of 2022.

Ráth Béal Ború—*County Clare*

Located near the large Lough Derg in the east of Ireland at the village of Killaloe, this massive ring fort is covered in a towering canopy of ancient trees from oak, beech, pine, hawthorn, and more. The quietness is deep here, even with the traffic of Killaloe and Lough Derg. Believed to be the birthplace of Brian Bóruma mac Cennétig (Brian Boru), the Irish hero and High King renowned for liberating Ireland from the Vikings' grip at the beginning of the eleventh century AD, this *ráth* has revealed artifacts back to the Neolithic Age and certainly contains a sense of timelessness. Thus, we stitch back together into the Neolithic.

An Invitation

At the close of the Neolithic Age, the advent of the Bronze Age into the Iron Age, something fundamental shifted on the planet. Climate change, the potential collapse of previous high culture, ocean levels rising, and the movement of people did not seem to ultimately disrupt the flowering of human spirit and ingenuity. Instead, it seems that Neolithic culture in Ireland was prepared for the changes. The essential universal peace that was sustained for almost 4,000 years across Europe, especially in the north, continued to allow for a burgeoning spiritually-focused Neolithic people. The people of the Age of Taurus created masterpieces of stone that are standing legacies of their relationship with the mysteries still today. And these ancient temples are often still alive and filled with the powerful, timeless forces they would have housed thousands of years ago.

There is an invitation here. We can stumble over the uprising of resource extraction-centered greed and the patriarchal-based culture that sprang up in the Middle East and northern Africa at the end of the Neolithic period, the dawning of the Age of Aries, or we can look to the sustained ancient harmonies of northern Europe and Asia that lasted well into the Bronze Age. The invitation is to recognize that though we have been in an era where wars of conquest are the fashion for almost 2,500 years, prior to this, even with massive climate change and sea levels rising over 300 feet—inundating cultural centers around the world—the Irish have over 4,000 years of history as a non-empirical nation. In that time, thousands of portals and gateways were created by our ancestors to help us unlock the codex that is in our spirit lineage, in our blood, and in our DNA. The ancient Irish created living temples to dissolve the time-space continuum. They created pathways of remembrance, and it is up to us in our present time to put the parts of the whole back together again in a dynamic universal harmony.

This is the Celtic path and the art of the *seanchaí:* to weave the threads of current in the universe into new and renewed harmonics. We are here to sustain, restore, remember, balance, harmonize, and track the songs of the universe, both in the heavens and on the Earth. Likewise, it is to focalize the probabilities of the multiverse to leave the best possible ripple across all realms and worlds, in this world and the other. This is part of the reason why the ancient megaliths are such strong beacons calling us home to Ireland (and other places): to recalibrate, heal, dissolve, and become emissaries of the living Light of Erin—and beyond all cultural forms and definitions. Let us prepare to walk in time and in the timeless between. The powerful forces, allies of *Tír na nÓg*, and the primordial essence of the Earth are all working in collaboration with us. We are not alone, and we are beyond time and on time for this confluence.

"In Ireland, this world, and the world we go to after death are not far apart."
~ William B. Yeats

Chapter Eighteen

LIFE WITH THE GOOD PEOPLE

Time is the landscape's fourth dimension. We are the unseen: ghosts of yesterday-tomorrow, caravanning through an endless labyrinth of riddles and haunted by our mortality. Need and desire become intertwined, leaving the tongue thirsty for the alchemist's draught. Drink the riddle and see what unfurls:

> *"I never was, am always to be,*
> *No one ever saw me, nor ever will*
> *And yet I am the confidence of all*
> *To live and breathe on this terrestrial ball."*[218]

I have been taken by the forest. I was taken long ago, in the days when the sun was young and nights were long. In that flower of the Golden Age, my tail was longer, stirring the leaves gently as I wound my way amongst the beech and oak, eating blackberries while scooping up mouthfuls of ice-cold water, salmon, and hazelnuts. My mother is quite sure that I am a Faë as I was born on a blue moon. The Good People love children born on a blue moon, for the child's blood is as blue as their own. A child of the blue moon can hear the *ceol sídhe* or fairy music arching across time, echoing in the mountains, and weaving between the sounds of falling water.

◇◇◇◇◇◇◇◇◇◇◇◇◇◇

[218] Classic Irish riddle...see if you can determine "what am I?"

Time is illusive. In the realm of the Good People, time is an irrelevant obstruction to the movement of our immortal nature—the soul. The closer we get to the Summerlands, the Land of the Good People, or to *Tír na nÓg*, the closer we come to knowing our *anam cara* and our *aislingí* across all the multiverses.[219] Our *anam cara* and *aislingí* are not something separate from ourselves but are instead our true soul's voice, calling to us from outside of time to know ourselves and thus to enter a living relationship and riddle with the mysteries. Our *anam cara* invites us again and again to a state of reverence, awe, and wonder, for it is truly only within the state of openness that life is inspired, and we can flourish. Whether we see the world through the lens of science, art, engineering, poetry, law, health, religion, or other indoctrination, our view of the world is static and flat without the animation of the invisible threads of our *anam cara* calling to us from across time. Our *anam cara* reminds us to embrace the mysteries.

For many of the spring years of my life, I had many reoccurring dreams and visions of sacred landscapes and places that I was called to commune with to further the evolution of my soul in a bright awakening. The flowering of a dream into the reality that we inhabit most frequently on a day-to-day basis can be exhilarating. At the same time, it can confirm that we are walking on our path or perhaps act as a warning bumper to nudge us back onto our paths. None of the reoccurring dreams have ever affected me as much as that of finding myself in the sacred landscape around Lough Gur as shared in the chapter on Bealtaine and Áine earlier in this book. True dreams and visions illuminate the path before us. Our *aislingí* and the song of our *anam cara* reveal the bright and true like Áine and Lough Gur did for me years ahead of ever making pilgrimage to Ireland. My *anam cara* was calling me away from unhealthy modern social constructs and inviting me home in Spirit. I was being "taken by the Faë" into a deeper relationship with the divine and the eternal reflection of paradise that still exists on planet Earth.

[219] *Anam cara* is Irish for "soul friend" as greatly popularized by the late and great John O'Donohue of County Clare, Ireland.

I will get deeper into the Good People and the Faë shortly, but what is most important is to remember that before going to Lough Gur for the first time with Sinéad in 2003, I had only seen the place in visions. In my mind, a landscape with four streams running roughly from the cardinal directions into a lake with no stream exiting could only occur in a magical landscape or vision. Yet, sitting in a 4,500-year-old *clochán* and sharing this reoccurring vision of an Otherworld landscape with Sinéad was compelling. She listened attentively. As I shared the vision of this place that I knew so well and visited so often, her smile and the light in her eyes grew brighter. The vision I had emerged in and walked through for many of my later teen years and early twenties was a real place. And this was only the first of many places that Sinéad helped me to find over the ensuing years. From vision to three-dimensional reality, my *anam cara* and *aislingí* were calling to me from across the fissure of time, through the void, and across the gap in the physical expanse from places I had never been in this lifetime.

This place that she took me to is one of the most potent sacred sites of the goddess Áine. Perhaps even more importantly, this place of my visions is one of the oldest sites in Ireland with continued human habitation. For at least 6,000 YBP to possibly 7,500 YBP, people have lived on the shores of Lough Gur in County Limerick. Some of the finest votive offerings ever found in Ireland have been discovered underneath the waves of Lough Gur. Many are now on display in the National Museum of Ireland in Dublin.

The lore of the lough is that Áine comes down from her throne on the mountain and removes her mystical cloak to bathe in the sacred waters of Lough Gur at Bealtaine. Perhaps she entered the site through the same ring of stones that I did, though I would hardly call the conical hill, or Knockfennel Hill (Cnoc Finnine), a mountain—they are one and the same. In some of the stories, she bathes and frolics in the forests near the lake for the duration of summer, returning to her other haunts in *Tír na nÓg* at Samhain. In others, she emerges from the cave beneath the lake every seven years on the back of a white horse and circumambulates the lake three or five times. Sometimes in the myth, this happens when the lake drains down into the cave. In some versions of the story, when Áine comes down from the hill to bathe, she is either captured by or falls in love with a mortal. The mortal then coerces her into being lovers and they have a child together. In these variations of the telling, the child becomes the one who lives beneath the lough and rides out on the horse every seven years.

And to be sure to tell the story true, everything I observed at Lugh Gur is as I had seen it in the visions with two exceptions. One, the circle of oak, beech, and ash around the stone circle on top of Knockfennel hill is absent. Second, the circle of stones is barely perceptible as they have been trampled by cattle for over one-hundred years. Only the tops of the stones are visible through the hearty Irish pasture grass and wildflowers. But the stone circle is still there. And after some inquiry at the museum near the lough, it seems that the trees had still been present until the early 1900s when they were cut down by the farmer tending that pasture due to storm blowdown. What I found upon arriving at this sacred place was the beginning of a journey of discovery—both in the bending of timelines, but also in the flowering of my *anam cara*, and the repeated appearance of many *aislingí*, calling through the veil from *Tír na nÓg* to my humble mortal human form wherever it happened to be. My immortal heritage was calling me home.

During the time that these trees were being cut down on the top of Knockfennel, the Irish Literary Revival, or Celtic Twilight, was in full effect. Not too far north of Lough Gur at Tulira Castle in County Clare, William B. Yeats, Lady Gregory, Æ Russell, Maude Gonne, Ella Young, and Edward Martyn were gathering in the summer months under the auspices of the Order of the Celtic Mysteries (OCM) to revitalize the ancient enchantments of our Irish heritage. They were also collecting the timeless oral legends from the Irish countryside and catalyzing Ireland's liberty from the British crown. Lady Gregory spearheaded the charge of collecting myths and legends without applying any poetic license. Her friend Yeats fully embodied the modern bard-magi and braided riddles and codices into the heart of his works. Edward Martyn, distant relative in my mother's family, was at the forefront of creating sanctuaries and underwriting the cost of the revitalization of the Irish-Celtic arts. Ella Young was braiding ancient tales of Celtic magic from recently translated documents into gorgeous prose and stories. This company of the Celtic Twilight was one of the first groves of modern *seanchaí* to publish, translate, or republish material that had so long been a part of the oral tradition of the bards or buried in the archives of forgotten texts. They relit the flame in the sacred heart of Erin for our contemporary times.

Whether it was by chance or not that the Order of Celtic Mysteries emerged at the same time as the cutting of the groove at Knockfennel at Lough Gur, it matters not. Yet, this is the wave that I remembered in the visions and still see when I go to the place within—even though I have been back to Lough Gur multiple times since that first visit, and I have seen the ring and hilltop without the trees. I believe that the keepers of the inner sanctum of the sacred grove we know as the Celtic Twilight were consciously sending out transmissions across time, from Lough Gur and Knockfennel, as well as other portals to *Tír na nÓg*. Did any sentient beings catch the call? Wake up and come home!

In sync with the immortal nature of the Good People, or the *sídhe*, the seed grove of the Celtic Twilight invites us to come home to our *anam cara*, and if we can, to come home to Ireland. There is an ancient light waiting for us there, the Light of Erin, that will illuminate our pathways through the darkness and the riddles of life.

The Good People

In Irish folklore, there are hundreds of "species" of little people, known as faëries, Faë, *sídhe*, or the Good People. Most of these little people begin to appear during the Christian era as localized spirits and diminutive gods. The ancient gods of sacred places had to be accounted for in some way while the Celtic people slowly began adopting Abrahamic traditions via the Christian faith from the fifth century AD. Cultivating a relationship with the Good People was a safe way to honor the ancient currents of the land and not offend the Christian God. With Ireland calling many of her children home and thousands upon thousands of stories of the Good People in Irish literature, many of which have never been translated into English, it would behoove us to track the evolution of the Irish relationship with the *sídhe* in order to better formulate our own understanding of these mysterious beings.

The origins of the *sídhe* in Ireland are rooted in the ancient divine race of the *Tuatha Dé Danann,* and in some cases, to the *Fomorians* and

Firbolgs. Time and Christianity have reduced the stature of the *sídhe* to what amounts for most people in the modern-day to "little fairies." I have never seen a fairy. I am fairly sure I never will see one because that is not the lens that I look through. I do not need the ancient deities to show up as Disneyland-style miniatures. I see them for what they are: immortals of a divine race that is beyond our normal understanding of time and stature. The *sídhe* are said to now live underground in "fairy mounds," in ancient forests, across the western sea, or in a parallel universe where they walk amongst the living.

I "see" these beings regularly around the world, not just in Ireland. Usually, I see or sense their presence at dawn or dusk, on misty days, or when the sun blindingly reflects off the water. Typically, they have a message for me that is usually encoded in a riddle, though sometimes they will be explicitly frank. As the years pass, I see them less and less as something outside of myself but instead as an aspect of myself outside of time—my *anam cara*—calling to me at pivotal moments in this lifeline to help me sync up more clearly with my eternal nature.

The Faë, *sídhe*, and *aislingí* typically appear as visions or embodiments outside of the observer. The term "faërie" is derived from the French words *fé erie*, meaning "the enchantment of the *Fées*." *Fé* is derived from the Vulgar Latin word *fata*, meaning "the goddess of fate," which is itself derived from the Latin *fatae*, referring to the classic Fates. "Faërie" originally applied to supernatural women who directed the lives of humans and attended births. Now it has come to mean a type of paranormal creature associated with the earth. In Ireland, the faëries classically are called the *Aes Sídhe,* though Yeats helped to popularize applying *sídhe* to refer to faërie, both as a place and the immortal beings inhabiting it. *Sídhe* written as "*sí*" also happens to be the name for the earthen mounds and hills that are found across the Irish landscape. Irish mythology, legends, and folklore claim the Faë live under these mounds, so the term *sídhe* has come to mean "Faërie" in general, but it more properly refers to the palaces, courts, halls, and residences of the Faë. However, they are known by a wide variety of euphemisms, including "the Fair Folk," "the Good Neighbors," "the Little Folk," "the Little Darlings," "the Good People," and "the People of Peace."

The Origins of the Sídhe

The origins of the *sídhe* can roughly be divided into three groups: an older race of people, ancestors, or diminutive gods and immortals.[220] The first category describes the Faë as an older race of people driven into hiding by invading newcomers through all the various settlements and invasions of Ireland both in the Mythological Cycle as well as the Historic Cycle. The Faë associated with the older races continue to survive in part by borrowing tools, food, animals, and even women and children from the newer settlers of Ireland. They are known to attack solitary travelers (especially when drunk) who wander into their territory or haunt isolated farms. Some of the Faë of this category are also known to do fair work in exchange for food and lodging, such as a *beantighe* and some *leipreachāns*.[221] In time, the new Irish come to think of these older people as having supernatural powers and develop traditions about them to protect themselves and try to stay out of their way. This may have occurred in Ireland when the Mesolithic hunter-gathers were supplanted by Neolithic farmers sometime around 4,500 YBP. Certainly, the Irish mythological history claims that defeated races retreated under mounds to become the *sídhe* in their many forms.

The second way of explaining the *sídhe* is that they are our ancestors. To outsiders, this would appear as a form of ancestor worship, and many legends seek to connect living Irish people with mythical forebears from a past golden age in Irish history or prehistory when things were more heroic and beautiful. Legends and folktales tell how kings, queens, and heroes entered *Tír na nÓg* when they died or were enticed there from the land of the living by *aislingí* to help establish new kingdoms or beget

220 See Walter Evans-Wentz book entitled *The Fairy Faith in Celtic Countries*, first published in 1911.

221 *Beantighe* is a *sídhe* that helps take care of a home or hearth. A *leipreachān*, or leprechaun, will help in the smithy, the shed, or with tools. They are also likely to create rainbow bridges to your silver and help turn it into mead, whiskey, or wild parties that last a whole night through filled with pipers, fiddlers, and more.

Faë children. Many Irish generally believe that the *sídhe* are either angels or spirits of the dead and that *Tír na nÓg* is the afterlife in heaven.

The third classification of the *sídhe* assumes that the Faë are diminutive gods or immortals, such as the *Tuatha Dé Danann*, *Firbolgs*, and *Fomorians*. The power of these ancient sovereign deities has thus been diminished with the evolution of time and the superimposed beliefs of other waves of immigration and faith traditions to Ireland. This is especially witnessed with the invasion of the Milesians and half a millennia later by the peaceful incursion of Christian mendicants in the fifth century AD. The ancient gods were eventually forced to retreat underground or emigrate to the Summerlands, and the gods who remained often became diminutive nature spirits connected to specific landscape features or regions.

I think all three of these classifications carry a portion of truth with respect to the origins of the *sídhe*. In the following sections, I outline some of the "species" of the *sídhe* as they are known in their modern, contemporary context in myths and legends across Ireland. The *sídhe*, in the form of *aislingí* and other signs or symbols, have offered invitations, procured contracts, and proffered doorways to help my *anam cara* come home and to live a more reciprocal life in relationship to Spirit. Perhaps some of the *sídhe* have called you as well. May you find a key or two herein to help you unlock your own riddles in the pursuit of Paradise.

Aes Sídhe

The *Aes Sídhe* are an immortal and divine race comparable to Scandinavian faëries or elves that inspired J.R.R. Tolkien's elves in the *Lord of the Rings*. These are not "little people," but instead are taller, brighter, stronger, and more beautiful than humans and are eternally youthful. The *Aes Sídhe*, also referred to as just the *sídhe*, live underground in caves, mounds, forests, and mountains and are often appeased with offerings or the completion of certain tasks. *Aislingí* are typically emissaries from this type of Faë, but not exclusively. As the *Aes Sídhe* are typically associated with the sovereign spirit of a place, it is critical to exonerate them with gifts of reciprocity while avoiding angering or insulting them. This becomes especially true when you agree to the completion of a task or contract with an *aisling*. As sovereign spirits of place, the *Aes Sídhe* are fierce guardians of a place, whether a forest, mountain, fairy hill, cairn, individual tree, lough, river, or cave. Since the veil between our world and the Celtic Otherworld is closer at times of dusk and dawn, this is the time of the *sídhe*, as are the changes in season at the cross-quarter festivals of Samhain, Ímbolc, Bealtaine, and Lughnasadh, as well as Midwinter and Midsummer.

The *sídhe* are most akin to our immortal human nature, beckoning us to leave behind the mundane trappings of the world, merge with the timeless, and invest in the eternal marriage of spirit and matter. The *Aes Sídhe* are often indifferent to human activities unless one of their sites is being disturbed, where they are known to invoke a *géis*, curse, or wrath upon the transgressor. Some of the *sídhe* are very curious about humans and love to invite us into relationships. They may request the completion of a task to maintain the larger harmonies of the planet or universe in a context outside of our normal human constructs while others like to tease us and draw us into their pleasures. Some of the *Aes Sídhe* have been considered malevolent, though it is easy to empathize with them, as humans have destroyed much of the original garden that they once called home.

Beansídhe (Beansí)

The *beansídhe* or *beansí*, typically anglicized as "banshee," is a song of the keening at the passing, or pending passing, of one from the world of the living to that of the dead. A *beansídhe* is the aspect of the Faë that calls the human soul home to the Summerlands. Traditionally, a *beansídhe* was a female ancestor spirit who has been appointed to forewarn members of Irish families of the impending death of a loved one. Traditionally, a *beansídhe* was a living female traditional wisdom keeper, more like an Irish priestess, seer, or *bean feasa*. Because of Christian and Romantic era influences on Irish mythology, the *beansídhe* are unfortunately most frequently depicted as a hag, a ghostly woman, or even a demon in modern films and stories. *Ban* or *bean* in Irish means "woman" and *sídhe*, or *sí*, refers to the immortal Faë. Thus, a *beansídhe* is a "woman of the immortal fairy," female immortal. During the Gaelic Revival (twelfth–fifteenth centuries AD), a *beansídhe* also became a name for highly trained *seanchaí* women who were carriers of ancient Irish-Celtic lore. After the Cromwell years, the term *beansídhe* began to be referred to a darker female spirit emerging from the Otherworld.

The appearance of the *beansídhe* is that of a beautiful young woman, a stately matron, or a withered old hag. These are symbolic of the triple aspects of the Celtic goddess of winter, war, and death, the three Morrígna—the Morrígu, the Macha, and the Cailleach. The garb of a contemporary *beansídhe* is a black, grey, or white hooded cloak, or the winding sheet (grave robe) of the dead. She will also appear as a woman washing blood-stained clothes belonging to those who are about to die. The only experiences I have had with the *beansídhe* have been positive, and they have either shown me a direction to turn in life or they have protected me from malevolent or vampiric human beings. I do not mean literal vampires, I mean vampires of human emotions, psyche, and/or masters of mental or emotional manipulation—the art of glamour.[222] You probably have met a few of those people along the path.

The *beansídhe* is not always seen—rather, she is most often only heard. As mentioned above, her mourning, wailing cry pierces the night before someone is bound to perish. It is said that in 1437, King James I of Scotland was approached by an Irish seeress or *beansídhe* who foretold his murder. Records speak of several human *beansídhe* or *bean feasa* counseling the great houses of Ireland and the courts of Irish kings. There are parts of Leinster where the *beansídhe* is called the *bean chaointe* ("keening woman") whose shrieking call is reportedly so sharp that it can shatter glass. In County Kerry, witnesses say that the cry of the *beansídhe* is a low, pleasant singing, while in County Tyrone, it sounds like boards being struck together repeatedly. In some parts of Ireland, the *beansídhe* call is described as the combination of the wail of a woman and the moan of an owl. In the northern country of the United States, the *beansídhe* song wavers like the wail of a loon. In the Southern Appalachian Mountains, we hear *beansídhe* keening within the scream of barn owls and bobcats.

222 The original meaning of "glamour" is the effect of a spell that causes one to see objects in a form that differs from reality, typically to make filthy, ugly, or repulsive things seem beauteous and attractive.

The Beantighe

The *beantighe* is a benevolent house *sídhe* that will look after a traditional family's hearthside. The *beantighe* is most often described as a small, elderly woman wearing tattered, old-fashioned dresses and has a wrinkled and kind face, though sometimes she can be a young maiden or beautiful matron. *Beantighe* translates to English as "woman of the house," and you may have recognized that the Irish is similar to that of the *beansídhe*. This is because both Faë beings are linked to old Irish families and are associated with feminine (*bean*) aspects of the *sídhe*. But in opposition to the sometimes frightening and ever-powerful *beansídhe* mostly found in the wilds, the *beantighe* is friendly, warm, and found in or near homes. Like the *beansídhe* association with the triple goddess of winter, the *beantighe* is associated with the triple goddess of spring, Brigid, and sometimes to Áine. The *beantighe* is a housekeeper, fire tender, and watches over the animals and children in the house. Some Irish folklore tell of mothers getting up in the middle of the night to check on their children and finding that they had an extra blanket already covering them or a window open or closed to adjust the temperature in the room. This was most assuredly the work of a *beantighe*. The *beantighe* loves cream and berries and therefore should be offered such. Other tales tell of old Irish women who were careful not to keep their homes too clean for fear of being accused of hosting a *beantighe* by their English puritan Christian neighbors and landlords.

I met a *beantighe* once while I was exploring an old inn ruin near a waterfall in a high mountain bog in the Gap of Dunloe in County Kerry. I did not see her watching me. I was loudly commenting on the ridiculous design of an old, pre-famine outhouse which had the seat hanging right over the stream near the waterfall behind the inn. I was rambling on about how it was the most ill-advised toilet I had ever seen when I heard a guffawing behind me. I turned to see no one there, but to hear the voice of an elderly woman telling me not to be so judgmental. I never did actually "see" her, but we got into an extensive conversation about hygiene, water quality, and hearths. She ended up deciding to leave the long-vacant hearth of the dilapidated inn and come with me across the Atlantic. She has been lovingly tending the fire in my home since 2015 with the promise that she will have the honor of tending the hearth of the mountain house and Haltia Haven, as she does love waterfalls and deep forests. She has already enjoyed helping with the fires in the valley as well as tending the *Tobar na mBandia*, the sacred spring.

Púca

Considered to be bringers both of good and bad fortune, a *púca* can have dark or staunch white fur or hair. As shapeshifters, they can take on the appearance of horses, foxes, goats, cats, dogs, hares, and humans, sometimes exhibiting various animal features, such as ears or a tail. *Púcaí* most commonly take the form of a sleek black horse with a flowing mane and luminescent golden eyes. If a human is enticed onto a *púca's* back, it has been known to give them a wild ride, oftentimes into the Otherworld. Typically, a *púca* will not harm its rider. The *púca* also has the power of human speech and has been known to give advice, especially near Samhain, leading people away from harm or malevolent forces. Though the *púca* enjoys confusing and often terrifying humans, they are benevolent.

Certain agricultural traditions surround the *púca*. It is a creature associated with Samhain when the last of the crops are brought in for storage and winter begins. Anything remaining in the fields after Samhain is considered *"púca"* or enchanted and thus rendered inedible by people. In many parts of Ireland, reapers leave a small share of the crop still standing, referred to as the *púca's share*. This is an offering to help placate the hungry creature and honor their gifts of forewarning from malevolent beings. Samhain is the one period of the year when they can be expected to behave civilly.

In some regions, the *púca* is spoken of with considerably more respect than fear and may be a diminutive form of the ancient god Crom Cruach. If treated with respect, a *púca* may be beneficial to those who encounter them. They most frequently inhabit mountains and hills, and in those regions, there are stories of *púcaí* appearing on Samhain and providing prophecies and warnings to those who consult it. The *púcaí* are the Faë who lived near and protect the ancient standing stones and stone circles and may be regarded as being either menacing or beneficent. It is always wise, therefore, to bring some milk, honey, and perhaps some bread and cheese to offer to the guardian *púcaí* of a stone circle before entering, especially at night.

These beings are highly tangible in the stone circles in the west of County Cork and in County Kerry, especially in stone circles surrounded by trees. There is a particular stone circle in the southwest of Ireland that I simply must keep secret where the standing stones are *púcaí*. One can see their individual character under the full moon, buried under ivy and the shadow of beech, hawthorn, and oak. Truly these stones come alive.

Merrows

The Irish version of the mermaid or merman is called a merrow or a *murdúch*. Sailors and people who lived by the extensive shoreline of Ireland had a whole gamut of merrow lore, and many still tell the enchanting tales today. In writer W.B. Yeats' collection of Irish folk tales, there is an entire section dedicated to stories of the merrows. Quite often in legend, the merrow is said to have a greenish tint to its skin with webbed fingers, the tail of a fish, and seaweed-green hair. One particularly frightening and prevalent legend of the merrow tells of male merrows who capture the drowned souls of sailors and put them into pots. These pots stay at the bottom of the sea, never to release the poor sailors' souls unless a willing human being was to release them. This tale is somewhat retold in the 2014 film, *Song of the Sea*, co-produced by Tomm Moore.

Male merrows are said to be downright malevolent and awfully ugly. Perhaps this is why we have so many stories of female merrows seducing human men—their choices among the male merrows left the females feeling left out from selective breeding. The female merrows seduce sailors and other young men by singing to them, like Greek sirens, and then drag them under the waves to the bottom of the sea. No one knows what happens to these men, though some believe they stay alive in a state of enchantment. Others believe they are drowned and killed.

One particularly interesting aspect of these Irish legends is that the merrows were only able to swim underwater with the aid of a magical talisman—a magical red cap to be exact. Perhaps the red caps were a type of fly agaric mushroom (*Amanita muscaria*). If a person were to steal this cap and not return it to the merrow, the merrow would then be unable to return to their home underwater. In one legend, an Irish man is granted use of the red cap so that he can visit a male merrow's home under the sea.

Selkies

My favorite of all the Faë beings are the selkies. The selkies are seal-people or a *sídhe* that can change forms between a seal and a human being depending on whether they are on land or in the sea. Selkies originate from the Orkneys and the Shetlands as well as across Ireland and Scotland, and even Iceland. As I mentioned in my writings of pre-visioning Lough Gur, it was a selkie woman who first held the portal open to me of *Tír na nÓg*. Some of my favorite haunts in Ireland along the west coast and in the islands are where selkies are known—or have been known historically—to frequent. I have watched them for hours bobbing on the surface of the sea, sometimes as seals, sometimes as women. They sing to my heart and frequently prompt deep soul longing and will draw full body crying out of me. I have swum with them off the coast of the Isle of Skye. I know that one day, they will invite me to stay under the waves with them in the Summerlands, or more specifically, *Tír fo Thuinn* ("land beneath the waves").

There are numerous stories about beautiful selkie women who are captured by sailors and taken onto land to be made into their loyal wives. The men hide the selkie's sealskin in order to keep her bound to the land. Unfortunately for these men, selkie women have an insatiable longing for the ocean. If a selkie finds her hidden sealskin, she will immediately slip the skin back on and swim back to her home under the waves, never to be seen again. The seal-men, or selkie males, are also said to be very attractive, and legend has it that if a woman wants to have a selkie-lover, she need only cry seven tears into the sea, and he will appear to her. Usually, these love stories are tragic and end in more tears for the human lovers. In some cases, selkies are malevolent and will seduce humans into the water and drag them under. Other stories tell of selkies saving drowning sailors.

There are theories of origin for selkies. One of them says that the selkies were merely women from Northern cultures that wore skins and used animal skins on their kayaks. They came from the sea, and so, therefore, the legend of the seal-woman was born. Or perhaps the legend comes from old sailor stories where indeed they had sightings of seals and imagined these seals to be beautiful women instead.

Leipreachán (Leprechaun)

The classic Irish *leipreachán* or leprechaun is a joyous expression of life—until you step on their toes or give them too much to drink. These beings are truly a reflection of the health of the land in that they are either super playful and friendly, or they are grumpy and crass when the land is not healthy. There are several possible origins of the term "leprechaun," including the term *leath bhrogan,* a type of shoemaker, and *luacharman,* a dwarf or pygmy. Leprechauns are often depicted as small, aged men with curly beards and thick hair and who may have had slightly too much to drink. Their drink of choice is rumored to be home-brewed hooch. Keep in mind that a leprechaun will never become so intoxicated that their hands become too unsteady to play the fiddle, their tongue become too tied to weave a yarn, or their handicraft marred or despoiled in any way. Leprechauns represent the diminutive form of the masculine deities of the *Tuatha Dé Danann*, especially the Dagda and sometimes Crom Cruach or Lugh.

Leprechauns have appointed themselves protectors of the treasure left by Vikings when they marauded through Ireland, and it is widely believed that they store it in crocks, pots, or souterrains. Leprechauns avoid contact with humans at all costs, as their gold is important to them, and they consider us to be greedy and foolish. If you manage to capture a leprechaun, so the legends go, they will offer immense amounts of wealth in exchange for their freedom. However, before you go leprechaun hunting, you should know that it is most likely not worth the trouble. Most of their gold coins turn to leaves or ashes when it is parted from the leprechaun, and silver will disappear after payment and return to the leprechaun's purse soon after their freedom has been obtained.

Leprechauns are the keepers of the gold at the end of the rainbow. The rainbow is a symbol of our heritage, specifically our DNA and the winding of our biology through time and the mysteries. The gold represents our *anam cara* or immortal nature. We must answer the riddling of the wise leprechaun or the bumbling of the wise fool in disguise to access the inner gateways to reveal the gold within.

Dragons

Dragons do not play into the Irish-Celtic mythology quite as frequently as in Welsh or English traditions. Dragons are often seen as allies of the *Fomorians* or the *Fir Bolgs*. Dragons are embodiments of the primordial currents running through the land in the ley lines, geology, and waterways. If you meet a dragon, it would be best if you are prepared for their riddles and tests, for just as leprechauns guard the inner treasure, the dragons guard the massive hordes of entire cosmologies, traditions, and cultures. Dragons are the rainbow light weaving through the multiple layers of consciousness simultaneously. They are the song of our DNA. Dragons are the guardians of treasure greater than any gold of the Earth—and they bite a little harder than a leprechaun.

Despite their lack of presence in Irish folklore, it is difficult to miss the dragon-like nature of Celtic knots. More so, it is difficult not to feel and see their timeless presence across Ireland. They are present in many places and frequent some of the wild and sacred sites for their own regeneration, nesting, training, and healing. Some of the favorite haunts of the dragons that I have visited include the nesting and training grounds for the westerlies in the glacial corrie loughs near Connors Pass in the Brandon Mountains.[223] Training grounds for water and cloud dragons can also be found near the westernmost tips of the Dingle Peninsula and Iveragh Peninsula in the southwest of Ireland, as well as between Glencolmcille and Portnoo in County Donegal. They originate both in the mountains as well as along the coast and are typically seen as mist or low clouds.

[223] A *corrie lough* or lake is a glacial mountain lake, pond, or pool that was excavated by a glacier.

Giants

While Ireland is well-known for its belief in the wee folk, it may come as a surprise to some to learn of the fondness the Irish have for tales of giants. Balor of the Evil Eye, king of the *Fomorians*, was a giant who locked his own daughter in a tower, had an all-powerful eye that wreaked havoc on his enemies, and had to be kept blindfolded in order not to hurt his allies with that eye. It took four men to lift his eyelid. In later folklore, the task of unveiling the eye is described by Alan Ward as such:

> *"It was always covered with seven cloaks to keep it cool. He took the cloaks off one by one. At the first, ferns began to wither. At the second, grass began to redden. At the third, wood and trees began to heat up. At the fourth, smoke came out of wood and trees. At the fifth, everything got red hot. At the sixth, blood begins to boil and heart become weak, the mind numbs and reality fades. At the seventh, the whole land caught fire."*[224]

Balor tried to kill his own grandsons and was successful at killing two of the three, but his grandson Lugh (child of a treaty marriage between the *Fomorians* and *Tuatha Dé Danann*) survived and eventually killed Balor in the war between the two races at the Second Battle of *Maige Tuired.*[225]

The giants were not all cruel behemoths like Balor. Fionn mac Cumhaill, the great leader of the *Fianna*, often became a giant in myth. He was credited with building the Giant's Causeway off the northeast coast of (Northern) Ireland. He used his wits rather than violence to defeat a visiting Scottish giant. Stories about giants in Ireland explained how natural features had been formed and why large megalithic structures could be found across the landscape. They were probably correct. A classic legend of the son of Fionn mac Cumhaill, Oisín, tells that upon his return from his three-century-long love affair with Niamh, a Faë woman, in *Tír na nÓg*, Oisín found the people of Ireland to be diminutive. They were so frail and weak compared to his

224 Alan Ward, *Myths of the Gods: Structures in Irish Mythology.* 2011

225 Second battle of Moytura or *Cath Maighe Tuireadh* in Irish.

old comrades that an entire village of men could not lift a standing stone back into its appropriate position. Oisín simply reached over from his saddle and with one hand, lifted the stone back into its standing position. Unfortunately, the girth or flank cinch of his saddle broke and he fell from his magic steed. Niamh had instructed him never to dismount the horse if he wanted to return home to her. Oisín lost his immortality, and age caught up with him rapidly in front of the bewildered eyes of the villagers.

Fairy Hounds & Lion Dogs

Also known as "hounds of the hill," fairy hounds are said to be the hunting dogs of the Good People who dwell in hollow hills. Fionn mac Cumhaill had two hunting fairy dogs, Bran and Sceolan. Intelligent and skilled in hunting, they displayed a great loyalty to Fionn. Dogs are often known for these traits but brother and sister Bran and Sceolan were related to Fionn. Legend has it that they were born to Fionn's aunt, Tuiren. Tuiren was married to Iollan Eachtach, but he had another lover who was a jealous *sídhe* woman. Out of her jealousy, the *sídhe* woman put Tuiren under a *géis* while pregnant which turned her into a dog. She remained in this form until the *géis* was broken, but by then, she had already given birth to the puppies who remained dogs and thus became Bran and Sceolan, the loyal hounds and cousins of Fionn.

Getting further into the Irish lore archives, many fairy dogs are known to live as long as the *sídhe*, and oftentimes, in the lore and Celtic art, are depicted as lion dogs. Lion dogs have a particular place of magic in the Celtic worldview since they are both lion and dog. They have the strength and vigor of a lion and the loyalty of a dog. In many ways, the lion dog is the fierce symbol of all things Irish: the fierceness of a lion in the fight whilst loyal like a dog to family and kin. The lion dog is near and dear to my heart and can often be found running in my dreams or leading me to a sacred well, and better yet, showing up while on vision quests around the world as tangible dogs that appear to guide or protect me.

Cú Chulainn is an Irish mythological hero who appears in the stories of the Ulster Cycle as well as in Scottish and Manx folklore. He is often depicted as a fairy hound or lion dog. He gained his better-known name as a child after killing the smith Culann's fierce guard dog in self-defense.

Cú Chulainn offered to take the dog's place guarding the smithy until a replacement could be reared. At the age of seventeen, Cú Chulainn defended Ulster single-handedly against the armies of Queen Medb of Connacht in the famous *Táin Bó Cúailnge* as the armies of Ulster were subject to the curse of the Macha. It was prophesied that his great deeds would give him everlasting fame, but his life would be a short one. He was known for his terrifying battle frenzy, or *ríastrad* (warp spasm), the Celtic berserker state sometimes called the "torque."

Changelings

Adult Faë admire beauty, and they have no wish to keep any of their own deformed children. They will attempt to swap them secretly with human infants. These beings are known as "changelings," and it is rumored that they can be ill-tempered and wise beyond their years. To amuse themselves, the changeling babies work magic in the human household. Some changelings are known to screech and wail all day and all night, and their cries will sometimes reach the point where they can no longer be heard by humans. Others are quaint little angels that seem sent from heaven, even if they are not the most attractive babies.

Will-O'Wisp

A Will-O'Wisp is a type of *sídhe* that appears as a soft light in wild places. They are often described as phantom lights that hover just above the ground in the wilderness, luring travelers away from the beaten path. Most of these lights haunt the moors and bogs of Ireland and the deep forests around the world. They are sometimes seen as a type of luminescent fairy that dances across lakes and bodies of water at night or drifts over the ground along a non-existent pathway deep through the forest. The light that these fairies give off tends to look like a flickering candle, a flickering orb of light, or like fireflies. Aside from their ability to dazzle and tantalize travelers, Will-O'Wisps are also powerful omens. They can predict the future, appearing to people before their deaths, flocking to the site of a tragedy before it takes place, announcing the birth of a mystery, revealing a surprise turn of events for the future, or showing someone with Faë blood how to navigate through the dark to find hidden secrets. Will-O'Wisps might also reveal buried treasure or forgotten interment sites—just do not tell the leprechauns.

I have followed Will-O'Wisps from dreams into enchanted night walks, sometimes not waking up fully until I found myself out of doors and in a strange location. While living in Ireland, a Will-O'Wisp taunted my dreams for weeks until I finally followed it to begin unlocking a riddle that had been pulling on me the entire time I lived there. I was shown where to dig for a buried key and found it. I was then directed to take the key into an ancient beech and oak forest to open a door. Once the door was opened, I was pitched back into a memory of a parallel or past life, revealing a deeper "why" behind my intrinsic motivation for ecological conservation and indigenous rights. Another time, I followed a procession of thousands of Will-O'Wisps in the Southern Appalachian Mountains on Midsummer to find an opening in a song that brought me to *Tír na nÓg* and to the celestial paradise of the regional slant-eyed giants. The Will-O'Wisps are one of the main *sídhe* inhabitants of Haltia Haven.

Lunantisídhe

The *lunantisídhe* are the Good People that guard the blackthorn trees, one of the sacred *ogham* trees, especially along hedges and edges of wild places. They do not allow the cutting of hedges on Samhain or Bealtaine. If someone cuts or trims a blackthorn during these times, it is believed some misfortune will befall them. The *lunantisídhe* are not frequently seen but can be heard laughing and giggling in the hedgerows along pastures, paddocks, and roads across Ireland. Many of them stowed away on immigration ships to the USA and settled in New England, the lower Midwest, and the Southern Appalachian Mountains.

I have only some experiences with the *lunantisídhe*, mostly in being privy to having roe and privet berries from the blackthorn hurled at me on the way to the school bus stop when I was a child. It is good to know when not to cut hedgerows and it is still a law in Ireland to not cut hedges from the first of March until the thirty-first day of August. This is purported to protect the birds and their nests, but I am sure the *lunantisídhe* had something to do with the implementation and regulation of this national policy in the Republic.

Take the Plunge

Whether they may be diminutive gods, nature spirits, ancestor spirits, angels, demons, or celestial beings, the Good People have many guises to wear to communicate with us mortals. Some people never "see" the Good People but instead feel a presence or a sense of deep and ancient magic. Others feel them as a sense of inspiration or illumination of consciousness through the complex riddles and puzzles in life. The purpose of this whole chapter is not to try to convince you whether they exist or not. That is neither here nor there. You have either contacted them or you have not in any of their various forms. Spirits and the divine will appear to you in the way that you need to see them. The Good People may appear as external beings, *aislingí*, beckoning us further along the journey. The Faë may also wear various skins of a Celtic cultural context like the different "species" described above. Truly, the *sídhe* are beyond time and language. They invite us deeper into respect for the self within the self…and yet to be here, fully committed to the Earth and the divine.

Interestingly enough, with all the visions that I have had and experiences with the Faë or the Good People, it is a rare thing indeed for me to actually "see" one. I have had many visions in the dreamtime, in trance, in meditation, while playing music, and more which have allowed for brazen appearances of the Faë. I have also had many experiences where the Good People show up in my peripheral vision and then promptly disappear as soon as I turn towards them. And yet, I will say that I have had many experiences where an elder, a child, a stranger, or even an old friend has temporarily become an emissary for the Faë. I am not talking about a spirit possession, but a temporary visitation through the soul of another akin to when we meet an angel along our path. Someone who has been an angel or a *sídhe* for me may never even know it, or perhaps they do. Perhaps you have had similar experiences where for a moment in time, someone is a direct channel to the immortal Faë, angels, or the divine. They may share a specific message or grant a talisman that is critical to recalibrate our path through life.

The Good People dwell in the liminal. They are eternally present. The Summerlands is a parallel universe to our own yet intricately interconnected. The Faë invite us to find portals and thresholds to not only cross over into the Otherworld but also to stitch our worlds together in deep beauty. The *sídhe* invite us to live in inordinate harmony with the natural world while also going out on a limb to help us get back on our path. And when we do stumble along the path, the Good People may help us up. Yet sometimes they do not, for in the timeless realm within which they inhabit, the *sídhe* are able to see greater patterns that we cannot. They know the fiery shaping on the anvils of life or the terrifying personal alchemy that we are dragged through. Sometimes they are part of creating these experiences in life. The *sídhe* ultimately are here to help us develop mettle, become durable, and become more effective guides. If we were coddled through all our personal trials and tribulations in life, then we will develop little substance to offer to the world. The Good People help form us into resilient emissaries for the eternal.

With that, I will leave you to wander the forests of your heart and countryside. Also, I will leave you with the craft of bard, poet, and *aisling*, Fiona Macleod. In this poem, she invokes the essence of time, the allure of the garden, and the subtle enigmas of *aislingí:*

Time
I saw a happy Spirit
That wandered among the flowers:
Her crown was a rainbow,
Her gown was wove of hours.

She turned with sudden laughter,
I was, but am no more!
And as I followed after
Time smote me on the brow. [226]

[226] Fiona Macloed, *From the Hills of Dream: Threnodies, Songs and Later Poems*, 2nd ed., p 197, 1913.

PARTING THE VEIL

Chapter Nineteen
AISLINGÍ & GRATITUDE

"Books too often are written out of other books, and too seldom from the life of [people]; and in... the Fairy-Faith... the Celt[s] [themselves are] by far the best, and in fact the only authority."

~ W.Y. Evans Wentz

I believe that the best version of this book would have been a blank piece of paper or an empty journal. I have often spoken to this effect while hosting programs, retreats, and pilgrimage. At the same time, I feel that it is important to leave a subtle little marker along the trails that I have found, rediscovered, or blazed on my own while Ireland has slowly revealed her mysteries to her wayward son. I am grateful for the authors, poets, mystics, holy sisters, and bards who have wholeheartedly believed in the path of the pilgrim through this world and *Tír na nÓg*. I am also grateful to the academic reviewers who specifically asked to see a better list of references and provide a bibliography of the resources in the annals of Irish literature where culturally specific information shared in this book comes from. I have done my best to provide that information herein, both in the footnotes as well as the bibliography and glossary. Let me be very clear on the order of operations here: the heart and soul of the journey with the *sídhe* began with dreaming, pilgrimage, and ancestral memory. The archives of Irish literature supporting this publication were only discovered years later under the direction of fantastic mentors, Irish mystics, *seanchaí*, and academics.

My hope is that the presentation herein of the human-*aisling* relationship via the Irish-Celtic lens will provide valuable catalysts to propel others' journeys forward in deep beauty and peace. The invitation is to climb a mystery every day. Allow the mind and heart to be soft when the world allows for it. The armor of knowledge and faith creates sanctuary for ourselves and others to blossom. When the soul's hunger for the majesty of life remains pliable and malleable, both the heart and mind may continue to learn and grow. Softness within allows divinity to grant us deep peace through all the storms, upheavals, and programming. The heart of the Irish-Celtic keys is stored in your ancestral memory. The heart of the codex is anchored in the very landscape of Ireland herself. The art of the pilgrimage home to Ireland is the marriage of ancestral memory and the vast landscape of Irish lore and traditions. You are one of the keys to unlocking the mysteries. You are also the door.

The divine *sídhe* will seek you out. They want to collaborate with you to bring healing to the Earth and to your bloodlines, as well as to bind the beauty of our worlds together in a dynamic harmony that benefits all beings in the highest and greatest capacity. Do not settle for less. There will be many times in life when contracts are offered that may sound appealing, both human and with aspects of the divine. You do not have to say "yes" just because someone asks you to do something. The same principle should be applied to working with spirit and the divine. If a spirit incarnate as a human offers you a substance to put in your body, you can say "no"—and most of the time, probably should. If a spirit offers for you to be their "host" or emissary as a priest or priestess, you do not need to say "yes" unless it is truly in the interest of the highest and greatest possible future outcomes. Many ancient and new deities do not have the best interest in mind for all of creation.

Discernment is the key to tracking the true essence of *aislingí* in our lives. As a seeker and adept, we must learn to separate fantasies created by nothing more than our dreaming minds from seed ideas that are planted in our hearts and minds by the *sídhe* and *aislingí*.[227] As with any relationship, our intentions and what we truly bring to that relationship are far more important than what we may be expecting in return. My friend, Steve

◇◇◇◇◇◇◇◇◇◇◇◇◇◇

[227] See Steve Blamires' book *The Chronicles of the Sídhe.*

Blamires, often says to me that a relationship with an *aisling* and the *sídhe* is dynamic. Sometimes they make requests that seem impossible, but they know that we can handle the tasks assigned with the resources we have available. Trying to get in touch with *aislingí* is just like trying to get in touch with a friend via phone or texting: sometimes they may answer right away, sometimes they may not answer at all, and sometimes they may not return the call for hours, days, months, or years. With *aislingí* and God alike, it is not about what you get out of the relationship so much as being of service: *"not my will, but thine be done."*

Our *aislingí* communicate most easily with us as their emissaries via three of the most common approaches. The first way *aislingí* communicate with us is via subtle insertion of ideas, hunches, callings, and random seed thoughts that suddenly illuminate the mind, seemingly at random and from nowhere. Often, these nudges or moments of awakening come when we are willing to conduct activities outside of our normal habitual patterns or via an invitation to do something outside of habitual patterning. The second way that *aislingí* communicate with us as their emissaries is via moments of synchronicity. Many people in the twenty-first century call this phenomenon "flow-state," and it reflects the miraculous moments of synchronicity that provide us with resources in the day-to-day world. These arrive when they are needed most or to promulgate the completion of a specific task, quest, or mission that an *aisling* has asked us to complete. The third way that *aislingí* communicate and give us guidance is through direct inner communication and via angels or visions. These communications can come in via audio, visual, and kinesthetic means or through a combination of some or all these modes of exchange.

Aislingí will communicate with you in the best way that you are able to receive. If you are a visual learner, their strongest form of communication will be predominantly through visual experiences such as pathworkings, meditations, visions, apparitions, and many more. If you tend to be more of an auditory learner, then *aislingí* will most likely communicate through music, undertones of everyday life, sounds of nature, the *ceol sídhe*, or even in specific phrases or quotes emoted by other speakers. As a kinesthetic learner, the *aislingí* may communicate with you via your dance, placing hands on megalithic structures, touching trees, swimming, and many more body-centric activities. A fourth way that every so often becomes a mode through which an *aisling* will communicate may be via reading and writing. In this context, the *sídhe* make themselves known and reveal messages through the writing of another person or via your own automated writing. We all receive information and messages through a combination of all these modes. Personally, I find I am first visual, then kinesthetic, then audio, followed by an occasional message twined in and between the written word.

Aislingí do not care how you get the message as long as it is received. As emissaries, we should not only be willing to receive messages but also act accordingly. *Aislingí* do not make requests that you are unable to fulfill. They also will not continue to make requests if previous ones have not been completed. Sometimes human blundering, missteps, or irrespective decisions will get in the way of completing a task. The Christian concept of "sin" is to transgress or err from the path of completing our unique tasks on behalf of the divine. Missteps and "sin" can be redressed through a realignment with the path via atonement or attunement. When we fall from Grace, let us rise again and find our feet on the path. We are only passing through life. We are the unseen unless we can surrender to the majesty of divine immortality in the brief mortal lives we are gifted. The *aisling* Fiona Macleod once wrote:

> *"Is it wholly unwise, wholly the fantasy of a dreamer to insist, in this late day, when the dust of ages and the mists of the present hide from us the Beauty of the World, that we can regain our birthright only by leaving our cloud-palaces of the brain, and becoming one with the cosmic life of which, merely as [humans], we are no more than a perpetual phosphorescence?"*[228]

May your journey from an unseen to the seen, from carnal to deep peace, and from emissary to *aisling* ever invoke a sense of wonder, awe, and reverence for deep beauty in this world and beyond. May coming home to Ireland illuminate the pathways before you: the paths that have been blazed by those who have gone before you and the paths that you will discover. You are an emissary of the Light of Erin.

[228] From a letter written by Fiona to confidant Catherine Janvier as collected by Steve Blamires in his research for *The Chronicles of the Sidhe.*

Chapter Twenty

CELTIC TREE MEDITATION ENTER THE LIGHT OF ERIN

"[The] Celtic phenomenon of shape-shifting [was] an effect that the Irish seem to have taken for granted as we take for granted molecular structures. I myself...am, like the rest of reality, essentially fluid—essentially inessential."

~ Thomas Cahill

Modern science tells us that all of life, biotic and abiotic, flows with a living electromagnetic field.[229] The Chinese call this life force *qi*, or chi. The Irish call it *fórsa beatha* or *fórsa. Fórsa* is the essence and energy of life present in all things. Much like the Force in the *Star Wars* film series or electricity-feeding homes, it is universal energy that is available to do work. How that energy is channeled into different uses when we plug in may take on different subjective labels according to the eye of the beholder, such as "good, bad, or neutral."[230]

◇◇◇◇◇◇◇◇◇◇◇◇◇◇

[229] Biotic—relating to or resulting from living things, especially in their ecological relations. Animals, birds, microorganisms, bacteria, etc. Abiotic—physical rather than biological; not derived from living organisms. Stone, organics, water, etc.

[230] Somewhat in the eye of the beholder, but there are inherent "black," "white," and "grey," "green," or "red" magics that are self-serving, selfless, and existent, in harmony with nature, or sensual in nature.

Fórsa is measurable as electromagnetic energy in the form of EMFs but is not typically visible to the human eye.[231] The flow pattern of the electromagnetic field of an object is similar in shape to a donut and is known in science and sacred geometry as a "tube torus." All *fórsa*, when it is correctly aligned, is continually cycling, up and down and around, between spirit and matter—interchanging and sharing with the seen and unseen universe.

The beauty of a healthy forest, especially an ancient forest, is that trees perfectly emulate the architecture and living technology of a tube torus. Our Celtic ancestors lived and breathed forests and trees, sustaining the timeless harmonies of the sacred groves and deep wood through song, devotion, scrying, and caretaking. When the hungry empires of the Sea of Middle Earth had burned most of their forests and ventured north to fuel empirical furnaces and navies, the Celts' forests fell.[232] Over time, the hungry empires adapted a similar humanmade technology to trees in the form of arches, columns, and flying buttresses of the temples and great cathedrals of Europe.[233] Whether through the original life-enhancing function of the trees or through emulation in architected cathedrals, they all function in creating an environment that can enhance or recalibrate the refinement and purification of the human body's biofield. Forest or cathedral, these are the sacred centers that help us to keep singing, praying, and coming together outside of time—to bridge the world of body, mind, and spirit for the betterment of all beings, biotic and abiotic.

Our *aislingí* will often invite us to revisit the sacred grove together. In the grove, you may find your heart listening deeply or your body moving in dance, qigong, or fluid yoga. As a practitioner of qigong for

◇◇◇◇◇◇◇◇◇◇◇◇◇◇◇

231 An EMF meter can measure AC electromagnetic fields, which are usually emitted from man-made sources such as electrical wiring, while gauss meters or magnetometers measure DC fields, which occur naturally in Earth's geomagnetic field and are emitted from other sources where direct current is present.

232 "Sea of Middle Earth" is a direct translation of the Latin root words of the *Mediterranean Sea.*

233 Different cultures have developed different sacred geometry in their holy places based on the core principles or inherent patterns of the universal harmony that their genetic heritage is/was responsible for upkeeping.

over twenty-five years, I would encourage the play of qigong at times to heighten awareness of the biofield, refine relations with *aislingí*, augment lucid dreaming, and more clearly connect with the world. Qigong is the closest thing that I have found that embodies the ancient art of the Celtic warrior's torquing practice—getting into the zone and raising the energy. I highly suggest exercising your awareness of *fórsa* through the daily practice of breathing, qigong, Celtic tree meditation, and whatever else helps you to come into harmony with your body, mind, and spirit. You will be of better service to the planet, your family, your home, your community, and to living a fulfilling and inspired life. Energy follows thought. Thought follows intention—but the intention is useless if it is never set into motion. The Celtic tree meditation will align you on all levels and help you reset your intentions if things are out of alignment.

Celtic Tree Meditation

To begin, try practicing in a forest where there will be no personal distractions. Once you have the practice down, you will be able to do it anywhere—around large crowds, in city parks, and on the move. But start with stillness and quiet in a healthy forest or with a tree that has caught your attention. I was taught by my teachers to begin coaxing the energy of the earth up through my feet, utilizing my breath as a vehicle to convey the intent.[234] As you breathe in, draw your breath slowly from the abdomen up along the spine into the top of the lungs. You can do this by imagining a balloon of energy filling directly in correspondence with your breath. Fill your lower abdomen like a balloon and slowly imagine it being lifted up your spine, through your lungs, back of your throat, and behind your eyes to the top of your head. Let it gently move through your head and open at the top of the crown to the heavens like a flower or branches of a tree. The energy can then flow in an arc up, out, and back down into the earth and back in through your feet.

When you breathe out, reverse the flow from the top of the crown and the cosmos beyond, down through your body into the earth. I was

[234] My teachers here are Craig Ellis, Dennis Thoman, Delfina Rose, Nicki Ferrato & Michael, and Roger Jahnke.

taught to imagine the exhale initially as a bubble being released at the top of the crown and then picturing a warm waterfall flowing down my face, chest, and belly across my loins and into the earth. Then, the *fórsa* can be allowed to arch up and out in a sphere toward the crown where it can continue to flow down through your central column.

Once you can get the basic breathing down, you may be able to take longer breaths where you encourage the energy to cycle in and through your body multiple times as you are breathing in, and then multiple times as you are breathing out. As you breathe in, allow the energy to continue cycling upward and out, recycling as it reenters your field in the bottom of your feet. Meanwhile, the breath and the tube torus grow stronger and brighter as you pick up the beautiful *fórsa* from nature around you, and vice versa. As you exhale, the *fórsa* moves down through the top of your skull through the central column and as it builds, it gathers the illumination of the cosmos recalibrating your body and mind.

Experiment. See how many cycles or turnings of the tube torus you can make before you need to reverse it to let the breath out. Then, try reversing the flow. Try breathing in toward the earth and breathing out toward the heavens or cosmos. Once you get the hang of it, you may "see" the energy flowing, or at the very least, notice how different muscles and organs come into play to assist the movement of energy and your self-awareness and control. I bet that you will feel amazing and want to keep experimenting. Practice and refine. See what qualities of the self are revealed. Notice how your own *fórsa* builds and the impact that this has on your work, relationships, and life focus. I bet that your ability to convey and articulate concepts will be increased, as well as amplify and enhance your magnetism.

Once you have it down, play with it. Play with trees. Play with singing in a church. See what grows from your awareness and how it shifts even your intentions in life. Welcome it. It is your heritage. In our grove, we will practice this together to see how our circle becomes a giant tube torus and the effect that has on us collectively and on the world. See how you become a tree and how a tree or a forest can become you. Then, you are ready to serve as an emissary for the *aislingí*, the living Light of Erin, the freedom of Kathleen ní Houlihan, and the spirit of Ireland.

∞

Appendix

IRISH *(AN GHAEILGE)* PRONUNCIATION GUIDE

A couple of helpful and critical rules for pronouncing *an Ghaeilge*:

Rule 1: Aspiration of Consonants—Denoted by a "dot" over the consonant in Middle Irish (also sometimes in Modern Irish). The dot denotes lenition where the sound of the consonant is spirantized or lost and is called a *ponc séimhithe* or *buailte,* "dot of lenition." (This is used in ḃ, ċ, ḋ, ḟ, ġ, ṁ, ṗ, ṡ, and ṫ). Most Modern Irish uses an "h" after the consonant to create the same lineation or aspiration, which is the format used in this book and can be seen with pronunciations here:

1. **bh** (or ḃ) = v
2. **ch** (or ċ) = k (as in "lock," though sometimes silent.)
3. **dh** (or ḋ) = y (as in "yore" or "Yule".)
4. **fh** (or ḟ) = silent
5. **gh** (or ġ) = y (as in "Yule," though sometimes silent and sometimes a "k" sound.)
6. **mh** (or ṁ) = w
7. **ph** (or ṗ) = f
8. **sh** (or ṡ) = h (as in "hill.")
9. **th** (or ṫ) = h (as in "hill.")

Rule 2: Eclipsis of Consonants—The omission, disappearance, or substitution of unvoiced consonants with a corresponding voiced consonants ("c" becomes "g," "f" becomes "bh," "t" becomes "d," "p" becomes "b"), or nasals ("b" becomes "m," "d" becomes "n," "g" becomes "ng"). Also applies to preceding a vowel by inserting an "n" or "h." Specifically:

1. "B" is eclipsed by "m" as in *mBandia* (pronounced "*mahn-dee-uh*").
2. "C" is eclipsed by "g" as in *gConnachta* (pronounced "*gun-nock-ta*").
3. "D" is eclipsed by "n" as in *ndoras* (pronounced "*nor-us*").
4. "G" is eclipsed by "n" as in *i nGaeilge* (pronounced "*nail-ghe*").
5. "F" is eclipsed by "bh" as in *bhfuinneog* (pronounced "*win-yoog*").
6. "P" is eclipsed by "b" as in *bpoll* (pronounced "*ball*")
7. "T" is eclipsed by "d" as in *dteach* (pronounced "*jack*")
8. An "n" or an "h" is the eclipsis in front of vowels as in *Tír na nÓg* or *Mná na hÉireann.*

∞ Glossary (Connacht Dialect) ∞

Abhainn (*ow-win*): Means "river" or sometimes "stream." Often anglicized as "owen," as in Owenmore, a river in County Mayo.

Ail na Míreann (*ehl nah mere-ahn*): Also known as the "Cat Stone," this is the Irish Stone of Divisions, the navel of Ireland, located at the Hill of Uisneach.

Aillte (*all-tcha*): Irish word for "cliffs" and *aillte mara* for sea cliffs.

Áine (*on-yah*): The Irish goddess of summer, wealth, and sovereignty and the matron sovereign land goddess of the kingdom of Munster with her seat at Lough Gur. Her name in Irish means "brightness, glow, joy, radiance."

Aisling (*ash-ling*): Vision or dream. Also refers to a vision of a goddess, *sídhe*, angel, or beautiful otherworldly elven woman seeking contact with a mortal emissary. Plural *aislingí.*

An Cailleach Bhéara (*on call-yack ver-uh*): *Cailleach* means "veiled/hooded" and *bhéara* may mean "bear" or "sharp." The "old woman" and goddess associated with winter—hence "sharp, old, hooded woman."

Anam cara (*on-um kahr-uh*): Means "soul friend" or "soul mate." Popularized by John O'Donohue.

Anu (*ah-new*)*:* Anu is sometimes considered a variant of Danu, the Mother Goddess of the *Túatha Dé Danann.* She is also considered one of the triple aspects of the summer goddess, the spring-maiden/lover aspect of Áine—also known as *Fenne.*

Aonbharr Mhanannáin (*en-var va-nah-non*): The legendary horse of Manannán mac Lir who could traverse both land and sea and was faster than the wind.

Badb (*bayv* or *bow*): Modern Irish is "Badhbh," also meaning "crow"—a war goddess who takes the form of a crow. One of the triple aspects of the winter goddess with her sisters, Macha and the Morrígu, also known as the three Morrígna.

Bean chaointe (*bahn kween-teh*): Means "keening woman." An intense spiritual song that communicates strong emotion.

Bean feasa (*bahn fah-suh*): A wise woman, knowledge keeper, and the closest thing the Irish have to a "shamanic" tradition for women. See *Fear feasa.*

Bean fhionn (*bahn fee-own*): Also spelled "*beanfionn.*" Literally means "white/beautiful woman/lady." A *sídhe* connected to bodies of water.

Beansídhe/Beansí (*bahn-shee*): Literally translates to "woman/female" (*bean*) and "immortal/Faë" (*sídhe*). In Christian Ireland, it came to mean a female spirit in folklore that was believed to presage, by wailing (keening), a death in a family.

Beantighe (*bahn-tee*): A *sídhe* that helps take care of a home or hearth, literally means "house woman."

Bealtaine (*byell-tin-eh*): Also frequently written as "Beltaine." From the Irish root words *beal* meaning "a mouth or entrance to ford across a river" and *tine* or *teine* meaning "fire." The third cross-quarter holiday in Irish tradition; typically celebrated between April 30 and May 2.

Bodhrán (*bow-rawn*): The traditional Irish frame drum typically played with a tipper or the thumb and forefinger.

Brigid (*bree-ja*): Also frequently written as "Bridget." Brigid is the Irish goddess of spring, celebrated at Ímbolc. She is a triple goddess of healing, poetry, and smithcraft. Her seat is in Kildare as she is the matron and sovereign land goddess of the traditional kingdom of Leinster in Ireland.

Caoilte (*kweel-teh*): Male name meaning "swift of foot." A figure in Irish folklore.

Céad míle fáilte (*kayd mee-leh foyl-cha*): A greeting that means "a hundred thousand welcomes."

Cessair (*kaws-sair*): The name of the high priestess from Canaan of the ancient Goddess tradition. One of the first settlers of Ireland in the pre-Diluvian period in the Mythological Cycle.

Cill Dara (*kill darra*): Anglicized as "Kildare." Traditional sacred and secular center of Leinster. Historically, Kildare was in competition with Dún Ailinne at Cnoc Ailinne (Knockaulin) in County Kildare as the sacred center of Leinster. Kildare literally means "church of the oak."

Claíomh Solais (*klee-iv shoh-lis*): The Sword of Light wielded by Nuada. One of the Four Jewels of Ireland bestowed upon the *Tuatha Dé Danann* and brought from the pre-Diluvian city or faëry city of *Findias*. Literally translates as "saber of light" or "lightsaber." It always strikes true.

Clochán (*kloh-kawn*): Usually refers to dry-stacked stone "beehive" huts but can also mean "steppingstones." Plural *clocháin*.

Clooties (*cloo-tees*): Ribbons, rags, and whatnots tied to trees and wells for the fairy folk. Literally means "a strip of cloth."

Cnoc Áine (*nock on-ya*): A hill that lies on the southern shore of Lough Gur. *Cnoc* means "hill." Named for the goddess *Áine*.

Cnoc Finnine (*nock finn-in-eh*): Anglicized as "Knockfennel." A hill located on the northern shore of Lough Gur. Named for the Goddess Fenne (or Finnine or Fennel), the spring aspect of the triple goddess Áine. Herein lies the cave of Finnine.

Coire Ansic (*coy-reh ahn-sik*): The Cauldron of Plenty. One of the Four Jewels of Ireland bestowed upon the *Tuatha Dé Danann* and brought from the pre-Diluvian city or faëry city of *Muirias*. Wielded by the Daghda and at Samhain by the Morrígu. The cauldron would never empty, no matter how many ate from it—and thus no one went away hungry.

Crom Dubh (*crawm doov*): Lord of the Earth, perhaps an ancient aspect of the Dagda. He wrestles/battles with Lugh at Lughnasadh (August 1) over the goddess Gráinne and the harvest.

Cruachán Aigle (*kroo-uh-kahn ay-guhl*): Transliterated as "Mountain of the Eagle." One of the original names for the mountain Croagh Patrick. Also, historically known as *Cruachan Aille.*

Cú Chulainn (*coo kwu-lin*): Irish for "Culann's Hound," an Irish mythological hero appearing in the stories of the Ulster Cycle as well as in Scottish and Manx folklore.

Darerca (*dar-urka*): Sister of Saint Patrick and mother of several saints and mystics. See *Daire na hErka.*

Dá Chích Anann (*daw hee-ugh ah-nahn*): Paps of Anu, two twin mountains in Country Kerry that look like "paps," or breasts. Ancient pilgrimage path for fertility and abundance.

Daire na hErka (*derry na urka*): "Derrynahierka," named after Saint Darerca of Kerry, Ireland. A deep and ancient oak forest found in Killarney National Forest in County Kerry. See *Darerca.*

Dagda (*dag-duh* or *day-dah*): The Daghda is one of Ireland's oldest gods and father to Brigid. He is associated with fertility, agriculture, and abundance. Frequently known as the "good god" for his lavish gifting, feasts from his cauldron of plenty, and the deep music from his magical harp.

Danu (*dah-new*): Ancient mother goddess of the *Tuatha Dé Danann*—Danann and Danu are interchangeable.

Dúchas (*doo-hiss*): Ancestral heritage or indigenous birthright.

Dún Ailinne (*doon allen*): Ancient sacred and secular center of Leinster at Cnoc Ailinne (Knockaulin) in County Kildare. Home of Fionn mac Cumhaill and the winter home of the *Fianna*.

Éire (*aye-ruh*): Irish for "Ireland," the name of the island and the sovereign republic. Named for Erin, the goddess of Ireland. Also synonymous with Ériu.

Emain Macha (*ah-mon ma-ha* or *ah-mon mock-ah*): The sacred center of the Macha in Ulster in County Armagh. *Emain* means "twins" in Irish. *Macha* means "plain" as in an expanse of lowland. Also known as Navan Fort.

Éolchaire (*eoh-lah-reh*): The longing of expatriate Irish, and those of Irish heritage, to come home to Ireland. While it can refer to a type of homesickness or grief for Ireland, it also refers to a "remembering"—an ancestral remembering—perhaps of places in Ireland that one has never seen with their own eyes, but is first remembered in dreams, visions, and apparitions. See *Aisling*.

Ethniu (*en-yoo*): *Eithne* in modern Irish. She is the mother of Lugh and the daughter of Balor.

Faë (*fay*): Fairy-folk. Synonymous with the *sídhe* but derived from French etymology.

Falias (*fa-lee-us*): One of the four ancient pre-Diluvian or faëry cities from which the *Tuatha Dé Danann* migrated to Ireland. Morfessa is/was the poet-druid sovereign at *Falias* and passed on the *Lia Fáil*, or the Stone of Destiny, to be stewarded at the Hill of Tara in County Meath by Nuada and Danu. Debates ensue over whether this city is in the Celtic Otherworld or now under the Atlantic Sea off the northwest coast of Brittany, or even up in the Arctic. See *Lia Fáil*.

Fear feasa (*far faw-suh*): A wise man or knowledge keeper in the Irish tradition and the closest thing the Irish have to a "shamanic" tradition for men. See *Bean feasa*.

Fear Uaine* or *Fír Uaine (*far win-yuh*): Literally meaning "man green," refers to the Greenman or wild primordial masculine spirit inherent in the very landscape of Ireland and the sea.

Feiseanna (*fesh-in-naw*): Ancient Irish public assembly. See *Óenach.*

Fenne (*fen-nuh*): One of the triple-form goddesses of summer along with Gráinne and Áine. She is also associated with Anu, the lover aspect of Áine. Upon her sacred mound at Cnoc Finnine at Lough Gur is where the sweet cave of this lover waits for the rays of the setting sun to pour in to impregnate her at Bealtaine.

Fial (*fweel*): The Macha's daughter from her set of twins. Means "modest" in Irish. Sister of Fír. See *Fír.*

Fianna (*fee-uh-nuh*): A small, semi-independent band of warriors, healers, bards, and druids in Irish mythology. They are featured in the stories of the Fenian Cycle where they are led by Fionn mac Cumhaill. See *Fionn mac Cumhaill.*

Findias (*fin-dee-us*): One of the four ancient pre-Diluvian or faëry cities from which the *Tuatha Dé Danann* migrated to Ireland. Uiscias is/was the poet-druid sovereign at Findias and passed on the *Claíomh Solais*, or the Sword of Light, to be stewarded by Nuada. Debates ensue over whether this city is in the Celtic Otherworld or now under the Atlantic Sea in the vicinity of the Faroe Islands, or even up in the Arctic. See *Claíomh Solais.*

Fionntán (*fyun-tahn*): From mythology, the first man to inhabit Ireland. Was said to have sailed to the island alongside *Cessair.* The masculine primordial shapeshifter, changeling—the Greenman. See *Cessair* and *Fear Uaine.*

Fionn mac Cumhaill (*fyun ma-cool*): Leader of the *Fianna* in Irish mythology; an incarnation of *Fionntán.*

Fír (*feer*): The Macha's son from her set of twins. Means "true" and "man" in Irish. Brother of Fial. *See Fial.*

Foraisí (*for-eh-sha*): Also written as *foraoise*. The Irish word for "forest."

Fórsa (*for-sah*): The essence and energy of life present in all things. Refers to a force or "to leverage." Also called *fórsa beatha* (*for-sah ba-ha*).

Gáe Assail (*gaia ah-suhl*): The Spear of Assal, or Spear of Victory. One of the Four Jewels of Ireland bestowed upon the *Tuatha Dé Danann* and brought from the pre-Diluvian city or faëry city of Gorias. Wielded by Lugh. Transliterated as "lighting spear"—it always strikes its target and safely returns to the hands of the wielder.

Gaeltacht (*gayl-tawk-d*): Areas of Ireland where the Irish language (Gaeilge) is still spoken.

Gaoithe Sídhe (*gwee-yeh shee*): *Sídhe* riding the wind or their wind horses. Also, can refer to a sudden gust of wind or a whirlwind that was thought to have been caused by the faëries.

Géis (*gas* or *geh-sh*): A taboo, obligation, prohibition, or vow. Specifically, it means "a spell prohibiting some action." If someone under a *géis* violates the taboo, the infractor will suffer dishonor or death. Plural *geasa*.

Go raibh an fórsa leat (*guh row an for-suh lat*): "May the force be with you." See *Fórsa*.

Goibniu (*gov-noo*): Metalsmith of the *Tuatha Dé Danann*, associated with hospitality.

Gorias (*gor-us* or *gor-ee-us*): One of the four ancient pre-Diluvian or faëry cities from which the *Tuatha Dé Danann* migrated to Ireland. Esras is/was the poet-druid sovereign at *Gorias* and passed on the *Gáe Assail*, or the Spear of Victory, to be stewarded by Lugh. Debates ensue over whether this city is in the Celtic Otherworld or now under the Atlantic Sea off the west coast of County Mayo or County Galway, or even up in the Arctic. See *Gáe Assail*.

Gráinne (*grawn-yuh*): Also written as "Grainne." Literally means a "ripe grain." She is the third aspect of the summer goddess with Áine and Fenne. She represents the harvest and fullness.

Grian Banchure (*gree-in bon-hoor-uh*): A name sometimes used for the Macha in parts of Ulster. *Grian* means "sun," *ban* means "woman," and *tíre* (pronounced *"chu-re"*) means "folk" or "people."

Grianán na nAileach (*gree-anon na nayl-ack*): "Grianan of Aileach," a hillfort located in Inishowen, Donegal.

Kathleen ní Houlihan (*Kathleen nee who-lin* or *nee who-leh-han*): The spirit of Ireland personified as a woman. Specifically, she is a mythical symbol and emblem of Irish nationalism found in literature, art, poetry, and song.

Ímbas (*eem-boss*): Transliterated roughly as "the light that illuminates," inspiration, illumination, or "from the darkness comes light." Similar to the popularized Welsh word *"awen."* See *Ímbas fiosaíochta.*

Ímbas fiosaíochta (*eem-boss fiss-ic-ta*): Transliterated as "the discipline of knowledge that illuminates" and means "clairvoyance" or "visionary ability." Sometimes provided directly by fresh springs and wells in Ireland or by relations with the *sídhe*—it also can be honed and developed due to deep discipline, ascetic practices, or through grief/ecstasy. Modern Irish variant of *ímbas forosnai.* See *Iomas.*

Ímbolc (*eem-bowlk*): Meaning "in (or of) the belly." The second cross-quarter holiday or fire holiday in Irish seasonal traditions—celebrated between February 1 and 4.

Inis Mór (*ee-nish moor*): Means "Great Island" in Irish. Sometimes spelled "Inishmore." One of the islands off the western shore of Ireland.

Inis na bhFiodhadh (*ee-nish nav fey-doe*): Ancient Bardic name for Ireland, literally means "Island of the Sacred Tree."

Iomas (*ah-mows*): "The light that illuminates." Traditionally *imbas* or *ímbas*. See *Ímbas fiosaíochta.*

Leath Bhrogan (*lah vro-gun*): A type of shoemaker; perhaps an origin for the term "*leipreachán*" or "leprechaun." See *Leipreachán.*

Leipreachán (*lep-re-cawn*): Anglicized as "leprechaun." A *sídhe.* A diminutive form of the Daghda and other ancient earth gods of Ireland. Frequently depicted as tricksters or riddlers.

Lia Fáil (*lee-uh fall*): The Stone of Destiny or the "speaking stone." One of the Four Jewels of Ireland bestowed upon the *Tuatha Dé Danann* and brought from the pre-Diluvian city or faëry city of Falias. It would cry out beneath the true sovereign who ascended into the high kingship of Ireland. Purportedly stolen from the Irish and Scots in 1296 and sits under the English throne.

Lough (*lock*): Irish word for "lake."

Lough Gur (*lock ger*): Lake that is about one hour south of the city of Limerick and part of the ancient sacred center of the Irish kingdom of Munster in County Limerick. After Sligo, one of the oldest inhabited locations in Ireland.

Luacharman (*low-ar-men*): Means "dwarf" or "pygmy." A possible origin for the term "*leipreachán*" or "leprechaun." See *Leipreachán.*

Lughnasadh (*loo-nah-suh*): The feast of Lugh in honor of his foster mother, Tailtiu. This cross-quarter fire festival demarcates the beginning of autumn and the harvest season. The fourth cross-quarter Irish holiday celebrated between July 31 and August 2. Often called "Reek Sunday" in contemporary Ireland for the annual Pattern Day pilgrimage to the summit of Croagh Patrick.

Lunantisidhe (*lewn-an-tuh-shee*): The Good People that guard the blackthorn trees, one of the sacred *ogham* trees, and the threshold between the Otherworld and ours. See *Ogham.*

Macha (*ma-ha* or *mock-ah*): Meaning "of the plain" in Old Irish. Macha is the Irish goddess of autumn, the harvest, family/tribe, and loyalty. Her ascent is celebrated at Lughnasadh. One of the triple aspects of the winter goddess with her sisters, Badb and the Morrígu, also known as the three Morrígna. Her seat is at Navan Fort (*Emain Macha*) as she is the matron and sovereign land goddess of the traditional kingdom of Ulster in Ireland.

Magh Meall (*ma mell* or *moy mell*): Also known as *Mag Mell*, meaning the "plain of honey" or the "delightful plain." One of the realms of the Celtic Otherworld, similar to *Tír na nÓg*, a type of Otherworld paradise inhabited by the *Tuatha Dé Danann* or the *sídhe*. Often the first realm that humans visit within the other realm. One of the "upper worlds" most frequently accessed by fire, asceticism, ecstasy (or suffering), and pursuit of a magical animal, or via the sea.

Manannán Mac Lir (*mah-na-non mack lear*): Son of the Sea (Lir), King Under the Waves, and protector of Ireland by way of the sea. His dominion is referred to by several names including *Mag Mell* (Plain of Delights), *Tír fo Thuinn* (Land beneath the Waves), or *Tír Tairngire* (Land of Promise). Attributed to many magical talents, including raising sea mists to protect that which he loves, as well as his kingly nature. Owner of the Wave Sweeper (crystal boat), Aonbharr Mhanannáin (a horse that can run over land and water), the Sword of Light (Fragarach), and the *Féth Fíada* (cloak of invisibility).

Mór Mumain (*moor moom-in*): Can be translated as the "Great Mother." She is the original goddess of the kingdom of Munster (*An Mhumhain*) and is often considered synonymous with Danu, and thus the mother goddess of all Ireland. Wife of the Irish god of the sea, Lir or Lyr.

Morrígu (*moor-ee-goo*): Also known as *the Morrígan*. The Morrígu is the Irish goddess of winter, candor/truth, fate, and conflict/war. Her ascent is celebrated at Samhain. One of the triple aspects of the winter goddess with her sisters, Badb and the Macha, also known as the three Morrígna. Her seat is at Ráthcroghan *(Ráth Cruachan)*. She is the sovereign land goddess and matron of the traditional kingdom of Connacht in Ireland.

Murias (*mweer-ee-es*): One of the four ancient pre-Diluvian or faëry cities from which the *Tuatha Dé Danann* migrated to Ireland. Semias is/was the poet-druid sovereign at *Murias* and passed on the *Coire Ansic* or the Cauldron of Plenty to be stewarded by the Daghda (and the Morrígu). Debates ensue over whether this city is in the Celtic Otherworld or now under the sea near Dogger Bank in the North Sea, or even up in the Arctic. See *Coire Ansic.*

Nechtan (*neck-ten*): Also spelled "Nectan." Ancient Grail god of Ireland. Keeper of the sacred archives of the sacred well atop the Hill of Uisneach, the *Tobar Segais*, or "Well of Wisdom" into which nine sacred hazel trees dropped their wisdom-bearing hazelnuts. He was the husband of Boann, the goddess of the Boyne River.

Niamh (*nee-av*): A woman's name in Ireland, refers here to Oisín's fairy lover in Irish mythology. See *Oisín.*

Nuada (*new-uh or new-uh-the*): Also known as "Nuada of the Silver Hand," he was the first king of the *Tuatha Dé Danann.* He lost his hand in battle but received a replacement hand made of silver. Represents the resurrected king, sovereignty, beating the odds. Nuada's great sword, the Sword of Light *(Claíomh Solais)* was one of the Four Treasures of the *Tuatha Dé Danann.* He is synonymous with Nechtan. See *Nechtan.*

Óenach (*ee-nock*): Ancient Irish public assembly. The pilgrimage to sacred and secular sites and an occasion for high ceremony, arts, trade negotiation, musical/athletic/combat competitions, celebration, entertainment, and where laws/alliances were pronounced and confirmed. Plural *óenaig*. See *Feiseanna.*

Ogham (*oh-um* or *ow-um*): The twenty sacred and indigenous "trees" of Ireland that were symbolized in an Early medieval alphabet used primarily to write the early Irish language.

Oidheadh chloinne Lir (*iya cloyn-yah leer*): Literally means "Fate of the Children of Lir." A legend in Irish mythology.

Oileáin (*ih-lawn*): Irish word for "islands."

Oisín (*oh-sheen*): Character from the story of Niamh and Oisín and his return from *Tír na nÓg* to Ireland. Son of Cuchulainn and later, after emerging back from the Summerlands, a companion of Saint Patrick.

Ollamh (*aw-love*): Literally means "most great," referring to a poet or bard. The senior-most druid in Ireland. The head *ollamh* of a province would have been the head of all the *ollamhs* in that province and would have been a social equal of the provincial king.

Oweynagat (*oh-way-naw-got*): Literally means "cave of the cats." Initiation chamber of the Morrígu as well as Connacht kings.

Púca (*poo-kuh*): Shapeshifters that are considered to be bringers of both good and bad fortune.

Ráth (*raw* or *raah*): Known as "ring forts"; circular fortified settlements built primarily around the Bronze Age through AD 1000.

Ráth Cruachan (*raw* or *raah crow-kin*): Traditional sacred and secular center of Connacht.

Ríastrad (*ree-stred*): A battle frenzy or a berserker-like state. Means "warp spasm."

Samhain (*saw-when*): Also spelled "samhfhuin"; *sam* meaning "summer" and *fhuin* meaning "end." First cross-quarter festival in Irish tradition that is celebrated between October 31 and November 1. Marks the beginning of the Celtic Year.

Sceolan (*sh-koh-lin*): In Irish mythology, one of Fionn mac Cumhaill's two hunting faëry dogs; Bran and Sceolan.

Seanchaí (*shawn-a-kee*): A traditional Celtic storyteller or knowledge keeper.

Sí (*shee*): Means "mounds" and is used to refer to fairy mounds. Pronounced the same as *sídhe.*

Siansán (*she-in-sawn*): Literally means "the humming winds"; the *sídhe* winds.

Sídhe (*shee*): Spirits or the Faë. Diminutive ancient gods of Ireland—the Tribe of the Mother Goddess Danu, the *Tuatha Dé Danann.* They are the immortal ones, the high elves, and/or the ancient deities of Ireland and our Irish ancestors. As immortals or "high elves," they are classically called the "*Aes Sídhe*" (pronounced "*ays shee*"). W.B. Yeats helped to popularize the shortened *sídhe* as the well-known name for the immortals in the late nineteenth, twentieth, and now the twenty-first centuries.

Sliabh an Iarainn (*shleev on eer-in*): Mountain in Ireland, sometimes written on maps as "Slieve Anierin," located in modern-day County Leitrim where the gods, the *Tuatha Dé Danann*, first landed in Ireland in their cloud ships or giant birds/eagles.

Sliabh an Iolair (*shleev on ee-oh-lar*): "Mount Eagle." A mountain in County Kerry, Ireland, on the Dingle Peninsula.

Sliabh Eachtaí (*shleev ock-tee*): Or "Sliabh Aughty." Glacier-polished mountains that stretch from County Galway through County Clare and almost to Limerick.

Sléibhte (*shleev-tah*): One of the Irish words for "mountains." Singular is *sliabh.*

Slua Sídhe (*slew-uh shee*): Fairy warriors of Ireland that ride with the Morrígu at Samhain and on their own at other times of year—especially ahead of storms. Often called the "Fairy Host." They clear the countryside of refuse, and many Irish know them well in late autumn and early winter as they can be quite destructive.

Solas Bhríde (*sew-lass breed*): Translates to "Brigid's Light" in reference to her eternal flame tended at Kildare. Also refers to a Christian Spirituality Centre in Kildare which welcomes people of all faiths and of no faith.

Solas geal na hÉireann (*so-las gehl na haar-on*): "Shining light of Erin (Ireland)" or "bright light of Ireland."

Suideachan Bean-tige (*shee-han ban-tee*): Translates directly as "the housekeeper's chair," and is typically written as "*Siodhachán bantí*" or "*Siodhachán bantigh.*" Áine's seat or "throne" at Lough Gur.

Tabhair neamh dóibh (*tyor neh-ave doh-ehv*): Phrase meaning "give them heaven" in Irish.

Tailtiu (*tow-choo*): Foster mother of Lugh; Firbolg and adopted member of the *Tuatha Dé Danann.*

Táin Bó Cúailgne (*toyn boh cool-nyah*): *The Cattle Raid of Cooley,* a classic tale in Irish mythology.

Tír fo Thuinn (*teer foh henn*): Meaning "Land beneath the waves," in reference to an aspect of the Summerlands and the home realm of Manannán Mac Lir. One of the "lower worlds" most frequently accessed by water (wells, streams, rivers, the sea) or dreams.

Tír na mBan (*teer nah mahn*): Literally means "land of women," but refers to a land or isle inhabited by women. One of the "lower worlds" most frequently accessed by water (wells, streams, rivers, the sea) or dreams.

Tír na mBeo (*teer nam byo*): Literally means "land of the living," and place of everlasting life and otherworldly paradise. Lugh's sword, Frecraid, or "The Answerer" came from this realm. One of the "lower worlds" most frequently accessed by water (wells, streams, rivers, the sea) or dreams.

Tír na nÓg (*teer non ohg*): Land of Youth, The Irish Otherworld, Summerlands, Land of Eternal Youth, Land of the Faë. A realm parallel to our own yet operating on a different time signature. One of the "lower worlds" most frequently accessed by water (wells, streams, rivers, the sea), dreams, or megalithic sites.

Tobar Beannaithe (*tober ban-ee-heh*): Irish word for "holy well." Singular is *beannaigh*, pronounced "*ban-ee.*" Plural is *toibreacha beannaithe.*

Tránna (*trah-nah*): Irish word for "beaches." *Trá* is singular for "beach."

Tuatha Dé Danann (*too-hawt de don-an*): Literally means the "Tribe of the goddess Danu." The immortals and ancient gods of Ireland of the Mythological Cycle.

Tuathail (*too-hill*): Irish word meaning "something reversed from its proper direction."

Tuiren (*teer-en*): In Irish mythology, Fionn mac Cumhaill's aunt. Said to have birthed Fionn's fairy hounds Bran and Sceolan.

Uaimh (*oo-av*): Irish word for "cave." Plural is *uaimheanna.*

Uisce (*ish-kuh*): The Irish word for "water"; also, the root of the English word *whiskey,* water of life.

Uisneach (*ish-naw*): The sacred center, geographic center, and the spiritual naval (*bellios*) of Ireland. A region of Ireland that literally means "place of the hearth."

Uragh (*yew-raw*): Mistranslated as "place of the yews" by author Patrick Weston Joyce; most likely translates to "place of the heather."

Bibliography and Cited Texts 

"Archaeological Survey of Ireland, National Monuments Service." *National Monuments Service*, https://www.archaeology.ie/archaeological-survey-ireland. Accessed 21 Jun. 2022.

Barkham, Patrick. "'Rarest Fern in Europe' Discovered in Ireland, Plants, The Guardian." *The Guardian*, The Guardian, 4 Oct. 2020, https://www.theguardian.com/environment/2020/oct/04/rarest-fern-europe-discovered-ireland.

Best, R.I., editor and translator. *The Settling of the Manor of Tara*, vol. 4, Royal Irish Academy, 1910. Translated from *Leabhar Buidhe Leacáin* (*The Yellow Book of Lecan*, 1391), pp 121-172.

Benham, Patrick. *The Avalonians*. Gothic Images Publications, 2006.

Black '47. Directed by Lance Daly, performances by Hugo Weaving, James Frecheville, and Stephen Rea, Elemental Pictures, 2018.

Blackie, Sharon. *If Women Rose Rooted*. September Publishing, 2016.

Blamires, Steve. *Celtic Tree Mysteries*. Crossed Crow Books, 2023.

———. *Glamoury: Magic of the Celtic Green World*. Llewellyn Worldwide, 2000.

———. *The Chronicles of the Sídhe*. Skylight Press, 2012.

Burke, Sir Bernhard. *A Genealogical and Heraldic History of the Landed Gentry of Ireland*, edited by Arthur Charles Fox-Davies, Harrison & Sons, 1912.

Byrne, Aisling. *Archipelagic Otherworlds, Otherworlds: Fantasy and History in Medieval Literature*, Oxford Academic, 2016.

Cabot, David. *Ireland: A Natural History*. HarperCollins, 1999.

Cahill, Thomas. *How the Irish Saved Civilization*. Anchor, 1996.

Carmichael, Alexander. *Carmina Gadelica: Hymns and Incantations*. Floris Books, 2006.

Colclough, Phil. *Song for Ireland*. 1981.

Collins, Will, and Tomm Moore. *Song of the Sea*. Directed by Tomm Moore, Cartoon Saloon, 2015.

Collis, J., *The Celts: Origins, Myths and Inventions*, Tempus Publishing Ltd., 2003.

Concannon, Helena. *Daughters of Banba*. 1st ed., M.H. Gill & Son, Ltd., 1922.

Cowan, Tom. *Fire in the Head: Shamanism and the Celtic Spirit.* HarperOne, 1993.

Curtis, Choate, et al. *The Little People of the Hills*. 1st ed., Harcourt, Brace & Company, 1928.

Dawson, Alastair G., et al. "Reconciling Storegga Tsunami Sedimentation Patterns with Modelled Wave Heights: A Discussion" *Shetland Isles Field Laboratory, Sedimentology, International Association of Sedimentologists*, vol. 67, issue 3, 2020, pp. 1344–1353.

Dinneen, Patrick S., *An English-Irish Dictionary, Being a Thesaurus of the Words, Phrases and Idioms of the Modern Irish Language*, M.H. Gill & Sons, Published on behalf of The Irish Texts Society, 1904.

Duffy, Seán. *Atlas of Irish History, 3rd ed.*, M.H. Gill & Company, 2011.

Evans-Wentz, Walter Yeeling. *The Fairy Faith in Celtic Countries*. 1st ed., Oxford University Press, 1911.

"Explore Natural Communities, NatureServe." *NatureServe, Unlocking the Power of Science to Guide Biodiversity Conservation*, https://www.natureserve.org/products/explore-natural-communities. Accessed 17 Apr. 2023.

Frazer, W. "O'Brazile or Hy Brazile," *Notes and Queries,* s6-VIII: 475, December 1883.

Gonne-MacBride, Maude. *A Servant of the Queen: Reminiscences, 1st ed.* Victor Gollancz, Ltd., 1938.

Gregory, Lady. *Gods and Fighting Men*. 1st ed., John Murray Publishing, 1904.

Gunn, William, and John Allen Giles (translators and eds.), 1848. *Historia Brittonum (The History of the Brittons),* originally written in Latin in AD 888 by Nennius.

Haggerty, Bridget. "Irish Landmarks: The Holy Wells of Ireland—World Cultures European." *Irish Culture and Irish Customs, World Cultures European*, https://www.irishcultureandcustoms.com/ALandmks/HolyWells.html. Accessed 24 Dec. 2020.

Hancock, Graham, *Fingerprints of the Gods,* Penguin Random House, 1995.

Hull, Eleanor. *Cuchulain: The Hound of Ulster*. 1st ed., George G. Harrap & Company, 1913.

Hyde, Douglas. *Love Songs of Connacht*. 4th ed., M.H. Gill & Son, Ltd., 1905.

Jackson, Peter Wyse. *Ireland's Generous Nature*. Missouri Botanical Garden Press, 2014.

Joyce, James. *A Portrait of the Artist as a Young Man*. B.W. Huebsch, 1916.

Joyce, Patrick Weston. *Irish Local Names Explained (1879)*. Createspace Independent Publishing Platform, 2017.

———. *Old Celtic Romances (1894)*. Forgotten Books, 2018.

———. *The Origin and History of Irish Names of Places Vol. 1-3*. 6th ed., M.H. Gill & Son, 1893.

Kessler, Benjamin, et al., *Doggerland—The Europe That Was*, National Geographic Society, 2023.

Kiernan, Thomas J. *The White Hound of the Mountain*. 1st ed., The Devin-Adair Publishing Company, 1962.

Koch, John T., *Celtic Culture: A Historical Encyclopedia*. ABC-Clio, 2006.

Kondratiev, Alexei. *Celtic Rituals: An Authentic Guide to Ancient Celtic Spirituality*. The Collins Press, 1999.

Laing, Lloyd Robert, and Jennifer Laing. *The Picts and the Scots*. Wrens Park Publishing, W.J. Williams & Son Ltd., Sutton Publishing Ltd., 1998.

Lennon, Joseph, *Irish Orientalism: A Literary and Intellectual History*. Syracuse University Press, 2004.

Lucas, George. *Star Wars: Episode IV—A New Hope*. Directed by George Lucas, Lucasfilm, 1977.

Lynam, Shevawn, *Humanity Dick Martin "King of Connemara" 1754–1834*, Lilliput Press, 1989.

Lynch, J.F. "The Legend of Birdhill," *Journal of the Cork Historical and Archaeological Society*, Cork Historical and Archaeological Society, vol II, 1896, p 188.

Macalister, Robert Alexander Stewart, ed. *Lebor Gabála Érenn: The Book of the Taking of Ireland Parts I–V*. Vols. 34, 35, 39, 41, 44, Irish Texts Society, Educational Company of Ireland, 1938–1956.

MacBride, Maud Gonne. *A Servant of the Queen: Reminiscences*. 1st ed., Victor Gollancz, 1938.

MacKillop, James. *A Dictionary of Celtic Mythology*. Oxford University Press, 2004.

Macleod, Fiona. *From the Hills of Dream: Threnodies, Songs and Later Poems*. 2nd ed., William Heinemann, 1913.

———. *The Washer of the Ford and Other Legendary Moralities*. 1st ed., Patrick Geddes, 1896, p. 49.

———. *The Divine Adventure: Iona, Studies in Spiritual History*. 8th ed., Duffield & Company, 1910.

———. *The House of Usna*. 1st ed., Thomas P. Mosher, 1903.

———. *The Immortal Hour*. 1st ed., T&N Foulis, 1908.

MacLysaght, Edward. *Irish Families: Their Names, Arms and Origins*. Crown Publishers Inc., 1957.

———. *The Surnames of Ireland*. 6th ed., Irish Academic Press, 1985.

MacNeill, Eoin, and Gerard Murphy. *Duanaire Finn: The Book of the Lays of Fionn, Parts I–III*. 2nd ed., Irish Texts Society, Simpkin Marshall, 1933, 1948, 1953.

Magan, Machán. *Listen to the Land Speak,* Gill Books, 2022.

Mann, Charles C. *1491: New Revelations of the Americas before Columbus*. Alfred A. Knopf, Random House, 2005.

Matthews, Caitlin & John. *The Encyclopedia of Celtic Wisdom: A Celtic Shaman's Sourcebook*, Rider Books, Ebury Press, Random House, 2001.

McAleese, Mary. "Commencement Address for Graduating Class of 2006," *University of Notre Dame,* 2006, https://news.nd.edu/news/mary-mcaleese-2006-commencement-address. Accessed 23 May 2023.

McAnally, David Rice. *Taming the Pooka and Other Popular Tales as Told by the People*. 1st ed., Ward, Locke & Company, 1888.

McCracken, Eileen. "The Woodlands of Ireland Circa 1600." *Irish Historical Studies*, Irish Historical Studies Publications Ltd., 1959.

McCraith, L. M. *The Romance of Irish Heroines*. The Talbot Press Ltd., 1910.

McCraty, Rollin, et al. "Synchronization of Human Autonomic Nervous System Rhythms with Geomagnetic Activity in Human Subjects." *International Journal of Environmental Research and Public Health*, 2017.

McManus, L. *In Sarsfield's Days: A Tale of the Siege of Limerick*. 1st ed., M.H. Gill & Son Ltd., 1900.

Meakin, Annette M.B. *Galicia: The Switzerland of Spain,* Methuen & Co., 1909.

Meehan, Cary. *The Traveller's Guide to Sacred Ireland*. Gothic Image Publications, 2002.

Megaw, William Rutledge. *Carragloon: Tales of Our Townland.* 1st ed., The Quota Press, 1935.

Michell, John. *The Sacred Center: The Ancient Art of Locating Sanctuaries.* Inner Traditions, 2009.

Minehan, Rita. *Rekindling the Flame: A Pilgrimage in the Footsteps of Brigid of Kildare.* Solas Bhríde Community, 1999.

Morris, Kenneth. *Book of the Three Dragons.* 1st ed., Longman, Green & Company, 1930.

———. *The Dragon Path: Collected Stories of Kenneth Morris.* 1st ed., Tom Doherty Associates, 1995.

———. *The Fates of the Princes of Dyfed.* Theosophical Book Company, 1914.

Murphy, Gerard. *Duanaire Finn: The Book of the Lays of Fionn, Part II–III.* 2nd ed., Irish Texts Society, Simpkin Marshall Ltd., 1933–1953.

Nutt, Alfred. *Studies on the Legend of the Holy Grail with Special Reference to the Hypothesis of Its Celtic Origin*, 1st ed, David Nutt, 1888.

Narby, Jeremy. *The Cosmic Serpent.* Penguin, 1998.

Ó Cléirigh, Mícheál. *Foclóir Nó Sanasán Nua: A New Vocabulary or Glossary.* St. Anthony's College, 1643.

O'Byrne, W. Lorcan. *The Knight of the Cave.* 1st ed., Blackie and Son, Ltd., 1906.

O'Curry, Eugene. *On the Manners and Customs of the Ancient Irish.* 1st ed., Williams and Norgate, 1873.

Ó'Dónaill, Niall. *Foclóir Gaeilge-Bearla/Irish-English Dictionary*, Oifig an tSoláthair, 1977.

O'Donohue, John. *Anam Cara: A Book of Celtic Wisdom.* Harper Perennial, 1996.

O'Keeffe, J. G. *Buile Suibne: The Frenzy of Suibhne, A Middle Irish Romance.* 1st ed., Irish Texts Society, 1913.

O'Lee. *The Book of the O'Lees (The Book of Hy Brasil),* Collections at the Royal Irish, Fifteenth Century AD.

O'Rahilly, T. F. *Early Irish History and Mythology.* Dublin Institute for Advanced Studies, 1946.

Academy, Dublin Institute for Advanced Studies, Dublin, Ireland.

Roberts, Jack. *The Sacred Mythological Centres of Ireland.* Bandia Publishing, 2016.

———. *The Sun Circles of Ireland.* Bandia Publishing, 2013.

Rolleston, Thomas William, and Stephen Reid. *The High Deeds of Finn and Other Bardic Romances.* George G. Harrap & Company, 1910.

Russell, Æ. *Song and Its Fountains.* MacMillan & Company, Ltd., 1932.

———. *The Avatars.* MacMillan & Company, Ltd., 1933.

———. *The Interpreters.* MacMillan & Company, Ltd., 1922.

Shannon, P., et al. "The Petroleum Exploration of Ireland's Offshore Basins," *Geological Society, London, Special Publications,* vol. 188, 2001, p355.

Sigerson, George. *Bards of the Gael and Gall.* 1st ed., T.F. Unwin, 1897.

Stewart, R. J. *The Way of Merlin: The Prophet, The Goddess, and The Land.* HarperCollins, 1991.

Stokes, Whitley. *Three Irish Glossaries: Cormac's Glossary Codex, A. O'Davoren's Glossary, and a Glossary to the Calendar of Oingus the Culdee.* 1st ed., Williams and Norgate, 1862.

The Bible, Authorized King James Version. Oxford Paperbacks, 2008.

Tacitus, Cornelius. *Agricola and the Germania.* Translated by H. Mattingly, Penguin Books, 1948.

Tolkien, John Ronald Reuel. *The Fellowship of the Ring.* HarperCollins Publishers, 2002.

Train, Joseph. *An Historical and Statistical Account of the Isle of Man.* Mary A. Quiggin, 1845.

U2. *Sunday Bloody Sunday.* 7 Nov. 1983, https://audio-ssl.itunes.apple.com/itunes-assets/AudioPreview125/v4/9d/0b/c4/9d0bc49a-8d43-cab3-9175-80dcc261e9a0/mzaf_2518944721220264522.plus.aac.p.m4a.

Ua Laoghaire, Peadar. *Bricriu.* 1st ed., Muintir na Leabhar Gaedilge, 1915.

Velasco, Francisco, et al. "Distribution, Abundance, and Growth of Anglerfish (*Lophius piscatorius*) on the Porcupine Bank (West of Ireland)." *ICES Journal of Marine Science,* volume 65, issue 7, October 2008, pp. 1316–1325, https://doi.org/10.1093/icesjms/fsn130.

Ward, Alan. *The Myths of the Gods: Structures in Irish Mythology.* CreateSpace, 2011.

Watkins, Alfred. *The Old Straight Track.* Bloomsbury Publishing, 2014.

Williams, Charles, and C. S. Lewis. *Taliessin Through Logres, The Region of the Summer Stars.* William B. Eerdmans Publishing Company, 1976.

Winsor, Justin. *Narrative and Critical History of America.* vol.1, Houghton, Mifflin and Company, 1889, p. 51.

Yeats, William Butler. *Cathleen Ni Houlihan.* 1st ed., Shakespeare Head Press, 1911.
———. *Irish Fairy and Folk Tales of the Irish Peasantry.* Metro Books, 1888.
———. *The Celtic Twilight.* A.H. Bullen, 1902.
———. *The Tower.* MacMillan and Company, Ltd., 1928.
———. *The Wind Among the Reeds.* Elkin Mathews, 1899.
Young, Ella. *Flowering Dusk: Things Remembered Accurately and Inaccurately.* 1st ed., Longmans, Green & Company, Ltd., 1945.
———. *The Tangled-Coated Horse and Other Tales.* 3rd ed., David McKay Company, Inc., 1967.
———. *The Unicorn with Silver Shoes.* David McKay Company, Inc., 1960.
———. *The Wonder Smith and His Son.* Longmans, Green & Company, Ltd., 1949.
Young, Ella, and Maude Gonne. *Celtic Wonder-Tales.* Maunsel & Company, Ltd., 1910.
———. *The Coming of Lugh.* Maunsel & Company, Ltd., 1909.

∞

∞ Index ∞

I

J

K

L

N

O

P

T

U